ROUTLEDGE LIBRARY EDITIONS:
PSYCHOLOGY OF EDUCATION

Volume 1

COMMUNITY PSYCHOLOGY AND THE SCHOOLS

COMMUNITY PSYCHOLOGY AND THE SCHOOLS

A Behaviorally Oriented Multilevel Preventive Approach

GEORGE J. ALLEN, JACK M. CHINSKY,
STEPHEN W. LARCEN, JOHN E. LOCHMAN
AND HOWARD V. SELINGER

Routledge
Taylor & Francis Group
LONDON AND NEW YORK

First published in 1976 by Lawrence Erlbaum Associates, Inc.

This edition first published in 2018
by Routledge
2 Park Square, Milton Park, Abingdon, Oxon OX14 4RN

and by Routledge
711 Third Avenue, New York, NY 10017

Routledge is an imprint of the Taylor & Francis Group, an informa business

British Library Cataloguing in Publication Data
A catalogue record for this book is available from the British Library

ISBN: 978-1-138-24157-2 (Set)
ISBN: 978-1-315-10703-5 (Set) (ebk)
ISBN: 978-1-138-28546-0 (Volume 1) (hbk)
ISBN: 978-1-315-26894-1 (Volume 1) (ebk)

Publisher's Note
The publisher has gone to great lengths to ensure the quality of this reprint but points out that some imperfections in the original copies may be apparent.

Disclaimer
The publisher has made every effort to trace copyright holders and would welcome correspondence from those they have been unable to trace.

COMMUNITY PSYCHOLOGY AND THE SCHOOLS

A Behaviorally Oriented Multilevel Preventive Approach

George J. Allen
Jack M. Chinsky
Stephen W. Larcen
John E. Lochman
Howard V. Selinger

UNIVERSITY OF CONNECTICUT

LEA LAWRENCE ERLBAUM ASSOCIATES, PUBLISHERS
1976 Hillsdale, New Jersey

DISTRIBUTED BY THE HALSTED PRESS DIVISION OF
JOHN WILEY & SONS
New York Toronto London Sydney

Lawrence Erlbaum Associates, Inc., Publishers
62 Maria Drive
Hillsdale, New Jersey 07642

Distributed solely by Halsted Press Division
John Wiley & Sons, Inc., New York

Library of Congress Cataloging in Publication Data

Main entry under title:

Community psychology and the schools.

Bibliography: p.
Includes indexes.
1. Community and school. I. Allen, George J.
[DNLM: 1. Child behavior disorders–Prevention & control. 2. Community mental health services.
3. School Health. WA352 C736]
LC215.C559 370.19'31 75-42469
ISBN 0-470-01368-0

Printed in the United States of America

Contents

PART II: TOWARD A THEORETICAL BACKGROUND FOR MULTILEVEL PREVENTION IN THE SCHOOLS

PART III: FROM PRINCIPLES TO A PROGRAM: THE COLLABORATIVE INTERVENTION IN ACTION

Foreword

Happily I have this opportunity—and ample space—to record my reactions to *Community Psychology and the Schools: A Behaviorally Oriented Multilevel Preventive Approach* by Allen, Chinsky, Larcen, Lochman, and Selinger. Had I been backed to a wall and told that I must condense these views into *the* single English language word that best captured their essence, I would surely have chosen "exciting."

I do not use the word "exciting" frivolously. As I apply it to a scholarly scientific effort, it implies a heuristic, qualitatively different advance in how thought is organized, how resultant programs are articulated, and how research questions are posed and studied. This volume does each of these things skillfully and refreshingly. It caps a concerted 18-month effort by an able, dedicated team of more than 100 people—80+, university based and 20+, school based—to develop a comprehensive program for improving young children's school experiences and strengthening their adaptive skills. This innovative program offers a clear, stimulating preview of concepts and approaches that will define the prime turf of tomorrow's Community Psychology.

The freshness and fascination of this work come not from the problem it deals with—human adaptation, which is virtually as old as humanity itself—but rather from *how* it conceptualizes and addresses the problem. Several recurrent themes set the book's tone and boundaries:

1. It is more sensible and fruitful to prevent maladjustment than to try to deal with it after it has rooted.
2. High-impact social systems such as elementary schools have a vitally important role to play in achieving that goal.
3. Teaching children specific skills and competencies, and strengthening their adaptive resources is first-line primary prevention.
4. A comprehensive effort to cut down the flow of dysfunction will require new roles and the combined effort of many people, including some not previously considered to belong to a classically defined mental health field.
5. As viable new intervention models evolve, professionals must work closely with host systems to help develop the internal resources and competencies needed to continue them. These are the *leit-motifs* of the volume; each is destined to be a central future theme in community psychology!

This important piece of work can be considered at two levels: (1) as a concrete, circumscribed program with its surrounding network of evaluations or

(2) as the prototype of a broader class of approaches that it both pioneers and models. Although the project makes significant contributions at *both* levels, my personal sense is that the second will be the more profound and enduring.

The following is a grossly oversimplified summary of the study's main profile. Mental health professionals have talked about, gold-plated and worshipped primary prevention for years. But they haven't done it! The present team successfully harnessed this concept through the development of a social problem solving curriculum designed to build competency, adaptive resources and skills in *all* children. Not only did they present evidence that children learned social problem-solving skills, but they also found that important, secondary benefits accrued to program youngsters.

Secondary prevention was undertaken by means of a behaviorally oriented, college-student staffed, companionship program for children identified by classroom teachers as socially isolated or maladapted. This program, with specific behavioral goals, was shown to improve the social interaction of the target children in a playground–recreational situation, where neutral observers recorded it.

"Tertiary" prevention (some might still call it secondary) was developed, in a workshop format, via a behaviorally oriented teacher-training and consultation program. This component was designed to improve teachers' skills in interaction and handling children experiencing more serious acting-out and learning problems. Once again, direct observation of classroom events demonstrated that the workshop-training approach led to positive changes in teachers' behavior and helped them to acquire useful new classroom management skills. Appropriate changes in the behavior of target children were noted as well. A novel, important subfinding was that these positive effects carried over ("radiated") to a second group of youngsters, not themselves prime target children but identified beforehand as having similar problems.

The comprehensiveness and internal harmony of this program are among its most unusual features. It has "something to please everybody." It is a conceptually sound, carefully thought out, fluidly interconnected program *network* that deals with a *whole* school, at multiple levels, ranging from *bonafide* primary prevention to restoration of seriously maladapting children. This comprehensive multitiered approach is qualitatively different from preceding program efforts in this field. Thus, the authors have significantly modified "ways of doing things" and, in the process, have identified a clear, feasible program paradigm, with much appeal for the future.

This was far from an antiseptic laboratory project. From start to finish the project was shaped by, anchored in, and addressed to a real world. That's the way the authors wanted it, and that's the way it had to be! The cost (in sheer planning, dirty work, dialoguing, endless base touching, hearing inputs and providing feedback) of doing this is enormous. But so are the potential rewards. Properly done, as in the present case, the payoff (that is, a host system's incorporation of a viable, innovative approach) is the highest form of tribute to a program's success.

The volume's format skillfully explicates and amplifies the program's good sense and internal consistency. Separate chapters for each intervention "tier" formulate underlying concepts, integrate relevant bodies of prior knowledge and develop a clear justification for what was done. Likewise, pertinent findings for each program tier are presented and discussed in individual chapters. Finally, the full set of findings is carefully interwoven into a final cohesive picture that points explicitly to needed next steps.

One of the program's (and volume's) strongest features is the imaginative way in which it brings together and blends approaches often seen in the past as opposites (sometimes to the point of mutual exclusiveness). Town versus gown has become town plus gown, together, working toward the well-being of kids. Behavioral objectives and procedures have been fruitfully applied to community problems. Not only are theory, research (indeed, some pretty "hard-nosed" research), and practice all respected; they are neatly cast into mutually supportive roles. Thus, the authors actively seek out and engage relevant theoretical issues, but never in a vacuum. And they give equal time to the program's nitty-gritty, "how-to-do-it" aspects. Such practical matters as how to engage systems, how to recruit and train volunteers, how to do problem-solving training, behavioral observations and recordings, each an essential part of their total package, are patiently treated. The resulting product is satisfying both to the scholar–scientist who is oriented to theory, concepts, and hard data, and to the front-line practitioner who, understandably, wants specific, practical information. Their handling of complex design and statistical issues permits the practitioner to follow the argument and, at the same time, is specific enough to allow sophisticated researchers to evaluate the data critically. Hence, the final product will be useful and attractive for the scholar–scientist, student, and practitioner in mental health and education.

The book's style is gracious and appealing. It is free of dogmatism or authoritarian pronouncements. Openness and candor are its hallmarks. The authors think out loud as they proceed. They share major dilemmas openly and frankly with the reader. Although decisions to follow particular options are justified, alternatives are fairly represented. The processes by which critical program decisions were made are a matter of public record. Not only were the authors willing to risk the dangers of this open approach, but they actively encourage the reader to accompany them on a thoroughly educative voyage through the school of hard knocks.

Far from burying their problems and skeletons, they identify them for the reader. Part of the book's (as well the program it describes) message is that we can learn from our misses as well as from our hits. Where the authors have no answer they say so. Where they might have done things differently, they identify alternatives. Where their findings can be interpreted in several ways, they explore these possibilities in the reader's full view. And, throughout, they are vigilant and thoughtful about new program and research directions that flow from the findings.

This study does not answer all the questions it posed, with clarity and finality. Indeed, its major bodies of data include several perplexing discrepancies. As one example, positive program effects were consistently clearer and stronger using direct behavioral outcome criteria as opposed to indirect, secondary outcome criteria, and test measures. Although that key difference cannot be reconciled within the present mass of data, the authors are fully aware of it and suggest the next logical steps to take.

Thus, my most accurate crystal-ball suggests that even though some of the study's specific line-by-line findings may not survive the test of time, its pioneering, modeling contributions to conceptualization, community program development, and research will be great, indeed. This project is an exciting harbinger of things to come in community psychology. It is therefore especially instructive and heartening to note that the oldest of the five authors is age 33.

EMORY L. COWEN
Rochester, New York

Preface

This book represents a response to the current challenges facing mental health professionals. The present demand for and growing sophistication with regard to mental health services has stretched the capabilities of existing help-giving agencies to the breaking point and has demonstrated the inadequacy of our current passive, pessimistic and pathology-oriented treatment models. We begin by describing a new conceptual framework, which provides a constructive alternative to the traditional crisis-centered conceptions that currently pervade the treatment of problemmatic behavior. The model integrates the preventive orientation of community psychologists with the empirical operations of applied behavior analysts.

To be maximally viable, programs stemming from this model must evolve from a sound theoretical base, include comprehensive and empirically focused evaluative components, and be embedded in those societal institutions that foster socialization. A major aim of the book is to describe a program that incorporates these important features: an attempt to improve the interpersonal functioning of elementary school children by constructing a three-tiered intervention within a school system. On the first level, children were taught social problem-solving skills. The second level was designed to ameliorate social isolation in selected children by providing encounters with college student companions. The third level provided teachers with the classroom management skills necessary to remediate more serious academic and disciplinary problems.

We view our program as among the first concrete products of the theoretical integrative efforts of community and behavioral psychologists, and a precursor of future interventions, which will be increasingly multidisciplinary in scope. Our model demonstrates how interlocking needs of those within a university and an elementary school may be satisfied, and also points out the many challenging difficulties that occur when theoretical formulations are concretized into operational health-enhancing strategies.

We have sought to describe both the theoretical background and practical operation of our program in language appropriate for psychologists, teachers, concerned educators and consultants as well as students who aspire to professional and paraprofessional careers in the mental health and teaching fields. In order to satisfy the needs of this diverse audience, we have sought to outline and clarify our theoretical foundations, and follow this with a description of the real operating components of our multifaceted program as they evolved from this guiding framework.

In the first chapter, we discuss the larger societal forces that molded our preventive orientation. Chapter 2 describes the many practical problems that might be encountered in establishing mental health enhancement programs in schools, and specifies principles for establishing a collaborative partnership. Chapters 3, 4, and 5 provide overviews of relevant literature and describe attempts to foster competence in social problem solving, develop rewarding social interactions, and improve interpersonal and academic deficiencies in classroom settings.

These chapters provide a theoretical basis for formulating the specific strategies employed in each level of the intervention, as described in Chapter 6. Chapters 7, 8, and 9 contain evaluations of each program component. Specific empirical outcomes are supplemented by detailed case histories and other qualitative insights. In the final chapter, we describe the more general impact of the program on the school system, speculate on the future potential of such endeavors, and address several important ethical issues unique to community interventions. The appendix represents a resource for those interested in implementing the problem-solving curriculum. The text as a whole is designed to highlight our belief that community psychology must integrate its theoretical, pragmatic, and empirical boundaries if it is to continue its growth into a cohesive and viable field of endeavor. These parameters must be interwoven so that derivative programs will simultaneously increase knowledge, mesh smoothly with the operation of social institutions, and provide a basis for promoting the accountability of the entire enterprise.

In the final analysis, however, community psychology involves concerned people willing to work toward enhancing the functioning of other members of society. Without the active support of many individuals, our theoretical framework would have amounted to empty rhetoric, and our program would have been a futile endeavor. Many undergraduates at the University of Connecticut served as volunteers. Their willingness to learn, their energy and their dedication served as a source of inspiration to us.

We are also extremely grateful to the staff and students of the Hicks Memorial School in Tolland, Connecticut, especially Principal Andrew Winans, whose commitment to fostering both intellectual and emotional growth is reflected in the concerned and humanitarian environment of the school. The willingness of his staff to scrutinize and improve their effectiveness within the affective domain is a testimonial to the dedication of concerned educators everywhere. Our success as community interventionists ultimately has resulted from the efforts of these individuals, who intuitively understand the basic tenets of community psychology.

We also owe a special note of thanks to Vivian Lesh, who meticulously typed our manuscript with good humor and conscientious effort. We also appreciate the copy-editing efforts of Donna Larcen, which meshed with the excellent work of the LEA staff in producing the final product. Linda M. Collins helped enormously in the preparation of the Subject Index. We also would like to thank Emory L. Cowen, Charles D. Spielberger, and Maruice Elias, whose thoughtful suggestions improved the quality of the manuscripts.

Authorship was determined by the alphabetical ordering of our surnames. The five authors take equal responsibility for all aspects of the text, including all sins of commission and omission.

GEORGE J. ALLEN
JACK M. CHINSKY
STEPHEN W. LARCEN
JOHN E. LOCHMAN
HOWARD V. SELINGER

To:

Lynne, Mariann, Donna, Linda, and Marilyn

With Love

Part I

COLLABORATIVE INTERVENTIONS WITH SCHOOLS: MAKING THE CHANGING SCENE IN COMMUNITY PSYCHOLOGY

1

A Guiding Framework for Community-Based Interventions in School Settings

The past decade has witnessed a movement in the field of mental health away from traditional treatment procedures and toward the creation of a variety of innovative service approaches. Much of this reconceptualization of psychological practices has occurred within the emerging realm of community psychology. Some aspects of this discipline are aimed at developing and evaluating alternative methods in the reconstructive or "treatment" domains of human functioning. These approaches deal with areas such as improving methods of service delivery, using new treatment modalities and settings, and training nontraditional service providers. The goals of such innovations are to extend the reach and effectiveness of our psychotherapeutic techniques and to increase the influence of the service recipient in determining the nature of treatment.

Other aspects of community psychology are not limited to individually oriented rehabilitative approaches. The focus of psychological intervention has been expanded to include the building of psychological strengths and competencies rather than solely the amelioration of weaknesses. One of the goals within this innovative framework is to improve the capacity of our social organizations to promote growth in the social and psychological spheres.

We believe that the key theme in community psychology is the need for a broad base of preventively oriented programs to augment the currently existing mental health service network. Prevention is defined as any social or psychological intervention that promotes or enhances the emotional functioning, or reduces the incidence and prevalence of emotional maladjustment, in the general population (Bower, 1969). We heartily endorse Schwartz's (1972) contention that most current treatment strategies are stopgaps until methods of prevention can be made viable.

The purpose of this book is to describe an attempt to integrate the various theoretical trends in the field of community psychology and to arrive at a model of intervention which can meet the need for preventive services. In pursuing such an endeavor, it quickly becomes evident that any truly comprehensive program must include multiple levels of prevention. First, it is important to develop new service models for those individuals already having clearly disruptive interpersonal difficulties. These models would stress the prevention of further emotional deterioration and would also include the rehabilitation of individuals so that they can function productively in their natural environments. This type of intervention approximates Caplan's (1964) notion of tertiary prevention.

Secondly, it is crucial to focus on emerging interpersonal difficulties that are still highly susceptible to change before they become clearly detrimental. This level is similar to Caplan's concept of secondary prevention in its stress of early identification and intervention. Finally, it is imperative to include attempts to improve the psychological competencies and strengths of well-functioning individuals. Such efforts are comparable to Caplan's descriptive model of primary prevention.

This book describes a multifocused community-based intervention in a school setting that incorporated these three levels of prevention. The broadest level of intervention, designed to enhance the psychological functioning of all children, was a training program in social problem solving. This involved the development of a specific curriculum aimed toward enhancing coping skills and taught by teachers in the classroom. The second level of intervention was designed to identify potential interpersonal deficiencies in high-risk children and to remedy these problems before they became socially debilitating. This intervention employed college students, trained in the use of social reinforcement and modeling procedures, as companions to socially isolated children. The third level was planned to create a service model for children having significant academic or interpersonal difficulties. The purpose of this model was to help these children function productively in their classroom environments, thus reducing the need for outside referrals and placements. This approach involved training teachers to employ positively oriented behavior change techniques and stressing their systematic use with problematic pupils. We view Caplan's (1964) tripartite distinction as a useful analogy for conceptualizing the complex interplay of personal needs and institutional resources within a society. Throughout the book, we follow Sarason (1971) in depicting the school as a small society, and, within this framework, we view the behavior management program as roughly analogous to tertiary prevention efforts on a larger scale. Since the function of rehabilitating those with severely dysfunctional problems is not typically the province of the schools, this third level may be more accurately described as also involving a secondary preventive focus.

Before looking at these specific interventions, however, we will trace the theoretical rationale for our general approach and will elucidate a number of practical principles that should guide school-based community psychology interventions. We will also review previous work in the areas of the three levels of intervention and will provide a more extensive rationale for each of these specific approaches. Later, we will describe our multilevel intervention in detail and include an evaluation of the efficacy of each component. Let us now consider a theoretical framework for preventive interventions in the schools and examine the orienting assumptions that guided the development of our program.

The Need for Preventive Services

There are various analogies in the literature which point out the common sense of reducing the incidence of problem-causing stressors on individuals, rather than attempting the seemingly endless and perhaps ultimately futile task of rehabilitation after the damage has been done. Bower (1969), a pioneering conceptualizer of early detection and prevention techniques, describes past efforts in the field this way: "For the most part, attempts have been made to promote mental health in our society by trying to deal with the consequences of mental illness and its allied manifestations. This, it has been suggested, is about as effective as trying to turn back the Mississippi at New Orleans [p. 113]."

Cowen (1973), another articulate spokesman for the preventive approach, has detailed the many problems of the "end state" conception of treating maladaptive behavior only in its more serious forms. Our manpower supply is inadequate, our reach is limited to fairly specific population groups, and our traditional models of treatment have not proven to be particularly effective.

Current treatment orientations center around the provision of immediate and intensive support to individuals who are identified as being in crisis situations. This perspective implies an essentially short-term, and we believe short-sighted, view of the etiology and the alleviation of debilitating processes. The development of entirely new attitudes on the part of helping agencies and individuals is required in order to move toward a preventive approach.

The exclusive continuation of traditional helping practices is contraindicated for four logical and empirical reasons. First, there is a growing body of evidence (for example, Cowen, Pederson, Babigian, Izzo, & Trost, 1973) which indicates that many people who have problems early in their developmental history tend to have problems later as well. Intervention earlier in the individual's life cycle offers the hope of ameliorating the problem with less intensive effort.

Second, preventive efforts may well prove to be more humane in decreasing the intensity and duration of personal anguish and dispair experienced by the troubled individual. The consequences of preventing just one individual's wasted lifetime in a mental institution certainly justify the initial expense of money and effort on humanitarian grounds.

Third, Dorr (1972) indicated that the maintenance of a single child in a special education class costs $3,500 annually. Internment in a state hospital costs at least $4,500 for each adult and as much as $10,000 per year for a child. More recent figures from the state of Connecticut indicate that a psychiatric hospitalization for a child can run as high as $23,000 per year (Commission to Study the Consolidation of Children's Services, 1975)!

Finally, the mandate of prevention as defined above is not only to reduce the incidence of detrimental behaviors, but also to enhance the functioning of all members of our population. The ever-increasing complexity of our technological age requires the development of more adaptive life styles, not simply maintenance of the status quo. Preventive techniques hold the promise of promoting a more resilient psychosocial development that we are all going to need to handle the ever-growing challenge of emotional survival in the future.

Utilizing Social Systems to Promote Psychosocial Adaptation

A second important theme in our work is that preventive intervention must address change in our major social systems. Community psychologists have advocated that change efforts aimed at specific individuals are short-sighted and temporary at best, and may take the form of "blaming the victim" (Ryan, 1971) at worst. Strategies for correcting this situation have taken many forms. Some follow the orientation of Alinsky (1972) and propose a radical restructuring of our social institutions. Others (for example, Schmuck, Runkel, Saturen, Martell, & Derr, 1972) focus on the organizational development of institutions and attempt to improve the functioning of their staffs in such areas as communication and problem solving. Still others are developing a body of literature aimed at understanding the ecology of human behavior in institutional settings and suggesting strategies for intervention (Trickett, Kelly, & Todd, 1972). These are all extremely important trends that will ultimately help us alter social systems effectively. All are considered complementary to our orientation.

The present approach, however, focuses on working with institutions as they presently exist and attempts to help the personnel produce positive changes in the mental and emotional functioning of targeted individuals currently in such systems. Our proposed programs were not developed to replace other preventive approaches. Rather, the hope is that these interventions can be eventually integrated with other perspectives such as organizational development and ecological assessment. Our interventions are planned as basic packages that can be incorporated into a variety of school settings concurrently with other systematic innovations.

The approach employed in our program most closely resembles the work of Cowen (1973), Fairweather (1967), and Bower (1969). The programs are proposed as carefully evaluated building blocks to be included in a comprehensive approach to the enhancement of one of our primary social systems. As Bower (1973) states, "What community psychology needs is specific but solid platforms in community programs from which they can begin to put their psychology to good use. The platforms need to be built upon or close to primary institutions and to be seen by them as aiding and abetting their goals and processes [p. 16]." In many ways, this book describes the beginning of the construction of one such platform.

Schools as Settings for Mental Health Delivery Systems

The focus of this intervention is in the schools. Again, several writers have articulated many beneficial reasons for working with school systems (for example, Bower, 1969; Cowen, 1973). Schools are one of the few primary socialization systems which involve almost all children. In 1970, 58 million children spent about 25 hours a week for almost half a year in a school (Bower, 1973). Viable and humane programs aimed at promoting the mental health of children would have enormous reach if they were implemented as part of the on-going routine in school systems. School-oriented programs provide a means of preventing further separation of problem children from their peers and reduce the possibility of stigmatizing side effects inherent in current mental health practices. Schools also provide a readily available helping resource in the form of teachers. In Part II, we discuss many other advantages of early intervention in this natural setting.

The focus on schools is not meant to imply that they have been inadequate in meeting their traditional educative tasks. Rather, schools provide a unique entry point for preventive endeavors because the personnel are approachable. Schools contain many progressive and concerned individuals who want to broaden their traditionally defined teaching tasks to better meet the larger psychosocial needs of their students.

The maximally effective mental health structure will ultimately include schools and families as well as recreational and religious institutions. Bower (1972) calls these organizations "Key-Integrative Social Systems" (KISS). These in turn must be linked to a clearly integrated network of secondary treatment agencies, which Bower terms "Ailing-In-Difficulty" (AID) institutions. These include mental health clinics, courts, housing authorities, and welfare services. The field is witnessing an increasing accountability of these AID resources, and there is a nationwide move to integrate such service networks (Broskowski & Smith, 1974). Through the coordination of these networks and the development of more precise and powerful treatment technologies, mental health services will become more effective, briefer, and more specifically goal-oriented.

Increasing the productive capacity of KISS agencies and the efficacy of our AID institutions will hopefully reduce the need for large storage facilities whose function is the more or less permanent removal of people from society. Bower designates these storage agencies as "Illness-Correctional Endeavors" (ICE). To paraphrase Bower, prevention is geared toward providing children with a personally enhancing KISS so that they will require less AID and fewer will ultimately have to put on ICE. Our work in the school represents only one component, albeit quite an important one, in this ambitious general plan.

Complementary and Nondisruptive Interventions in Schools

A number of reviews examining school programs (Levine & Graziano, 1972; Zax & Specter, 1974) concur that the major problem with such interventions involves matching the sometimes conflicting needs of the school personnel and those of the interveners. This difficulty crops up in two areas, the initial implementation of proposed procedures and the subsequent assimilation of the program into the continuous operation of the school system. Zax and Specter's (1974) conclusion to their chapter on primary prevention in the schools summarizes this issue succinctly:

> The goal of establishing primary prevention programs in existing schools is difficult to achieve, but is worthwhile to pursue. The two challenges facing the interventionist are the need to demonstrate that his effort will have substantial positive effects, and the need to implement his approach by gaining entry into an institutional setting where workers may fear or discount his efforts. Although several of the programs described . . . offer evidence of positive effect, none has been widely sought or accepted within the educational community. Successful future efforts may depend upon an increased sophistication in the techniques of analyzing the social system of the school and of designing preventive interventions that fit the needs and tolerances of school personnel [p. 170].

A majority of programs conducted in institutions are billed as "demonstration projects" designed, implemented, and evaluated by consultants from outside the host organization. The consultant often has access to independent sources of financial support (such as federal or state grants), which can be used to organize resources for an attack on the presumably stultifying aspects of the current institutional environment. The influx of outside manpower can often produce dramatically promising short-term changes. However, maintaining such programs involves increasingly exhaustive efforts on the part of the outside investigator, particularly when factors such as staff ennui and fiscal cutbacks combine with the pressure (caused by short-term funding priorities) to produce positive outcomes. In all too many cases, the only fact that is demonstrated to the institutional personnel, who are notably resistent to innovations (Dunham & Weinberg, 1960, Ullmann, 1967), is that they can successfully withstand the change efforts of whoever follows in the seemingly endless flow of outside consultants into the institution.

Without the active collaboration of the school personnel, even the impact of powerful interventions gradually will fade. The ultimate question for any school intervention thus centers on whether such programs are conceived and established in such a way that they are seen as useful to the integral functioning of the system itself. We certainly do not claim to have perfected the most effective intervention in this regard, but all our strategies, from initial conception to final data collection, were designed with this goal continually in mind. Our efforts toward integrating the program into the school system are dealt with in Chapters 2 and 6.

Multifaceted Intervention Programs in Schools

A preventive endeavor should employ multiple levels of contact with the school so as to reflect the diverse needs of those who might be influenced by the program. Various intervention strategies should not be selected on purely pragmatic considerations but rather should be integrated so as to provide a theoretically cohesive framework for treatment.

To insure a cohesive and comprehensive program, we developed the three-level model of intervention mentioned earlier. The first stage addressed itself to antecedent conditions affecting the individual in the school setting. The goal in this phase was to enhance the functioning of all the individuals in the system. The concrete program reflecting this first phase of the project dealt with the development of a social problem-solving curriculum, which will be fully described in Chapters 3, 6, and 7. This intervention was carefully selected as one of the few classroom-wide programs that could be effectively implemented with broad acceptance by both the children and school personnel.

The teaching of social problem-solving strategies is a positive, growth-enhancing approach that does not invoke traditional conceptions of mental "health" or "illness." It is also one of the few interventions which has a built-in safeguard against fostering conformity behaviors because of its stress on self-development and independence. The approach is relatively value-free as it stresses procedures for solving one's own problems, rather than defining what these problems should be or what "socially acceptable" solutions might be envisioned.

On a more practical level, the curriculum is simple to implement, and it does not require role changes in the teacher or involve altering the classroom environment, as sensitivity groups or other affect-building programs often do. The program thus fulfills Fairweather's (1972) contention that "an intervention is acceptable to a society in direct proportion to the degree that the innovation does not require a change in the roles or social organization of that society [p. 77]." The social problem-solving curriculum appears to be readily adaptable to school settings and, thus, is more likely to be adopted. Finally, since the curriculum presents a sequential process for solving problems, it holds the hope of preparing children to handle unanticipated future difficulties and may prove to be one source of enhancement for "coping with tomorrow" (Toffler, 1970).

The second level of prevention in our trifocal model deals with the process of developing interpersonal relationships. This approach most closely resembles the work of Cowen (1973) and Bower (1969), and approximates Caplan's (1964) concept of secondary prevention. It focuses on carefully identifying children who may be developing interpersonal difficulties and matches them with resourceful, energetic adult models who attempt to help each child improve the quality of his or her peer relationships. The identified children are not labeled as "ill" or "abnormal." Rather, the program utilizes the active environmental contingencies that operate as influences on the behavior of the children. This is accomplished by having the companions involved with the identified children in natural group play situations on the playground.

The involvement of the modeling figure is consciously minimized and aimed at promoting the child's participation in general social interactions. The adult serves as a constructive and sensitive facilitator of social encounters, and interactive episodes are limited to nonstigmatizing situations such as playground or lunch activities. Although carefully trained adults work primarily with individual children who are targeted, the ultimate goal of this endeavor is the psychosocial enhancement of the play environment of the children on the school grounds.

The third level of intervention trains teachers in techniques for systematically rewarding positive behaviors and ignoring undersirable activities of children already identified as having significant academic or interpersonal difficulties. It is a consultee-centered approach which resembles Caplan's (1964) tertiary level of prevention. Although the ultimate benefits of this program are aimed toward the child, the focus of change is on the behavior of the teacher.

This aspect of the program introduces concepts of "objective teaching" (Meacham & Wiesen, 1974) to teachers. In particular, the approach emphasizes the appropriate use of praise, the specification of particular behavioral problems, and a focus on finding effective controlling contingencies. This strategy deemphasizes casting blame on the child or engaging in stigmatizing labeling practices. A "problem student" or "intractible child" is viewed as a person who has specific and modifiable behaviors that annoy others.

Although a number of writers (for example, Andrews & Karlins, 1971; Chorover, 1973) have castigated this approach as a form of "big brotherism," we believe that the methods of such training need not be coercive, nor the end products docile and dependent. Any set of potentially powerful behavior control strategies can be misused. However, this approach provides the teacher with a set of procedures that can be employed to increase the behavioral competence and self-control of all the children in a class. The ethical considerations raised by an intervention such as ours will be more fully elaborated in the final chapter. The major points to be emphasized here are that each program was designed to be functionally adapted to fit the on-going routine patterns of the typical elementary school, to be effective, and to be humane.

Increasing the Scope of Mental Health Manpower Resources

We readily acknowledge that the number of mental health providers is presently, and will continue to be, inadequate to meet the ever-increasine need for effective service. Mental health professionals can expand their service reach in two ways. The first is to develop orientations based on various forms of indirect consultation models. A general design for a collaborative intervention model has been described by Chinsky (1975). The specific collaborative strategies employed in this project are outlined in Chapter 2. Approaches such as these allow the mental health professional to expand his or her reach geometrically.

Teachers in the school system are an excellent resource for the provision of preventively oriented services. In addition to expanding the impact of the professional, utilizing members of the school has two other positive consequences. First, including these individuals in the intervention insures their active involvement and promotes their sense of ownership of the project. Second, such participation enhances the likelihood that such programs will be maintained in the system once the "outside" interventionists have left. In summary, their inclusion via the consultee-centered model provides the necessary pool of expert resources within the institution necessary for the growth and further development of the original intervention.

Cowen (1973) and others have documented the effectiveness of a wide variety of nonprofessionals in a variety of settings. Utilization of these individuals is a second method of meeting our ever-growing mental health service needs. One of the most frequently used nonprofessional groups has been college students. Our intervention was designed to include this valuable human resource as well. College students, organized and trained as described in Chapters 2 and 6, are an invaluable asset to a comprehensive intervention in school settings. They are a large, energetic, and flexible group that can serve a variety of functions including supervision and research evaluation as well as provision of direct service.

It is important to emphasize that the utilization of both these novel helping resources is not intended to replace traditional service providers. Instead, their role involves enhancing the work of the professional. We believe that a union of this type has a mutually beneficial outcome for the psychologist as well as for the nonprofessional. Such extensions of manpower will eventually have a profound effect on the role of professionals by increasing their use as consultants, conceptualizers, and evaluators of community interventions (Rotter, 1973). In many ways, this book describes the effective integration of a collaborative mental health team in action.

Linking Community Psychology with a Behavioral Orientation

Another major theme stressed in this book is the combination of a community or systems perspective with a behavioral approach. A complete model of community intervention includes two elements: a strategy for approaching potential problems and a systematic framework for describing human functioning (Rappaport & Chinsky, 1974). The preventive orientation defines our approach as one of actively seeking potential problems rather than waiting for their appearance in more severe forms. The second facet of our model derives from the behavioral-analytic framework, which developed relatively independently of the community movement (Maley & Harshbarger, 1974).

The systems approach stresses the broader social perspective and organizational focus of mental health interventions. Recent literature (Harshbarger &

Maley, 1974) has cited the downward extension of this approach toward a more direct emphasis on influencing the individual within this system. Behavior analysts, on the other hand, have traditionally been concerned about promoting environments that favor the maintenance of adaptive behavior, but they have not developed a systematic body of knowledge for altering social systems to achieve this goal (Reppucci & Saunders, 1974).

A mutually beneficial "marriage of convenience" between these perspectives seems to be slowly emerging in the field. The effort described in this book is one of the first experimental attempts to examine the feasibility of this combination. The broader implications of the systems perspective have been noted above. The consequences of the merger from the behavioral-analytic viewpoint are the following:

1. The intervention emphasizes changing specific behaviors of key persons in the system and providing meaningful payoffs for such changes.

2. The training techniques are designed to be specific and are oriented toward the achievement of behavioral criteria. This does not necessarily mean the adoption of a strict behavior modification stance, but it does imply a utilization of current knowledge about behavior change procedures to improve the efficacy of training both staff and students.

3. The intervention focuses on behavior change as the most salient of all possible outcome criteria. Chapter 2 provides a rationale for including multiple channels of outcome information. Verbal reports of changes in behavior, attitudes, and personality attributes are considered to be important. However, the actual documentation of behavior change is considered to be the sine qua non of demonstrable efficacy within any preventive endeavor.

4. The final adaptation from the behavioral perspective is the rigorous methodological tradition of this approach. While this point will receive further elaboration later in the chapter, we want to stress the idea that the empirically oriented methodological position of the behaviorists is perhaps their most useful contribution to the community movement.

Use of a behavioral approach does not carry an implicit assumption that changing individuals within a system will automatically result in improvements in the organizational structure. Our intervention is developed from a wider, combined perspective and is aimed at enhancing the health-providing functions of the system as a whole. In this case, we are attempting to introduce new curricula, enrich the quality of peer interactions, and facilitate the teacher's effectiveness in dealing with problem children. These areas were chosen, as noted above, from a careful consideration of maximally productive and practicable points of impact in the school setting.

The actual implementation strategies and outcome criteria of the program, however, are developed within a behavioral framework. The utility of *any* system-focused intervention must ultimately be measured by its effect on the behavior of the members of that system. Behavior analysts have been developing a wide variety of assessment techniques that can be applied for such purposes. Likewise, any system-oriented intervention must be implemented with the help and cooperation of the members of that system. Behavior analysts have developed clear and practical guidelines for training new behavior and rewarding people for adopting new role functions.

Changes in student and teacher behaviors are the major focus of this assessment. However, we assumed that a multitude of other individual and organizational changes in the school system resulted from our intervention. These changes will not be stressed in detail, but they are implicit in our description of the implementation and results of the project, and they will be summarized in the last chapter. Each of these could be operationalized and assessed objectively (for example, number of class minutes spent in the new curriculum, modes of interaction in the problem-solving classes, and so on). Further development of naturalistic and systematic observational procedures emanating from ecological and applied behavioral research will facilitate this process in the future.

The point to be stressed in this section is that a focus on *the individual in the system* necessitates a combination of these two perspectives. Community interventions can be made at broader organizational levels and still maintain clear and precise behavioral objectives and outcomes. This contention is emphasized because of the potential for misunderstanding between researchers in the two separate fields of community psychology and behavioral analysis. Another goal of our project, then, is to demonstrate that the two approaches can be productively integrated without compromising the strengths of either one.

The Need for Experimentally Rigorous Interventions

The final interlocking theme reflected in this program is its experimental orientation. As mentioned elsewhere (Chinsky, 1975; Lachenmeyer, 1970), psychologists often have had to choose between engaging in methodologically sound but trivial research or conducting less rigorous investigations that promised socially useful outcomes. One mandate of this intervention was to close this artificial gap. We believe that, if psychologists are to have any meaningful impact on societal functioning, they must be able to apply their research skills to real systems which affect the lives of real people. This requirement presents the field with numerous and often seemingly insurmountable difficulties.

The elusive and contradictory criteria of mental "health" and "pathology" currently available in the field dictate choosing a criterion that embodies the highest visibility, the least conceptual ambiguity, and the fewest procedural complications. Hospital administrators can point with pride to the fact that their institutions "processed," for example, 5800 "cases" in a given year. This sort of information constitutes highly visible evidence of providing service to any who demand accountability from the institution and can be used to justify requests for increased fiscal support in the future. The "bending," "folding," or "mutilating" of a few of the cases is regarded as an unfortunate but practically inevitable side-effect.

One of the special problems of preventive endeavors is that the effects of such efforts are invisible. Preventive strategies provide much more ambiguous criteria of success, the most notable being the absence of behavioral deficits or pathologies, however they may be defined. Criteria of this type provide low visibility evidence, involve conceptual confusions, and are administratively complex. Thus, practitioners of preventive enterprises become increasingly hard-pressed to justify the continuation of the endeavor to those with fiscal and political power. The more successful a preventive endeavor is, the more it contributes to its own eventual demise.

One excellent method of insuring that preventive efforts have clearly interpretable outcomes is by employing clearly interpretable experimental designs. The use of various types of control groups, however, involves an ethical dilemma which centers on the denial of treatment to those who need it. We believe that our current ignorance of truly effective treatment variables justifies any short-term exclusions that will increase our knowledge of relevant psychotherapeutic parameters. Even when well-designed interventions produce unequivocally promising outcomes, the visibility problem still may hamper attempts to implement the program on a wide scale.

No preventive program can demonstrate its efficacy in reducing the incidence or prevalence of variously defined disorders in the population without long-term follow-up. Unfortunately, even longitudinal research cannot provide unambiguous evidence of such reductions because of the multitude of other factors which might influence the outcomes over long periods of time (Paul, 1969).

A partial solution to these dilemmas involves using what Flanagan (1971, p. 119) calls "intermediate criteria" of adjustment. These dimensions may be behaviorally assessed within the time constraints of a preventive intervention, and their presence is viewed as indicative of more consequential and far-reaching criteria of social adequacy. Thus, increases in intermediate criteria as a result of participation in a preventive program provide high visibility evidence of efficacy. We return to this topic in the next two chapters.

We have already pointed out what the behavior-analytic tradition has to offer a community orientation. One long-standing drawback to the behavior modification literature has been the failure to adequately deal with problems of entry into social systems (Reppucci & Saunders, 1974). Tightly designed and well-controlled case studies and small-scale interventions are crisply reported, but seldom does this literature discuss the more general characteristics of the settings in which the endeavors were conducted. The community psychology movement has provided such information and, in addition, has taught behavioral psychologists to become more sympathetic to the problems faced by the applied researcher.

Because of legitimate concerns for the rights of every participant, researchers are obligated to insure that no damage or serious misunderstandings result from their work. Interventions must be carefully planned so as to ensure the ultimate welfare of all who are involved. The results obtained from preventive programs must be a valid reflection of whatever changes took place and must be as widely disseminated as possible to insure maximal information for future researchers and social planners.

A Review of the Basic Orienting Assumptions

In summary, our intervention is founded on eight broad and interrelated guiding principles. These points have been presented at the outset to assist the reader in clearly understanding our operating framework. They are briefly restated below:

1. There is a need to supplement existing mental health services with a wide and varied range of preventive programs.
2. These preventive programs should be addressed to meeting the mental health needs of those within our major social systems.
3. Schools, as primary socializing institutions, can be employed to develop specific and functional services aimed at promoting the social and psychological well-being of children.
4. Preventive mental health services in schools must contain components that complement the usual role functions of administrative and teaching personnel.
5. To be maximally effective, these services should be multifaceted so as to provide a comprehensive set of strategies for ameliorating the wide variety of potential problems that can beset children.
6. The reach of professional mental health manpower can be expanded by using consultative techniques and through the recruitment, selection, and training or nontraditional helping resources.
7. Community psychology can be productively linked with a behavioral orientation in terms of both methodology and behavior-training procedures.
8. Preventive interventions must be experimentally oriented and evaluated by means of precise behavioral data.

In Chapter 2 procedures are outlined for developing collaborative efforts between professional consultant groups and the school system. It considers issues of entry, as well as the preparation and organization of school personnel and outside paraprofessional resources. It also discusses the problems with and strategies for integrating the two groups and establishing the communication network necessary for a successful program. It concludes with a general overview of our conception of the evaluation component necessary for inclusion in any school intervention program.

2

Establishing a Partnership: Problems and Principles

We pointed out in Chapter 1 that behavior change strategies are likely to produce efficacious and durable effects to the extent that the procedures encompass a dual concern for both the organizational structure itself and the individuals within that social network. Practitioners in the area of community psychology have focused their efforts on changing social systems, whereas the emphasis in more traditional mental health practices (including behavioral analysis and behavior modification) has been on fostering change within individuals.

Malott (1974) has provided a theoretical framework for improving the delivery of mental health services within a social structure through what he calls a "systems design" approach. He views the analysis of a social organization as involving six states: studying the existing structure; specifying innovative behavioral goals and outcomes; designing, implementing, and evaluating the new system, and recycling (that is, continually revising the system on the basis of previously obtained evaluative information). This chapter draws upon Malott's framework as a starting point for considering the kinds of practicable strategies that can be employed to form truly collaborative interventions with school systems. The specific methods which were actually employed in the development and evaluation of our real-life mental health delivery system are presented in Chapter 6. Both chapters involve an integration of the deductive-conceptual approach of the organizational analyst with the inductive and empirical orientation of the behavior analyst (Maley & Harshbarger, 1974).

The task of transforming the intervention strategies from a conceptual model into workable procedures in a real-life setting is a formidable one and generates a number of problems. Since the success of any intervention program ultimately depends upon the resolution of such difficulties, this chapter also presents a summary of the practical issues which are likely to arise and proposes guidelines for their successful resolution. The problems may be conceptualized as falling into five distinct areas relating to the following:

1. obtaining access to and administrative support within the institution;
2. organizing paraprofessional resources outside of the host institution;
3. training members of the host organization;
4. developing communication links between the paraprofessional and institutional staff;
5. evaluating program effectiveness in a realistic yet comprehensive manner.

Gaining Access to and Support within School Systems

Like other institutions, schools are complex systems that function in accord with both formal and informal networks of norms (Sarason, 1971; Schmuck *et al.,* 1972). Investigators (for example, Goffman, 1961; Ullmann, 1967) have demonstrated that members of institutions often resist innovations, especially if the source of change is located outside of the organizational structure. Both the consultants and volunteers tend to be viewed as "outsiders." The implications of being an outsider are largely negative; teachers may initially view the proposed change program as requiring extra work on their part, as involving few meaningful incentives for themselves, and as serving the self-interests of the outside intervening agents. If these perceptions are not modified, any implementation endeavor will be either actively resisted or sabotaged in a subtle manner.

This problem will almost always appear, although careful consideration of potential entry difficulties can often minimize negative repercussions on the proposed intervention. One particularly useful strategy involves entering the institution slowly and gradually. Innovative programs contain both exciting and frightening aspects from the viewpoint of the organizational staff. Excitement derives from anticipating the potential benefits of a successful intervention; caution is dictated by an often healthy fear of unanticipated consequences produced by the change effort. Developing a series of planning meetings prior to the intervention with a few important staff members of the institution can serve to increase acceptance and diminish apprehension. The focus of such meetings should be to gain the trust and confidence of key administrators, for without their active and enthusiastic support, any project is doomed to failure before it even begins.

Trust may be developed most quickly by maintaining a frank and honest approach to the potential benefits and liabilities of the proposed intervention. This point may seem so self-evident that one wonders why it is even mentioned. However, the failure of many potentially useful programs is often due to a cavalier disregard for pinpointing the rights, responsibilities, and rewards of all participants. Clarification of such issues with administrators allows these individuals to gain personal knowledge of the outside change agents, which hopefully will reduce antagonism toward the change project. Some consultants (for example, Wood & Bland, 1971) advocate drawing up a formal contract between the collaborating parties involved in the project, even if no form of financial remuneration is provided to the consultants.

Research conducted within residential treatment institutions (Schmidmeyr & Weld, 1971) indicates that administrators and the personnel providing direct services have widely divergent views of the importance of potentially useful innovations. Negotiating with administrators is a necessary first step in implementing an innovation. Discussions, however, must also be gradually extended to the individuals who will be actively involved in the day-to-day operation of the program. Once adminstrative approval has been obtained, meetings with teachers should be organized. The focus of these meetings should again be toward clarifying the advantages and drawbacks of the program in order to reduce apprehension.

Potential teacher antagonism can be most effectively reduced if the consultants bill themselves as experts in the general principles of behavioral prediction and control, and if the teachers are treated as experts concerning the specific setting in which these principles are to be applied. When both the outsiders and the inside staff members view themselves as having expertise in separate yet complementary areas, a truly collaborative effort is almost certain to result.

True collaboration has three distinct advantages over the imposition of the proposed program by higher administrative officials. First, teachers will be more willing to offer concrete suggestions about the needs of the child population as well as the mechanics of implementing the specific change strategies. Teachers really are extremely knowledgeable about the school environment and adherence to their suggestions by the consultants will save much aggravation and wasted effort during the implementation stage of the project. Secondly, once the inside staff realizes that they actually do have some impact in determining the operation of the project, they will be more likely to invest greater effort to achieve a successful outcome. Finally, this approach helps ensure that both the consultants and the teachers remain task oriented, instead of wasting their resources on unresolvable issues such as personality conflicts. By utilizing a problem-oriented approach, the consultants can more quickly destroy the distinction between insiders and outsiders, which inhibits the free and honest flow of important information.

Organizing Outside Paraprofessional Resources

Most practitioners would agree that numerous difficulties will be encountered when moving from the preliminary planning stage to the execution of the formal procedures of the project. These problems will vary in terms of their complexity, magnitude, and duration. With regard to building an extramural paraprofessional structure, most problems can be expected to occur during the selection, organization, and training of volunteers. Careful consideration of potential problems in these areas can considerably strengthen the efficacy of using these nontraditional human resources.

Selection of Paraprofessionals

One major cornerstone of the community mental health movement has been the use of qualified volunteers in various paraprofessional treatment capacities (Goodman, 1972; Rappaport, Chinsky, & Cowen, 1971). This use of human resources magnifies the impact of the professional by freeing him or her from having to conduct individually focused psychotherapy. The geometric increase in a consultant's effectiveness as a change agent, as a result of using paraprofessionals, will be described in Chapter 5. The activities of the professional in this type of mental health delivery system are directed toward the selection and training of volunteers, as well as toward more general issues of program conceptualization and evaluation (Rotter, 1973).

Volunteers have been drawn from many diverse sources. One problem faced by the consultant who employs others in various treatment capacities is the fact that any program is only as good as the volunteers who staff it. College students represent an extremely large, energetic and enthusiastic source of volunteers. This heterogeneous group of young adults has been quite maligned as a result of the protests against the war in Vietnam, which severely shook the educational system of this country several years ago. However, we found the college volunteers to be bright, altruistic, deeply committed to developing an egalitarian society, and willing to work toward helping less fortunate others achieve better lives. They also possess the energy and optimism that age begins to rob from the professional.

Using students from nearby colleges to staff programs for the delivery of mental health services has several advantageous aspects which involve, first, the satisfaction of complementary needs of the volunteers and the host organization, and, secondly, control over the quality of the performances of the volunteers. Colleges have an abundance of students who are seeking exposure to relevant practical training experiences outside of the classroom. Elementary and high school systems, on the other hand, have a continual need for volunteers to help run supplemental extracurricular programs, which often receive only marginal budgetary support. Such schools can provide a utilitarian training locale for students who wish to obtain relevant educational experiences.

Academic courses can be built around on-going volunteer programs in outside agencies to combine didactic learning with practical opportunities to apply what is taught in the classroom, thereby making the learning process more efficient and enjoyable. From the student's perspective, field work often provides experiential information which is helpful in making an intelligently informed decision about a future career. For example, many undergraduates express a desire to work with children after graduation. This somewhat vague career goal is often based on what the student has learned in academic courses. A semester spent actually interacting with children provides the student with a better perspective of his or her capabilities in this area and may serve to strengthen or negate the initial career decision. Students who hope to obtain postgraduate educational training often find that participation in volunteer programs allows faculty supervisors to learn more about them as individuals. Their instructors are then able to write more discriminating letters of recommendation that enhance their chances of gaining admission to graduate programs.

The satisfaction of engaging in volunteer activities is often not enough of a payoff to maintain high quality performances by paraprofessionals over an extended period of time. Many students in volunteer programs become disillusioned when confronted with the obstacles that can block the occurrence of meaningful and rapid changes in institutional settings. Attrition of a substantial proportion of the initial volunteers can be fatal to the success of an intervention project. Attrition can be reduced by carefully explaining the mechanics and goals of the project to potential volunteers so as to insure that their expectations are realistic. Providing continual feedback about each volunteer's performance is another excellent method of ensuring long-term participation. Offering academic credit for supervised volunteer work allows the consultant to exert greater control over the quality of the performances provided by the participants. Ideally, feedback ought to be provided frequently, and suggestions for doing this are presented later in this chapter.

Although careful selection of participants is crucial to the ultimate success of the volunteer project, not much research has been directed toward delineating effective volunteers from those whose nuisance value outweighs their usefulness. One major approach, which involves attempting to predict performance from measures that purport to assess stable personality characteristics of volunteers, has been notably unsuccessful (Mischel, 1968). In one important example, Rappaport *et al.* (1971) failed to find a relationship between the degree of accurate empathy manifested by student volunteers and the quality of interactions between these students and long-term hospitalized mental patients. These same authors reported that assessment techniques, which involve behaviorally rated samples of interpersonal situations, such as the Group Assessment of Interpersonal Traits (Goodman, 1972), provide a more promising approach to the selection of volunteers.

In summary, since the volunteers will almost always be asked to interact with others in a variety of formal and informal social situations, well-developed interpersonal skills, verbal fluency, and tact appear to be extremely important selection criteria. Ratings of such characteristics may be obtained through a variety of procedures including interviews with project administrators, peer ratings following brief social interactions, or actual observation of work-related samples of social behavior.

Organization of Paraprofessional Resources

Selecting a group of interpersonally skilled and enthusiastic volunteers is obviously the first necessary step in effectively utilizing paraprofessional resources for treatment. However, even the most highly qualified volunteers will not function well unless they are properly trained. Before training per se can begin, however, the consultant must decide how the volunteers are to be organized. Five factors dictate the extent of organization necessary for maximum efficiency and effectiveness. The first of these is the general level of competence manifested by the volunteers. While the authors believe that certain behaviorally oriented training procedures can be used to increase the competence of almost any volunteer, large individual differences in skills and abilities will initially exist and must be taken into account. The four remaining factors encompass the size and complexity of the actual intervention program. These determinants include:

1. the number of volunteers needed for participation;
2. the quantity of different functions in which the volunteers will be engaged;
3. the complexity of the training procedures to be employed; and
4. the need for new volunteers as a result of either expansion of the project or extension of the duration of the actual program.

In many cases, all four determinants will be interrelated. Projects that employ a small number of volunteers permit a great deal of interaction between the student participants and the consultant, and each volunteer may be asked to engage in several different activities such as observing, scoring assessments, and so on. In addition, small programs usually involve implementing techniques that are easily learned, and such projects typically have short lifespans. Addition of an evaluative component to service projects often necessitates a more complex organizational structure.

One particularly efficient method of using volunteer resources in a large project is grouping participants into small teams and arranging these units into a hierarchy to facilitate training and supervision. Although the complexity of the framework will be directly related to the size of the project, many organizational hierarchies can be patterned after the model presented in Figure 2.1. For purposes of clarity, the roles described in the model have been associated with specific functions within the hierarchy, although in real-life settings the occupant of any given role could theoretically carry out tasks other than those described. The general structure of the collaborative intervention model has been described by Chinsky (1975). The specific applications of this model in an intervention are outlined below.

The consultants have overall responsibility for all phases of the project. The first major function of these individuals is to gain entry into the host organization. Issues of program design and evaluation, staff recruitment, and training

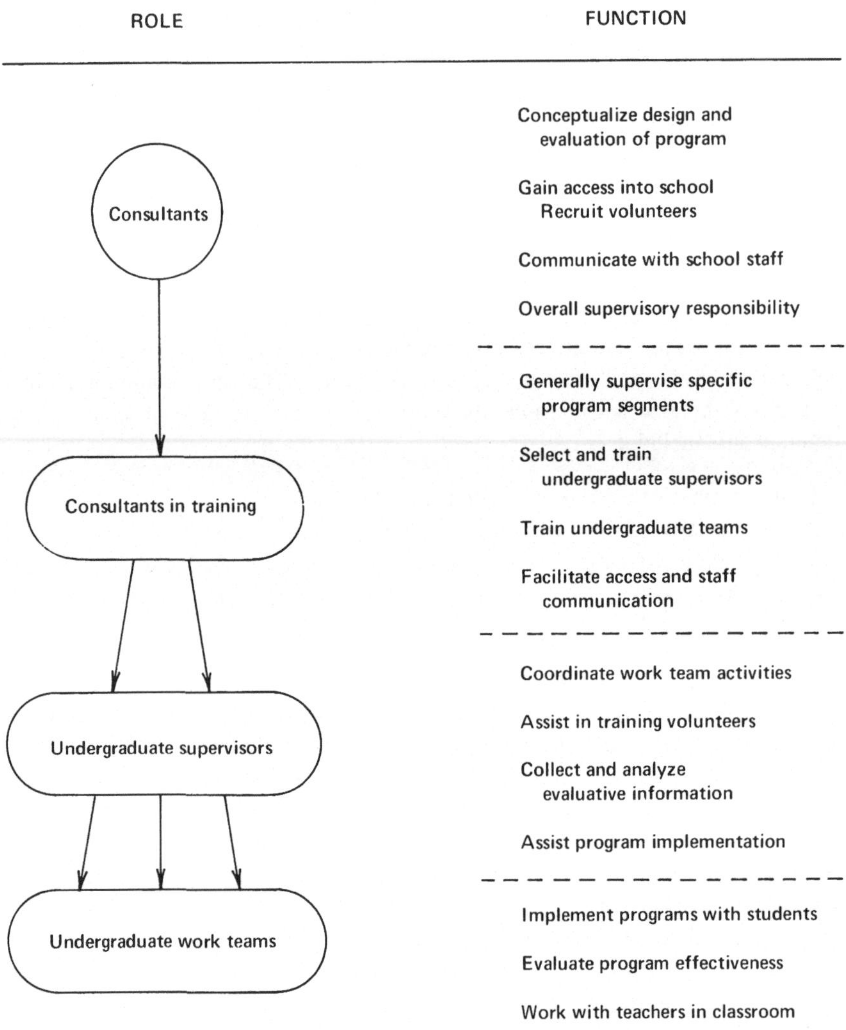

FIG. 2.1 Roles and functions of the participants in a collaborative intervention model.

may be unilaterally decided by the consultants, although resolving them in conjunction with school administrators and consultants-in-training is preferable. Graduate students make excellent program administrators at the level of novice consultants, and their participation provides them with opportunities to evaluate socially meaningful interventions while fulfilling graduate research requirements.

Undergraduate supervisors may be drawn from the larger pool of volunteers on the basis of demonstrating well-developed administrative and interpersonal skills, a sense of responsibility, and commitment to the success of the intervention. These individuals can serve a wide variety of functions which include working out assignments for the undergraduate team members, resolving scheduling conflicts, assisting in the training of volunteers, and coordinating the collection of evaluative data. In long-term projects, students who demonstrate superior skills while working on undergraduate teams often make excellent candidates for supervising the training of new volunteer recruits.

Most of the undergraduates will be assigned to teams, and each team should have a specific function in terms of implementing assigned procedures or evaluating the effects of the intervention. It is these individuals who will have the greatest daily contact with the target children in the school. Ideally, those undergraduates who are engaged in evaluation should not be allowed to interact extensively with those participants who conduct the treatment. Separation of teams helps prevent inadvertent bias on the part of the evaluators because of their having knowledge of the goals of the project.

Training of Selected Paraprofessionals

Proper training is obviously essential for conducting the intervention in an effective and nondisruptive manner. Training procedures will vary with regard to both format and content, depending upon the precise nature of the planned intervention. This section deals with how what is known about human learning can be utilized to develop effective and efficient training procedures. The authors assume that the principles articulated below have general applicability to many diverse content areas. These same strategies can also be employed in training participating staff in the host organization, although status differences between the student volunteers and teachers necessitates some changes in application. The suggested procedures are based on the application of Skinner's (1968) operant learning theory to teaching environments.

Several community-based interventions have used volunteers who received minimal training. Among the most notable examples was a large-scale project conducted by Rappaport *et al.* (1971). These investigators sent student volunteers into the "back wards" of a large urban mental hospital with instructions to interact with long-term patients. The volunteers were instructed to "act naturally" and "be yourself" and, armed with only these instructions, were able to promote substantial improvement in the social and emotional well-being of the target population. Although training was minimized, volunteer morale was kept high through requiring participation in a series of meetings during which the students discussed their experiences and ventilated their fears and concerns. This research project points out the importance of carefully selecting potential volunteers so as to obtain a high quality source of potential help.

Although the enthusiasm and spontaniety of such volunteers does have a positive impact on those being serviced in community interventions, a certain amount of formal training is obviously desirable for providing the participants with a framework for their activities. Adequately trained volunteers will be able to enter the school system with more confidence, and perform their duties more effectively, than service providers who have received minimal practice in using the techniques they will ultimately be expected to employ. Specific training procedures have been demonstrated to increase both the efficacy and efficiency of intervention efforts with children (Ross, Ross, & Evans, 1971). Effective training involves consideration of three basic areas: (1) developing adaptive attitudes toward learning, (2) organizing the learning environment, and (3) rewarding progressive improvements in performance.

Attitudes toward learning. Analysis of the psychosocial aspects of the typical learning environment found in college classrooms has relevance for training volunteers from this population. Horn (1969) has specified the operational attitudinal factors in the form of nine student expectations of what constitutes "proper" classroom behavior. Two dominant themes underlying these expectations are (1) students are relatively passive recipients of the learning content provided by an instructor, and (2) learning is a competitive rather than a cooperative enterprise. These themes suggest that trainees will manifest many characteristics of passive learners (for example, not asking questions for fear of appearing ignorant or stupid) unless steps are taken to promote a more active orientation. A less competitive and more active learning atmosphere can be fostered by stressing the viewpoint that making mistakes is an integral part of the learning process. This attitude can be conveyed both verbally and nonverbally, but this initial message must be bolstered by continually employing remediable and nonpunitive methods of assessing trainee performance. This raises the second issue which concerns developing a learning environment that is conducive to learning.

Organizing the learning environment. During initial training sessions, the importance of the contribution of every trainee should be clearly specified. Emphasis should be placed on the cooperative nature of the training enterprise. Specifying the functions of each participant within the context of the overall project increases enthusiasm and helps the volunteers gain clearer insight into the relevance of their personal assignments. Since the intervention will be only as strong as its weakest members, the likelihood of ultimate success is heightened if all participants come to feel a personal involvement with the program.

Communicating the importance of personal commitment can be accomplished only through ensuring that the trainees experience the enthusiasm of the training staff. Trainer commitment must also be evidenced by the investment of time and effort in the training process. The trainees will rightfully disbelieve statements concerning the value of their contributions if they view the consultants as distant and uninvolved in the training procedures.

Much research has indicated that learning new skills can be greatly facilitated by (1) breaking the material to be learned into small steps, (2) sequencing the steps into a progressive order of difficulty, (3) establishing clear standards as to what constitutes mastery of each step, and (4) providing feedback about performance at every step. Using these procedures can help nullify student competition and passivity in practicum-learning classes. The authors also believe that the four procedures can be more efficaciously used in conjunction with a teaching format that combines didactic presentations with practical exercises. When trainees are aware that they will be asked to perform tasks that are described via lectures or demonstrated by the consultant, they are likely to pay better attention and ask more questions. The actual performance of the practical tasks allows trainees to learn about the real-life problems inherent in implementing the techniques and provides multiple opportunities to remedy errors and receive corrective feedback.

Any task which a participant may be asked to perform can be broken into simpler components. For example, the task of training observers to rate the behavior of elementary school children involves at least five components: memorizing definitions of the behaviors to be rated, using a stopwatch, learning symbolic recording notations for the behaviors, accurately marking the notations on rating sheets, and quickly and accurately identifying target children. After these discrete skills have been learned, they must be combined so that the observer can handle the stopwatch while watching the children and marking the coding sheets.

The smooth integration of these behaviors during the rating occasions decreases the interruption of classroom activities. Fumbling around with the watch, pens, and coding sheets causes disruptions which annoy teachers and may sensitize the children to the fact that they are being observed. Mastery of these basic skills is also necessary before more complex procedures, such as gathering synchronized ratings with other observers for reliability estimates, can be made. Ideally, each component skill should be defined in measurable terms so that progress is readily observable by the trainees. No rules exist for determining how many steps a behavioral-training hierarchy should have. If the hierarchy contains too many redundant steps, the training process becomes very slow and boring to the trainees. If the transitional steps are too far apart, improvement might not be apparent and discouragement might result. The consultant is forced to employ a trial-and-error approach in continually revising the training sequences as a result of feedback provided by trainee performance. The trainer is very likely going to make some judgemental errors while doing this. By freely admitting these mistakes, the consultant can provide a graphic demonstration to the trainees that errors are indeed part of the learning process. This strategy will help strengthen the original attitudinal set toward learning and further reduce passivity and competition among the trainees.

Rewarding improvements in acquired skills. Skinner (1958), Howe (1970) and many others have demonstrated that specific feedback about mistakes in performance reduces the rate of subsequent errors. Feedback is crucial in teaching new skills, and it ought to be essentially positive. Employees in institutions often find that they receive no feedback unless they perform at a subpar level; acceptable job performance is the expected norm and virtually ignored. This type of feedback arrangement is very ineffective for teaching new skills or even maintaining acceptable job performance, since trainees are given no information that is useful in discriminating adequate from unacceptable completion of tasks.

One additional strategy for enhancing learning needs to be discussed. The training environment should be organized so that every trainee is given many trials to learn a new skill. Feedback about prior performance is useless unless it can be immediately applied toward improving the particular skill being trained. If the learning environment has been properly designed, it is easy to build in rewards for improvements in trainee performance.

Three specific procedures exert powerful impact in this area. First, keeping permanent records of the improvements manifested by trainees allows these individuals to view a summary of their progress over time. Research in many diverse areas (for example, Broden, Hall, & Mitts, 1971; Loeber, 1971; Thomas, 1971) has indicated that graphs of prior performance serve a rewarding function that makes subsequent improvement more likely to occur. Such charts have two additionally useful functions. Every human being has "bad days"–periods of time when nothing seems to go right. One psychological consequence of having a bad day in a training situation is to become discouraged and doubt one's abilities as a trainee. When an individual feels like this, he or she is likely to extend the feelings of discouragement into the past and future, assuming that nothing has been learned and that meaningful learning will not occur. Reference to graphs can demonstrate to a discouraged trainee that progress has in fact been made toward achievement of the training goals.

The second function of permanent records involves their use as diagnostic instruments. It may be that a trainee has realistic difficulties in mastering a particular skill. Reference to the charts may help the consultant develop a remedial strategy for alleviating the problem.

Another useful procedure involves placing rapid learners into positions where they help teach those trainees who learn more slowly. This technique allows more training trials for the slower learner, and provides the quick learner with a test of his or her skill acquisition. Contrary to some popular opinions, you must know something well before you can teach it adequately. Overlearning the skill certainly cannot hurt a trainee, and some evidence (Pagano, 1970) indicates that overlearning improves the performance of people in stressful situations.

The final strategy involves the liberal use of praise. Our society in general, and bureaucratic structures in particular, seem to rely more on punishment and negative reinforcement procedures than on positive feedback to teach new skills and to maintain behavioral control. The common complaint of many employees in institutions that "everybody (administrators) ignores me unless I mess something up, and then I really hear about it" is a typical example of this tendency.

Most people are not very skilled at either praising others or receiving praise in a graceful manner. Children and adolescents are often ridiculed by their peers for praising the work or efforts of others, and many view the praiser as attempting to improperly influence others for selfish reasons. "Browning," "teacher's pet" and "apple polisher" are some of the less derogatory labels which are applied to individuals who frequently use praise. Most other labels would require deleting expletives. As a result of peer disapproval, people often stop praising, and, as adults, we become suspicious of and uncomfortable around those who praise often.

Praising others is a skill, and like any other skill, it improves with practice. Teachers who are asked to praise improvements in the academic performance of their students as part of behavioral intervention programs (for example, Breyer & Allen, 1975; Thomas, Becker, & Armstrong, 1968) often report that their initial efforts sound "phony." This same research has indicated, however, that even phony praise is effective in improving student behavior. In addition, as the teachers become more proficient in praising their pupils, their concerns about this issue disappear. This finding suggests that those who view their efforts to praise others as insincere are probably reacting to their own initial discomfort in using this technique.

Praise has positive information value for trainees since it provides feedback about what they have accomplished. Negative statements inform trainees about what they have *not* done well, and exclusive reliance on this form of feedback certainly does not enhance rapid learning of skills. Liberal use of praise, however, does allow supervisors to provide occasional critical feedback without encountering defensive or hostile reactions. In addition, praise generally makes people feel good about themselves and competent about their abilities. Such positive feelings will often increase a trainee's willingness to exert extra effort to ensure the success of the program.

Training Participants from the Host Organization

The processes of fostering positive and dynamic attitudes toward learning, developing an efficient organizational format for training, and making the progression toward mastery of specific skills highly visible for the participants may also be generally applied to training teachers in the participating institution. As has been stated previously, the effectiveness of any training procedure may be augmented by:

1. stressing the idea that making mistakes is an integral part of the learning process and minimizing the negative consequences of errors while using them as examples from which to learn;
2. organizing training sessions so that general information is presented didactically and every participant receives many trials in mastering the specific practical tasks that pertain to the general presentations;

3. providing systematic feedback so that each participant may fairly and easily judge his or her progress toward mastery of the required skills;
4. setting up a positive learning atmosphere through the consistent use of praise.

However, teachers are quite dissimilar from college student volunteers on a number of important characteristics, and some additional guidelines for training these staff members should be considered. The two groups of trainees usually differ in three aspects: teachers are not as docile as students nor as ready to automatically accept the expertise of the consultant; they are more concerned about having to perform additional extracurricular duties and tasks; and they are less concerned with or influenced by academic rewards (such as grades) that a consultant can provide for diligent participation in the project. Since the consultants and their treatment team are essentially guests of the host institution, their control over the behavior of the staff members is tenuous and can only be strengthened by providing a pleasant learning experience and, more importantly, meaningful incentives for involvement with the program.

Fortunately, many potential payoffs for participants can be found within the school system and these can be used by the consultant through the mediation of school administrators. Most schools, for example, have budgeted money to pay for substitute teachers. Rather than have teachers attend training meetings after regular school hours, some form of release time from the classroom or from other supervisory chores might be arranged during the school day. While such arrangements might cause initial administrative problems, teachers would be more likely to attend training sessions. School administrators may also note voluntary participation in the project on a teacher's permanent record, or involvement may be favorably commented upon in the administrator's annual report of the teacher's performance.

If the consultants are affiliated with a university, academic credit may be offered for teacher involvement. Teachers usually are required to earn additional academic credentials throughout their careers, and successful completion of graduate courses has short-term reward value with respect to salary increments and professional advancement. This latter option also provides the consultants with a great deal of control over the extent and quality of the teachers' participation through the assignment of grades.

Before ending the section on training participants, two additional points need to be made. Both deserve consideration if training is to be conducted in an effective and rewarding manner. The first theme is that competent individuals are often punished when working in institutions, while mediocrity or even incompetence is inadvertently rewarded. Administrators may unintentionally contribute to this problem by assigning difficult tasks to organized and efficient individuals, as the selection of these people ensures proper disposition of the chores without involving further activity by the administrator. It always seems as though the most competent teachers are assigned to instruct the most difficult students, the secretaries who type most proficiently are asked to prepare the longest and most exacting reports, additional bus and cafeteria duties are given to teachers who are the strictist enforcers of discipline, and so on.

This arrangement has obvious payoffs for those in charge, since assignment of difficult tasks to competent individuals usually means that the administrator can forget about those particular chores and do other things. However, the payoff for the competent person is more difficult to comprehend, probably because none exists in most instances. The tendency to overload competent people with work may breed resentful feelings, especially when their efforts are not rewarded in some meaningful manner. Resentment may increase if less competent individuals are perceived as doing less work. Since consultants have a vested interest in assuring the smooth operation of the intervention, they might also tend to inadvertantly overwork their most competent staff members. Public acknowledgement of the contributions made by such individuals through praise or promotion to supervisory positions often will help to alleviate resentments about being exploited.

The final consideration is to remember that both volunteers and teachers are human beings having needs and feelings. Brammer (1973) points out that people who engage in helping relationships often have value conflicts over their adequacy to provide meaningful aid to others, the extent of their proper involvement with the helpee, and other issues involving their power over and control of helpee behavior. In addition, members of the treatment teams often have private concerns revolving around practical issues (such as personal health, family or peer conflicts, and so on) which may place them under a great deal of stress.

Full explanations of all aspects of the project and the roles of all participants can help the trainees resolve some initial confusions regarding their responsibilities and duties. However, it is even more important to promote an atmosphere of warmth, honesty, and trust in which trainees can discuss their problems and concerns with a sympathetic other person. Such a climate can only be developed through frequent interactions between supervisors and trainees, which have a personally relevant focus. If trainees feel that a supervisor can be trusted, they will be more likely to share their problems. Since some trainees will be reluctant to take up even a trusted consultant's "valuable" time, specific hours for discussing concerns of the trainees should be planned into the supervisors' schedules and made public.

Establishing trust and rapport with members of the school will require at least the time and effort as is necessary to achieve rapport with student volunteers. Time spent drinking coffee and discussing what may seem to be mundane topics with teachers is definitely not wasted time. Out of such interactions comes increased knowledge of the personal characteristics and concerns of each participant, and this knowledge forms the basis for developing trusting and mutually rewarding relationships.

Establishing and Maintaining Channels of Communication

Trust and enthusiasm are difficult to build and very easy to destroy. Even one or two unpleasant misunderstandings which embitter a small minority of the participating teachers can have increasingly disasterous repercussions over time. Disillusionment is like a cancer: unless it is quickly diagnosed and completely removed, it will grow until it has destroyed the project. Legacies of ill-will as a result of misunderstandings often endure long after a particular project is terminated and make future implementations of innovative mental health programs more difficult. This section presents strategies which are designed to help prevent the growth of antagonism between members of the volunteer organization and the school system. The first area of discussion involves the clarification of role confusions and the reduction of evaluation apprehension. A model for channeling the flow of information among participants from both organizations is then presented.

Clarifying Confusions and Reducing Apprehensions

Although initially viewed as outsiders, the consultants and other volunteers are expected to learn about the school system and to fit unobtrusively into its on-going functioning. Ambiguity as to the duties and responsibilities of the various volunteer teams may initially cause occasional interpersonal friction. Teachers, for example, may ask volunteers to assume disciplinary or managerial chores while in the classroom. From the consultants' viewpoint, however, assuming these tasks may reduce the effectiveness of the volunteers in carrying out their specifically assigned duties vis-à-vis the project. Refusal to engage in such activities can lead to resentment on the part of the teachers and may cause them to regard the program in a negative light.

Interpersonal friction between volunteers and teachers may also occur because the volunteers question either the educational values espoused by the teachers or their specific teaching methods. Even if the volunteers do not make unjustified comments about these issues, another source of apprehension very often involves concern expressed by teachers about being observed while in the classroom. This apprehension usually is expressed in three ways. First, teachers may appear overly anxious to obtain immediate feedback of the information that has been collected in their rooms. Secondly, they may be fearful that the information might be used by school administrators to adversely influence formal evaluations of their teaching performance. Finally, a small minority of the school personnel might utilize a passive–aggressive strategy by making a verbal commitment of cooperation yet behaving so as to sabatoge the completion of the actual procedures being employed. A teacher, for example, might ask an observer to return at another time, then dismiss the class for recess when the volunteer returns.

Since the occurrence of these problems cannot easily be anticipated, the consultant should assume that such confusions will inevitably happen and ought to attempt to turn these misunderstandings into learning opportunities for the parties involved. A number of procedures to clarify the role behaviors of participants and to reduce evaluative anxiety in the institutional personnel exist.

The consultants need a thorough understanding of the school system with regard to its personnel and its operation, and this knowledge should be imparted to the volunteers who will be working within the system. All outside participants need to be taught the basic rules of etiquette that apply to the school and should be instructed to be as nurturant and as positive as possible. It is also a good idea to have the administrators make clear that any information that is collected during the project will not be used to evaluate the teaching staff. Training volunteers to refer teachers' questions to their supervisors often avoids many misunderstandings. Volunteers should appraise their supervisors of such requests so that meaningful feedback may eventually be provided. Finally, attempts to incorporate the teachers as active collaborators in the planning of the program should be initiated early and continued throughout the duration of the project. The teachers will be continually learning more about the target children, and the knowledge they gain throughout the year can be vital in modifying the planned interventions so as to increase their applicability.

Directing the Flow of Communication

While it is true that "many hands make light work," it is also true that "too many cooks spoil the broth." Balancing the truisms contained in these adages involves carefully analyzing the communication patterns which facilitate the flow of useful information between participating volunteers and teachers. A detailed analysis of the communication patterns both within and between the volunteer structure and the school system is difficult to provide because of the many diverse forms that interpersonal encounters may assume. Despite this problem, three general types of communication can be distinguished, and properly directing these classes can enhance the intervention. The roots of this approach stem from the efforts of Patterson and Reid (1970) to provide a functional analysis of communication patterns in smaller social units. Figure 2.2 presents a general overview of an effective communication system.

One major source of communication involves feedback about the program. Feedback is defined as being essentially positive in nature and as having practical value for the participants. Teacher suggestions concerning improvements in the planned interventions is one form of feedback. Other examples include discussing the results of specific remedial procedures with those who have conducted them, providing members of the various teams and teachers with reports of their individual performances, and praising exemplary or improving performance on assigned tasks. It was previously noted that feedback can help keep interest in the program high and increase commitment toward the faithful implementation of the planned procedures.

Feedback has been somewhat arbitrarily distinguished from a related type of communication, which involves expression of complaints and grievances. In a

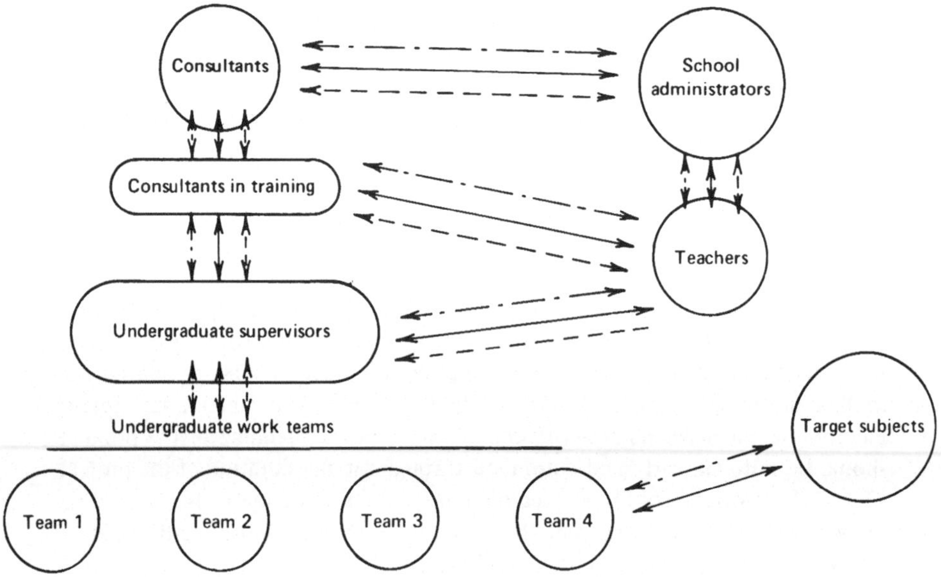

Note: Arrows represent the direction of communication flow, such that ______ = Feedback, _ _ _ _ = Complaints, and _ . _ . _ = Rapport-Building comments.

FIG. 2.2 Effective channeling of feedback, complaint, and rapport-building messages.

large project, it is impossible to meet the needs of all participants at all times. This class of comments serves a useful diagnostic function since these call attention to inadequacies in the project or to failures by individuals to carry out their assigned tasks. Dealing with complaints is usually an unpleasant task. However, complainants very often feel more positively inclined toward those who listen to their grievances, particularly if their expressions lead to noticeable improvements in the offensive situations. The consultant can more easily handle complaints by actively seeking them out rather than hoping none will be made and then being forced to react to their inevitable occurrence.

The third distinguishable pattern has been labeled general rapport-building communication. Any statement which serves to increase the mutual liking and respect of the communicants falls into this category. Many volunteers view such interactions as a nonfunctional waste of time because they are not directly related to the direct provision of services to the target population. This is simply not true, however. Frequent discussions between volunteers and teachers, which center on issues unrelated to the project, can have a strong and positive impact on teacher involvement in the program.

The flow of all three types of communication presented in Figure 2.2 is reciprocal in most instances. Certainly, within the consultant–volunteer pyramid, full and honest communication can be accomplished if participants at every level attempt to provide positive feedback to one another, voice grievances, and participate in rapport-building discussions. Ideally, there should be a "fallout" of feedback from the higher to the lower levels of the volunteer structure. The value of praising has already been discussed, and, while everyone likes to receive positive evaluative messages, the undergraduates are more likely to profit from the information contained in these comments than are the consultants. These latter individuals also are more likely to receive feedback from the administrative and teaching personnel of the school than are individual undergraduates.

Figure 2.2 also indicates that the teachers occupy a central role in the communication network, as would be expected given their power and status in the school. Their pivotal position dictates that communications to and from these persons should not always be reciprocal. The status of the volunteers and the consultants as guests within the school and the evaluative apprehension manifested by many participating teachers suggest that the flow of feedback and rapport-building statements should heavily outweigh the complaints directed toward the teacher. It is simply impolite for a volunteer to criticize a teacher for engaging in particular classroom activities that are perceived as distasteful. Volunteer grievances about teachers should be passed on to the consultant who may then decide to inform the teacher of the complaint in conjunction with or through the school administrators. On the other hand, teachers should be actively encouraged to discuss their dissatisfaction about any aspect of the program with any member of the volunteer team. Unanticipated problems can usually be satisfactorily resolved if the involved parties can communicate their feelings about the dispute in good faith. If a teacher mentions a grievance to a volunteer, the latter should immediately discuss the issue with a supervisor or consultant who can then contact the teacher to clarify and hopefully ameliorate the problem.

An additional insight can be derived from Figure 2.2. Consistent and honest exchanges of all three types of communication must be maintained between the consultants and school administrators. These individuals have the responsibility for supervising the functioning of all members of their respective staffs and the power to rectify misunderstandings that arise on the lower levels of their organizations. They also have the greatest prestige, and this provides them with the power to foster constructive changes. Adherence to the guidelines presented in this section will help ensure the smooth operation of the program and will aid in the development of a congenial atmosphere so necessary for promoting constructive change.

Comprehensively Evaluating Program Effectiveness

A deep conceptual chasm exists between researchers and practitioners in the mental health fields. The former are primarily concerned with demonstrating the existence of causal relationships between treatment manipulations and changes in behavior, while the latter are interested in applying relevant knowledge about psychological treatments to improve the lives of suffering human beings in specific settings. Frequently, these two aims are in conflict with one another.

Researchers use the tools prescribed by the so-called "scientific method" and other statistical procedures in order to make sense out of the phenomena they study. They realize that the behaviors of targeted individuals in a treatment program may change for many reasons that are unrelated to the focal procedures themselves. The operation of many extratherapeutic factors can cause inferential errors when a researcher concludes that participation in a treatment was indeed responsible for observed behavioral changes. In order to reduce the likelihood of such errors, the researcher attempts to control as many extraneous sources of influence as is humanly possible.

Sometimes the methods used to remove such influences (for example, denying people treatment by placing them into control groups, utilizing pseudotreatment procedures) conflict with meeting the needs of those individuals who desperately desire psychological service. In addition, since they work in the public domain, researchers are taught to be cautious about drawing conclusions and conservative when generalizing their findings. The task of the practitioner is to provide available treatments to those in need. The techniques utilized by professional psychotherapists are generally viewed as personalistic and artistic rather than scientific (Matarazzo, 1973). The practitioner simply cannot wait for the researcher to produce unambiguous answers about how to best provide psychological services and treatments. However, in their concern to provide concrete help to all who need it, practitioners may often inadvertently shortchange their clientele by employing inefficient and ineffective methods of treatment. One concern of this book is to demonstrate that it is feasible to combine the dictates of scientific method with a powerful behavior change technology which can help alleviate human suffering, without sacrificing the essential elements of either approach.

In community mental health, evaluation serves two related functions: advancing general knowledge about the effectiveness of interventions and providing information for improving the operation of our social systems. Investing effort in developing and implementing a program without incorporating adequate assessment procedures is a short-sighted approach. Without evaluation, the true utility of individual helping procedures and organizational functioning remains in doubt and no rational basis exists for developing new techniques and delivery systems or improving current ones. Evaluation also provides the basis for feedback to participants in mental health service projects.

The goal of any empirical investigation is the derivation of unambiguous explanations about relationships between the manipulable (independent) variables and measurable (dependent) variables under study. The strength of the conclusions advanced by the researcher is inversely related to the number of probable alternatives which can be postulated as explanations of the observed phenomena (Campbell & Stanley, 1963). Obviously, from this perspective, it is always possible to articulate alternative explanations of the results obtained in any experiment simply by invoking wild flights of the imagination.

However, the existence of possible alternative conclusions about an empirical finding does not destroy the value of the research which led to the investigator's interpretation. Campbell (1969a) points out that, in order to conclude that an experiment or body of knowledge is conceptually flawed, two criteria must be met. The alternative explanations must (1) make theoretical sense or be empirically justifiable, and, more importantly, (2) operate in a systematic manner throughout the study or across several related research investigations. In order to eliminate the systematic influence of potential biases in their assessment techniques, scientists attempt to ensure that their measurement procedures satisfy four interrelated criteria; they should be (1) comprehensive, (2) reliable, (3) unobtrusive, and (4) nonreactive. The first two criteria are relatively independent of the others and are extremely important to consider.

Obtaining a Comprehensive Evaluation

A comprehensive assessment is one which allows determination of program effectiveness from several different perspectives. Figure 2.3 presents four major parameters which circumscribe this dimension of the evaluation process. The first factor involves the source from which the observations are obtained. Participation in mental health programs can theoretically have impact on the

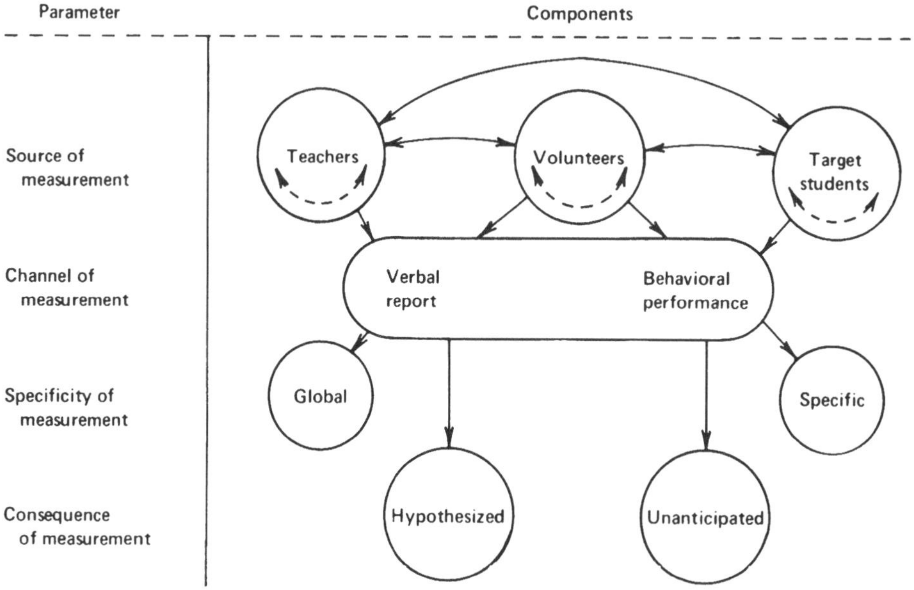

FIG. 2.3 Four parameters affecting the comprehensiveness of program evaluation.

change agents as well as on the targeted helpees. Changes in the behaviors and attitudes of adult participants in many types of intervention programs has been well-documented (for example, Allen, 1973; Breyer & Allen, 1975; Rabkin, 1972). Assessments from any source may be directed at that source itself or at the perceptible functioning of any of the other sources. For example, if we assume that a typical intervention involves three discrete groups, namely, volunteers, teachers, and target students, then six possible rating combinations exist. Self-ratings by members within each group may be obtained at different times before, during, and after the program. Self-ratings are designated by dotted arrows in Fig. 2.3. Members of any group can also rate the performance of those in other groups, as designated by the solid arrows.

The second factor to consider has been labeled "channel of measurement." All human behavior can be conceptualized as falling into three large classes, with each class being amenable to measurement through fairly distinctive channels. The first channel involves verbal report. The most common instances of this domain include verbalizing subjective states of feelings and attitudes to others and marking responses on questionnaires which tap emotional or attitudinal constructs. The second channel allows assessment of overt behavioral performances. Examples of measurements made within this domain include observer ratings of attentive and disruptive classroom behavior, frequency counts of aggressive interactions, peer ratings of a target person's dispositional characteristics, academic grades, attendance in school, and scores on standardized aptitude and achievement tests. The reader should note that although the format of some second-domain measures is identical to those of the first channel, their focus is different. For example, peer ratings are essentially verbal reports provided by these raters, but these reports are based upon their observations of the ratee. Third-channel measures assess relatively minute changes in physiological functions (for example, heart rate, respiration, skin conductance), and are typically not used in community mental health interventions.

It has been consistently noted by many investigators (Bernstein & Allen, 1969; Lang, 1968) that measures from different channels are statistically independent of one another and are differentially effected by particular sources of bias. For example, a child can deliberately and easily manage the impression he wishes to present to another through the verbal report channel ("Yes mother, I was a very good boy in school today. . . ."), but finds it difficult to present a socially desirable impression when being monitored by second-channel devices ("Ms. Smith, our classroom observations indicated that your son hit three students, kicked his teacher 12 times, and was attentive only 5% of the time.")

If an intervention program is truly effective, changes assessed across several sources of measurement and through different channels should be consistently in the same direction. One would question the utility of an intervention which led companions to view socially deficient children as improved without finding a corresponding increase in behaviorally rated interactions between the targeted youngsters and their peers.

The third criterion for comprehensiveness involves a content dimension that specifies the scope of the measurement to be obtained, and this has been designated as "specificity of measurement." Both verbal report and performance rating measures can be designed to tap very specific instances of behavior or more general characteristics. Global ratings within either channel tend to be more susceptible to systematic distortions (such as deliberate faking, halo effects, response bias, and selective forgetting) than are the more specific assessment devices. On the other hand, exclusive use of specific measures may increase the likelihood of concluding that an intervention had no impact on the participants when in reality some meaningful changes did occur. Both global and specific assessment devices have their place in a comprehensive evaluation of a mental health program, and they should be used in conjunction with each other.

The fourth parameter has been labeled as "consequence of measurement." In an effort to reduce the capriciousness of reality, psychologists have emphasized a nomothetical or hypothesis-testing orientation toward research. In this paradigm, hypotheses about the phenomenon under study are deduced from currently available knowledge and tested experimentally. Some philosophers of science (Kaplan, 1964; Lachenmeyer, 1970) have argued that reliance on this orientation produces well-controlled but trivial research findings. Experimental control is much harder to obtain in community mental health field studies than in laboratory-based research, thus making inadvertent conceptual confusions more likely to occur. The "quirkiness" of real-life phenomena has a humbling effect on researchers but can also produce rewards in the form of serendipity, or the discovery of important scientific relationships as a result of accidents, equipment failures, or oversights in the experimental setting. In a notable article, Skinner (1959) has pointed out the important consequences that serendipity has produced on the development of operant principles of behavior.

Obviously, it would be foolish not to anticipate certain outcomes while conducting any mental health project. Our nomothetical orientation toward research guides us in this endeavor. However, in the course of a long-term project, certain unanticipated processes and consequences are likely to be observed. These side effects of the intervention often provide extremely useful explanations of the anticipated measurable outcomes. The enterprising researcher will attempt to develop methods to assess unanticipated consequences so that they may be utilized in a systematic manner. Even if such spur-of-the-moment assessments do not meet all of the requirements imposed by scientific dictates, they can still serve to explain incongruities and may have heuristic value for future research projects.

Assessing the Reliability of Evaluative Observations

Reliability of measurement is the second criterion of adequate evaluation. In its most basic form, reliability refers to the consistency of information provided by a research instrument, and several types of reliability may need to be determined. If a measurement device contains multiple items that are presumed to measure a single attribute, then all of the items should theoretically show a moderate degree of agreement with the others. If this criterion is met, the scale is said to be internally consistent.

A second form of reliability involves the extent to which total scores on an assessment device that is administered to the same individuals at one time correspond to scores obtained following subsequent administrations of the measure. This agreement is designated as test–retest reliability. If the assessment device measures relatively stable characteristics, then a high test–retest correspondence over time would be expected in the absence of interventions designed to change the particular attributes being measured. This procedure necessitates repeated testing of individuals who do not receive the intervention under study. If the test–retest reliability of scores obtained from such nontreated samples is low, it is difficult to validly conclude that changes in treated target groups are due to the intervention procedures.

It is also legitimate to use assessment devices to measure immediately perceived feelings, moods, or other momentary states. These instruments are often useful in determining the effectiveness of clearly specified manipulations in tightly controlled laboratory experiments. Such measures typically manifest increasingly lower reliability coefficients as the time span between administrations increases. Their use in complex field studies having long life spans is inadvisable because of the many extraneous sources of influence which may operate in real-life settings.

If the design of a program necessitates measurement of certain momentary states, one acceptable procedure is to obtain a large sampling of the attributes over an extended period of time and derive average scores which correspond to different phases of the project. An increasing number of researchers argue that averaging state measures provides valid estimates of trait characteristics. One problem with this approach, however, is artifactual reactivity caused by repeatedly administering state measures, which is discussed later in this chapter.

A third type of reliability, called interrater reliability, refers to the extent that observers can agree in their simultaneous categorization of environmental events. Observers in classrooms, for example, are trained to use coding systems in order to reduce the jumbled multitude of ongoing behaviors to a describable level. In general, specific behaviors can be more reliably rated than more global summary terms. Two independent raters are more likely to agree that a particular child has kicked or hit another child than they will when asked to decide whether that child has been aggressive. However, specific behavior-rating systems are harder to learn, more cumbersome to use, and may not be molar enough to pick up meaningful changes.

Several procedures exist for insuring that assessment devices are used in a reliable manner. Careful initial training of observers and test scorers is crucial, and no evaluative data should be collected until all evaluators have demonstrated their ability to interpret the assessments reliably. However, even when pairs of raters obtain agreement within a dyad, the problem of "criterion drift" still exists. This is a process whereby acceptable reliabilities are obtained between consistently matched pairs while agreement across pairs becomes increasingly attenuated. Criterion drift can be avoided by rotating partners in varied pairwise combinations (O'Leary & Kent, 1973). Research also indicates that reliability checks should be continually performed throughout the duration of a project. Reid (1970) found that, when observers believed that their ratings could not be checked against those of another rater, reliability coefficients dropped to a median of .51 from a median reliability of .76, which was obtained when checking was thought to be possible.

A final consideration involves whether observers should be informed of the anticipated outcomes of the project. Orne (1962) and Rosenthal (1966) have pointed out that both subjects and student experimenters wish to help senior researchers validate their hypotheses. As a result of this tendency, they will produce data which is congruent with their perceptions of what the experimenter is looking for. Investigators have made the tacit assumption that obtaining high levels of interrater reliability avoids sytematic distortions from creeping into the raters' observations. Kent, O'Leary, Diament, and Dietz (1974) reported that deliberately biased observers' expectations of therapeutic change created more directional reactivity on globally defined impressionistic ratings than on specific behavioral rating categories. However, O'Leary, Kent, and Kanowitz (1975) demonstrated that even specific behavioral observations can be biased by exposing raters to the experimenter's verbal reactions to the obtained data. Dunlop (1974) also found that trained raters could systematically bias specific behavioral ratings of a videotaped segment of classroom interaction so as to portray the teacher and students in a positive or negative manner. Dunlop reported that this systematic bias occurred even though his observers continued to maintain high levels of interrater reliability. Thus, it is important not to communicate too much information about intended project outcomes to the student raters.

Gathering Unobtrusive and Nonreactive Observations

These two aspects of the evaluation process are intricately linked and are only slightly less important than the other two parameters. Obtrusiveness refers to the visibility of the assessment procedures to those who are being evaluated (Webb, Campbell, Schwartz, & Sechrest, 1966). Reactivity means that the act of measuring a phenomenon causes changes in that event (Skinner, 1953). Generally, the more obtrusive an assessment technique is, the greater will be the reactivity it produces. Since all measurement devices are both intrusive and reactive to some extent, all the researcher can do is minimize these influences and prevent them from operating in a systematic manner.

A number of procedures can be used to reduce these two influences on the observation process. The best method, which has already been discussed, is to employ multiple channels of measurement in a comprehensive fashion. Verbal report and behavioral performance measures are reactive in different ways and therefore less likely to produce unidirectional bias. Psychologists always try to disguise the purposes of their verbal report questionnaires by adding irrelevant "filler" items, building in inherent validity checks for "faking good" or "faking bad," and counterbalancing the socially desirable nature of questions to avoid response biases.

Even when the purpose of a verbal report measure is adequately disguised, repeatedly administering the measure over time to the same individuals often has reactive effects. Suinn (1969) asked undergraduates to rate their anxiety on several commonly used measures and found that retesting after five weeks led to a substantial reduction in verbally reported anxiousness. This reduction was most likely attributable to properties of the scales used, since no systematic intervention had been employed to reduce anxiety.

Behavioral ratings, on the other hand, tend to be initially more intrusive, hence making them more reactive with regard to ongoing routines in the observational setting. The very presence of strangers in the classroom will cause some disruption and may result in an artifactual inflation or depression in the rate of the target behaviors being measured. The best defenses against reactivity involve ensuring that the observers do not act in a disruptive manner and using the same pool of observers to rate in specified classrooms over long time spans. The ultimate goal of the observers is to blend into the natural landscape of the class environment.

Training observers in the proficient use of rating materials is obviously the first step in minimizing intrusiveness. Observers who noisily fumble around with their paraphenalia call attention to themselves and the resulting disruptions may well antagonize participating teachers and bias the data collected. Observers should sit in places where they can view their target children without being conspicuous to the members of the class. The best vantage points are toward the front and along the sides of the classroom.

Since the function of observers is to gather information in an unobtrusive manner, interactions between the students and raters should be avoided, unless a clear danger to the physical well-being of a pupil or a teacher exists. The saliency of the observations can be further reduced by requiring the observers to categorize the behaviors of other students in addition to the designated target pupils. This latter procedure has two advantageous aspects. First, it avoids the focusing of attention on the selected targets thereby decreasing the likelihood that these particular pupils will be stigmatized by their peers. Secondly, it helps ensure that the raters remain "blind" with regard to what children are the objects of the intervention procedures. Over time, adherence to these procedures will help to reduce reactivity in behavioral measurement processes.

Many other types of useful overt behavioral performance measures may be derived from the naturally occurring events in the school (Webb *et al.*, 1966).

Information such as the frequency of visits to the principal, absentee days, and the number of library books a pupil signs out may provide a basis for potentially important outcome measures. Written work of students could also be rated over a period of time for qualities such as neatness or number of errors. The colorful charts and graphs teachers often use to demonstrate students' progress in mastering academic and social skills may have utility in this regard.

An evaluation scheme which incorporates the four previously discussed components will enable consultants to draw clear and unambiguous conclusions about the efficacy of the procedures employed in an intervention. These conclusions can provide a means of accomplishing Malott's (1974) final goal of recycling a program. All too often, intervention projects are viewed by all participating parties as short-term demonstrations that disappear after the external sources of support have been withdrawn. The ideal community intervention program is one which influences the host organization to the extent that inside staff members continue to use and modify the procedures initially supplied by the outside consultants. The best method of ensuring maintenance of the intervention is to provide meaningful feedback regarding the outcomes that are ultimately obtained. Information can be properly employed to achieve this end only if the evaluation procedures are as comprehensive, reliable, unobtrusive, and nonreactive as possible.

Guidelines for Consultant Survival in a School System

This chapter has hopefully provided some useful insights and strategies that a consultant can employ to implement an intervention in a school gracefully and effectively. The pioneering and excellent work of Sarason and his colleagues (for example, Sarason, 1971; Sarason, Levine, Goldenberg, Cherlin, & Bennett, 1966) illustrates the complexity of entering the "culture" of the school as well as the difficulties inherent in effecting change in such settings. The major strategies we derived have been formulated into 17 behavioral guidelines, which are summarized below. These are very similar to those developed independently by Murrell (1973) for interventions in a variety of open systems. They are also in accord with Fairweather's (1967) suggestions for implementing what he called "experimental social innovations." Although the suggestions cut across the content areas of the chapter, the first five relate to entering a school, nine deal with training participants, and the final three concern themselves with communication and evaluation issues. We found that adherence to these rules aided us in coordinating a smoothly functioning program and, more importantly from our point of view, helped us avoid Excedrin headaches 103 through 286.

1. Take time to learn about the needs of all in the host institution. Talk with administrators, teachers and students.

2. Enter the system slowly. Gradually work toward developing a truly collaborative enterprise by obtaining and using suggestions and help offered by school personnel.

3. Be honest in specifying the benefits and liabilities of the proposed program. Clearly define your objectives before beginning the intervention, and never promise more than can be delivered.

4. Clearly define the roles, duties, rights, and responsibilities of all participants before beginning to implement the program.

5. Define and respect the role of the teacher as an expert in the operation of the school. Make this role explicit and incorporate teacher expertise throughout the program.

6. Screen potential volunteers and select those who appear to be hard working, socially skillful, and committed to the success of the program.

7. Develop an integrated and socially cohesive organizational structure for participating volunteers. In large projects, organize volunteers into hierarchically arranged work teams.

8. Combine didactic teaching methods and practical exercises while training participants. Emphasize a criterion mastery approach so that improvement in the acquisition of necessary skills is readily apparent to those being trained.

9. Endeavor to make training sessions useful and enjoyable. Promote the attitude that mistakes are part of the learning process and systematically focus on progressive successes.

10. Demonstrate enthusiasm by taking an active and highly visible part in training participants.

11. Continually praise the efforts of the trainees and staff. Positive comments lead to improved performances and make people feel good.

12. Provide meaningful payoffs for teachers and administrators who faithfully participate in the program.

13. Try to avoid inadvertently punishing competent participants by overloading them with work.

14. Develop a warm, trusting atmosphere that will encourage all participants to discuss troublesome personal concerns. Schedule time for this important function.

15. Emphasize clear and consistent communication. Build a network to transmit feedback, grievance, and rapport-building messages among all participants.

16. Design comprehensive, reliable, unobtrusive and nonreactive methods of evaluation so as to reduce the possibility of making unwarrented conclusions because of systematic biases.

17. Provide feedback about program outcomes to school personnel in the hope of making those components found to be effective self-sustaining.

Part II

TOWARD A THEORETICAL BACKGROUND FOR MULTILEVEL PREVENTION IN THE SCHOOLS

3

A Strategy for Primary Prevention: The Social Problem-Solving Curriculum

The major thrust of primary prevention is toward the most adaptive ecological match between people and their environment. There are two general strategies in current primary prevention research designed to achieve this goal. The first concentrates on modifying the environmental factors that influence psychological development. The second focuses on enhancing a person's skills to deal effectively with the environment (Caplan, 1964). Primary prevention is concerned with creating change within the primary socializing institutions rather than the identification and treatment of specific disturbed individuals within these systems. As mentioned in Chapter 1, the school has been identified by several authors as an appropriate socializing institution to develop effective strategies for primary prevention (Cowen, 1973; Hunt, 1968; Minuchin, Biber, Shapiro, & Zimiles, 1969).

Primary Prevention in the Elementary School

A review of studies dealing with primary prevention in the school reveals a dearth of research. Of the vast number of investigations in the field, few have reported empirical evaluation of program effectiveness. The majority of reported articles are speculative and deal with one or more of the following areas: (1) the need for and role of preventive mental health programs in the school (for example, Bower, 1965; Gottlieb & Howell, 1957); (2) the variables postulated to be important in such preventive programs (Cartwright & Biber, 1965; Hollister, 1965); and (3) the conceptualization and description of programs (for example, Klien, 1965; Lambert, 1965). The lack of empirical validation of procedures stemming from these concerns is the most serious drawback in primary prevention (Cowen, 1971; Flanagan, 1971; Garmezy, 1971; Van Antwerp, 1971).

Cowen (1973) has supported this conclusion with his recent comprehensive review. Chronicling the reports in the *Community Mental Health Journal,*

1963–1971, he indicates that the ratio of speculation to research (which was broadly defined by Cowen as any use of numbers) is three-to-one, with less than 3% of all articles falling into the general area of prevention. Golann's (1969) *Coordinate Index and Reference Guide to Community Mental Health* reflects a similar ratio of speculation to research (nearly four to one) with less than 2% of the 1500 works indexed dealing in the broad area of primary prevention.

The literature is replete with speculation as to the types of variables that contribute to positive mental health and adaptive functioning. Caplan (1964) spoke of psychosocial and sociocultural supplies, Hollister (1965) introduced the concept "strens," and Lambert (1965) discussed "ego builders." Jahoda (1958) cited six elements in an attempt to define positive mental health, Biber (1961) indicated seven, and Scott (1968) identified ten criteria for "normalcy." Walzer, Richmond, and deBuno (1975) delineated no less than 34 biological, sociocultural, and psychological factors that interact to affect the "psychosocial adaptation" of children. There is considerable complexity, a great deal of overlap, and often a lack of specificity to these variables, as well as difficulty in anchoring them to empirical referents that can be defined and measured. Yet, to properly evaluate programs in primary prevention, it is essential that we develop criteria for positive mental health that can be defined operationally and quantitatively.

However, it is these very complexities that account, in part, for the derth of evaluative research in prevention. As discussed in Chapter 1, we must consider the particular methodological difficulties involved in such research. Flanagan (1971) has generated a set of criteria which are particularly relevant for the interpretation and evaluation of research in primary prevention. While there are methodological concerns common to all evaluative research, Flanagan has attempted to relate these concerns to preventive research in particular. A discussion of some representative evaluative research in primary prevention, using Flanagan's criteria, will help to articulate some of the specific methodological problems evident in such research.

The first criteria are concerned with the sampling procedures employed. In addition to standard experimental techniques of random selection or matching to achieve equivalence between groups, the sample must be of sufficient size and representativeness to permit inference to the population it is expected to represent. For example, the *Woodlawn Mental Health Center Program* (Schiff & Kellam, 1967) was designed to prevent school adaptation problems of first graders. The representative sample included all first graders in the community (N = 2000), and the experimental and control schools (N = 12) were selected randomly. In contrast, studies often employ different criteria for selection of experimental and control groups, which raise questions of group equivalence (*see* Doyal, Ferguson, & Rockwood, 1971).

The second set of criteria require that the treatment rationale and procedures be clearly defined and detailed enough to permit replication and interpretation by other investigators. This includes clear specification of rationales and the procedures used to determine expected outcomes. For example, Susskind (1969) detailed the techniques of training and assessment used in his intervention to increase creative verbal behavior and questioning in the classroom. In the Woodlawn project, rationale was clearly articulated, but treatment procedures were broadly defined, and this characteristic inhibits interpretation by other investigators. Shore, Milgram, and Malasky (1971) reported the effectivenss of an enrichment program on the child's sense of powerlessness or locus of control as an innovative preventive strategy. But their report does not include specific or detailed descriptions of the treatment procedures of this program, limiting efforts at replication or interpretation by others.

The ultimate effectiveness criteria of primary prevention are reduced incidence rates of disordered behaviors in the population, yet time and sample limitations often dictate the use of "intermediate criteria." As defined by Flanagan, these intermediate criteria represent performances or behaviors that can be specified and measured. As intermediate criteria, these behaviors or performances should be desirable outcomes in themselves, as well as presumed indicators of more remotely anticipated reductions in the prevalence of disorders. In measuring these criteria, two methodological problems exist: (1) retrospective identification of potentially useful criteria limits the degree of causal inference that can be made between the intervention and the outcomes, and (2) reports of criteria change or improvement by those involved in such programs present problems of measurement bias, as was discussed in Chapter 2. The global adjustment ratings made by the teachers involved in the Woodlawn project are an example of the difficulties in measuring outcome by participants (Kellam, Branch, Agrawal, & Grabill, 1972; Schiff & Kellam, 1967). In an attempt to deal with this problem, Susskind (1969) employed behavioral measures of teacher and student behaviors obtained in the classroom by raters independent of the treatment program.

Finally, accurate determination of the effects of the intervention must be based on psychological as well as statistical significance. This is particularly true for studies with large samples, like the Woodlawn project, where small differences may produce statistically significant results. Further, replication was cited by Flanagan as an excellent procedure for strengthening causal inferences about program effectiveness. Of the studies discussed thus far, only the Woodlawn project, which has reported data over a five-year period, has included replication procedures in its methodology.

As the reader can surmise, most of the programs reported in primary prevention are fraught with methodological problems. One series of studies by Ojemann and his colleagues have not yet been discussed. These studies satisfy most of Flanagan's methodological criteria and they warrant our close examination. As a pioneer, Ojemann's innovative approach to prevention in the school provided a model for this phase of our project.

The *Program for Education in Human Behavior* (Ojemann, 1969), over 20 years in development and experimentation, is based on the causal-surface distinction in understanding human behavior. Ojemann defined causality as the awareness of the complex and variable nature of human behavior, without necessarily requiring knowledge of any specific cause. He further explained that a causal understanding of behavior includes awareness of the effects of emotions, feelings, environment, heritage, and learning on behavior. He predicted that an understanding of the multiple factors influencing human behavior enables one to deal effectively with others.

In the initial, well-controlled study (Ojemann, Levitt, Lyle, & Whiteside, 1955) the sample was selected from fourth through sixth grades in several elementary schools, and later studies (Ojemann, 1963; Ojemann & Snider, 1964) expanded sampling to include the entire elementary grade range. The treatment program described in the initial project has subsequently been further elaborated. The treatment approach included teacher training in the causal understanding of human behavior and techniques for teaching this approach in the classroom, with a detailed curriculum and materials for each elementary grade. Treatment objectives became more clearly specified as increased understanding of the causal nature of human behavior emerged. These are measurable by the Causal Test and the Problem Situations Test. Ojemann and his colleagues found significant increases in performance on these measures, and these findings have been replicated (Ojemann, 1963; Spano, 1965). More recently, the criteria of a causal understanding of human behavior has been related to level of social adjustment (Larcen, Spivack, & Shure, 1972; Spano, 1965). Others have similarly used education about human behavior as a preventive program in the elementary school, but data concerning their behavioral effectiveness are limited (Long, 1970; Roen, 1967).

Despite the fact that Ojemann's work has spanned two decades, there is no long-term analysis to date of the effectiveness of his preventive program on actual incidence of behavior problems. Ojemann infers that a causal understanding of human behavior enables one to cope more effectively with everyday living. However, the nature of his intervention is to provide an *understanding* rather than any active behavioral *skill* that would enable one to solve everyday problems. Despite these problems, we agree with Levine and Graziano (1972) that "Ojemann's approach, whatever its present deficiencies, is still the closest to a truly preventive methodology we have [p. 561]." Further, this approach suggests that training in active problem-solving skills is potentially a useful strategy for primary prevention.

The Problem-Solving Approach

Problem solving satisfies Flanagan's requirements as an intermediate criterion if it can be operationally and quantitatively defined. D'Zurilla and Goldfried (1971) viewed problem solving as a behavioral process, whether overt or cognitive in nature, which (1) makes available a variety of potentially effective response alternatives in a problem situation and (2) increases the probability of selecting the most effective response from among these various alternatives. Preliminary evidence also supports problem solving as a presumed indicator of social adjustment (Larcen *et al.*, 1972; Shure & Spivack, 1972a; Spivack & Levine, 1963; Spivack & Shure, 1974). Problem solving appears to be an excellent choice as an intermediate criterion and as an active skill that individuals can use independently to deal with the critical problematic situations that confront them in daily living.

Research in Problem Solving

Quite some time ago, Dollard and Miller (1950) pointed out the need for researching the process of solving interpersonal problems. However, research and theory in human problem solving for the past 25 years has been focused predominantly on physical and conceptual problematic tasks such as water jar or mathematics problems, jig-saw puzzles, anagrams, and discrimination tasks. Major reviews of human problem solving by Davis (1966), Duncan (1959), and Simon and Newell (1971), which examined hundreds of studies, failed to report even a single study which dealt with problem-solving skills in real-life situations involving interpersonal parameters. There is little evidence to indicate that problem-solving performance on impersonal tasks will predict interpersonal functioning. When researchers have tried to integrate data obtained from these physical and conceptual problem-solving tasks with personality variables or adjustment criteria, their findings have been generally inconsistent (Mendelsohn & Gall, 1970; Stevenson, Hale, Klein, & Miller, 1968).

Several studies have attempted to relate problem-solving flexibility to personality or adjustment variables. The flexibility–rigidity dimension is defined as the ability to generate more than one solution to novel problems as compared to persistence at the same solutions regardless of changes in the problem. Schroder & Rotter (1952) demonstrated that problem-solving flexibility was a learned behavior and modifiable, and the findings have been replicated by Jamieson (1969). Research on the relationship between flexibility and interpersonal functioning has produced ambiguous results, partially as a result of definitional problems with the criterion personality variables, for example, Minnesota Multiphasic Personality Inventory (MMPI) or Rorschach responses. In addition, none of the problem-solving flexibility tasks reported use material dealing with social problem situations, yet research findings have been generalized to infer behavioral tendencies in social situations (Bringmann, 1967; Goldner, 1957; Kurz & Capone, 1967).

Another trend in the research of problem solving is represented by studies in the area of creative problem solving. Guilford's (1960, 1967) emphasis on divergent rather than convergent problem solving has resulted in focus on the generation of alternate solutions and consequences in problem situations. Torrance (1962) has extended this emphasis on divergent problem solving to develop a whole series of creativity tests for children. Renzulli (1970) has applied these concepts in an innovative training program to increase problem-solving creativity by children. However, the tasks employed in these procedures are generally impersonal conceptual tasks, showing limited relation to the problems found in daily social and interpersonal situations. Also, studies that have attempted to relate divergent thinking or creativity to social adjustment variables have produced inconsistent results (Anderson, 1966; Casey, 1965; Greenberger, O'Connor, & Sorenson, 1971; Hinton, 1970, 1971; Stanwyck, 1974).

A third area of investigation has considered problem-solving programs in the framework of organizational development (Bennis, 1966; Schmuck *et al.*, 1972). Projects using these approaches have focused primarily on group problem solving with the aim of increasing institutional effectivenss. These studies have seldom included empirical components.

The research reviewed so far, indicates that the referents used to measure problem solving in physical and conceptual tasks, as well as those in creativity and flexibility tasks, are not functionally related to those dealing with how personal and interpersonal problems are solved in everyday living. Organizational studies in problem solving have seldom considered this approach in terms of individual enhancement or empirically examined the relationship between a system's effectiveness and the usefulness of this approach for the individuals within the system. It is necessary, then, to develop and articulate theory and research specifically focused on problem-solving behavior in personal and interpersonal problematic situations. Only with such a knowledge base can a strategy for preventive interventions using training in social problem solving be designed.

A Theoretical Basis for Social Problem Solving

Spivack (1973) proposed a theory of problem solving which presents a multidimensional thought process including the consideration of a variety of options to reach a goal, as well as the development of a step-by-step progression toward goal attainment. In a similar vein, Rotter (1974) and his colleagues (Rotter, Chance, & Phares, 1972) stress the importance of individual expectancies in successful problem solving. Rotter's theory predicts that individuals with high expectancies that alternative solutions can be found will evidence better social adjustment. D'Zurilla and Goldfried (1971) have integrated a variety of problem-solving theories within a sequential framework. Their model is useful for the general understanding of component behaviors in problem solving and will be outlined in some detail.

A first consideration is the *general orientation* or set that encourages independent problem-solving behavior. This set includes: the expectancy that most problems can be dealt with effectively, the recognition of problematic situations when they occur, and the inhibition of impulsive responses or the tendency to do nothing.

Members of the second class are called *problem definition* and *formulation* behaviors. These allow the individual to identify the problem and specific components, and to seek out additional information to aid in problem resolution. It is in accurately defining and identifying the problem that one can begin to solve it.

The *generation of alternatives* is perhaps the most crucial component behavior in finding the most effective solution or response. Osborn's (1963) method of "brainstorming," with its emphasis on producing a large quantity of solutions and withholding immediate criticism, is important in fostering this component behavior. The usefulness of this technique relies, in part, on the principle that "quantity breeds quality." That is, a child's effectiveness in problem solving depends upon generating a variety of alternatives. Although this principle has been supported by data (Parnes & Meadow, 1959), there is evidence that the diversity of solutions, nature of the problem and problem-solving group are critical moderators of the usefulness of simply producing a large number of solutions (Aldous, Condon, Hill, Straus, & Tallman, 1971; Hoffman, 1965).

The *decision-making* component implies that to maximize the effectiveness of the problem-solving behavior one must consider the outcomes or consequences expected as a result of the solution, as well as any potential obstacles. In addition, one should consider the specific ways in which the solution can be elaborated and implemented to maximize its effectiveness.

The *verification* component concludes the problem-solving process. After one has identified the problem, generated the possible solutions, decided on the best solution, given its probable outcomes, and implemented this solution, it is essential that one compare the available feedback and the actual outcomes in order to make the necessary self-corrections and modifications.

A schematic model, which adapts and expands D'Zurilla and Goldfried's conception of problem solving, is shown in Fig. 3.1. This model starts with a general set or expectancy that one can solve problems. Such a competency set orients the individual to expect that problem resolution is a function of his problem-solving behavior. Given this competency set, another important expectancy is that looking for divergent or alternative strategies will lead to successful problem resolution. Such an expectancy encourages divergent and creative strategies, rather than convergent, single-solution approaches to problem solving. Once one has identified and defined the important aspects of the problem, the individual begins to generate alternative solutions to the problem. As solutions or strategies are generated, their potential consequences are evaluated and specific steps or elaborations are considered that will maximize the success of the solution. The problem solver will continue to engage in this set of related behaviors until a satisfactory solution has been selected. After one has selected

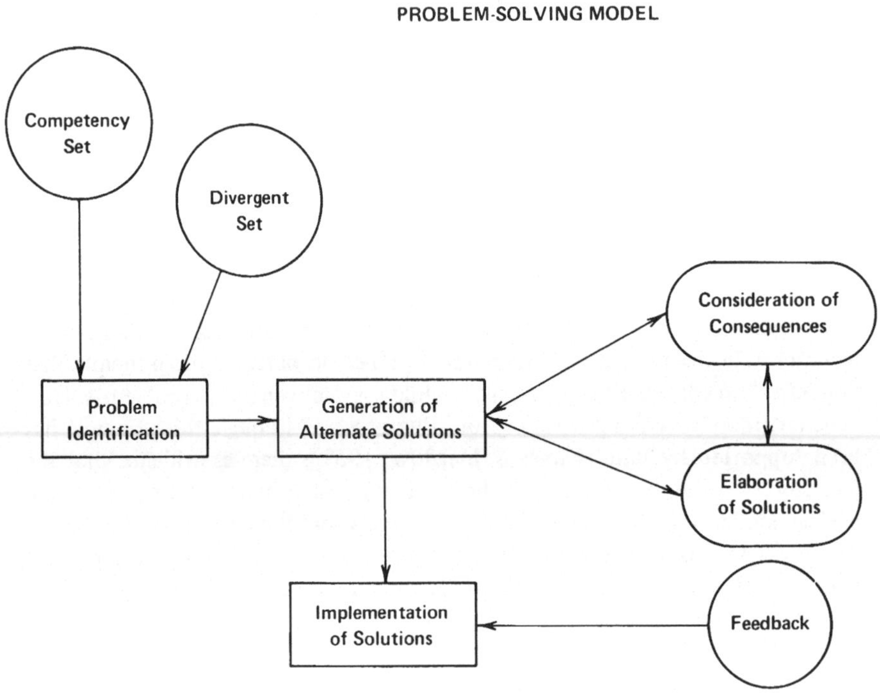

FIG. 3.1 Problem-solving model.

and implemented the solution, it is crucial to incorporate actual outcomes and feedback for future effective problem solving.

The techniques of implementing the components of this model in a training curriculum are discussed in Chapter 6 and further detailed in the Appendix. We will now focus our discussion on an examination of empirical issues related to our model of social problem solving.

Measurement Issues in Social Problem Solving

Little research exists on the development and validation of measurement procedures of problem-solving skills in interpersonal situations within this theoretical framework.

Morton (1955) used Thematic Apperception Test protocols to help adult clients in brief psychotherapy define their specific problems, generate alternative solutions, and weigh their successes and consequences. Hamburg and Adams (1967) used a modified TAT for college students, which attempted to assess the problem-solving competency of college freshmen. While the measure was used to successfully predict dropping out of college, the fact that no specific problem-solving referents, no explicit scoring criteria, and no reliability data are reported critically limits the utility of this assessment technique.

There have also been attempts to use interviews and global ratings of social problem-solving skills (Heilbrun, 1968; Heyder, Strickland, & Hayes, 1968), but again these methods are based primarily on clinical judgement and lack specificity, reliability, and generalizability.

Lundsteen (1970) developed a battery of social problem-solving tests for use in the language arts curriculum of fifth graders: an oral test, a written device, and an open stories method. The first two methods required the child to name three problems in his or her personal life, then to pick one and tell how it could be solved. Lundsteen presented an elaborate twelve-step process in the problem-solving sequence including, for example, problem definition, search strategies, and evaluation. The stories were then evaluated at each step of the process on a complex set of nine criteria (including elaboration, originality, multiple alternatives, causality) A child's score consisted of the total number of points received for each criterion at every step of the process.

The open stories procedure presents a series of stories to the child and asks twelve stimulus questions based on the twelve-step process. A child's score on this measure was calculated on the basis of the number of points received on each of the nine criteria for each stimulus question. Total score interrater reliability for all three measures was reported, but there were no reliability coefficients reported for the separate criteria. The author also indicated that a high relationship existed between IQ scores and these measures. However, no interrelationships between the measures were reported, and likewise no relationships to other problem-solving referents or performances were discussed, limiting inferences about the construct validity of the technique.

Feldhusen, Houtz, Ringenbach, and their associates have been developing the Purdue Elementary Problem-Solving Inventory (PEPSI), a measure designed to assess the social problem-solving skills of elementary school children. This is accomplished by presenting children with slides depicting real-life social situations (specifically chosen for their relevance to children of diverse ethnic and socioeconomic levels), an accompanying verbal description, and questions about the situations to be answered in a test booklet. A description of the measure (Feldhusen, Houtz, & Ringenbach, 1972), and a detailed outline of the guiding principles employed and component problem-solving skills measured (Feldhusen, 1975) are available for the interested reader.

Psychometrically, the PEPSI has demonstrated internal consistency with over 3000 elementary school children (Feldhusen, 1975). Preliminary construct validation efforts have utilized factor analytic methods. These data indicate that the PEPSI reliably measures six component problem-solving skills (Speedie, Houtz, Ringenbach, & Feldhusen, 1973), and taps certain abilities which other existing cognitive measures do not (Houtz, Ringenbach, & Feldhusen, 1973). While the measure demonstrates adequate relationships with other tests of logical thinking and conceptual abilities, its relationship to "real-life" behavioral indices of social problem solving has not yet been reported. Further, while we feel that this technique has many promising features, we wanted to use a measure that provided for more open ended and spontaneous forms of social problem-solving behavior.

The Means–Ends Problem-Solving Measure (MEPS) consists of story stems describing a hypothetical but typical real-life problem (Shure & Spivack, 1972a; Spivack & Levine, 1963). Using the "open middle technique," both the beginning and the end of the story are presented, and the subject is then asked to "fill in the middle" or "tell what happens in between." In scoring, three criteria were used: *means, obstacles,* and *time.* A *mean* was defined as any new relevant unit of information deemed useful in helping the testee to reach a goal. This included both alternative solutions and the elaborations within each solution. An *obstacle* was defined as any event which interferes with reaching the stated goal, and *time* statements identified propitious moments as a necessary aspect of an instrumental act (for example, at night when he can't see . . .). Reliability was demonstrated between independent raters both for total scores and the three separate criteria.

Some validity data has been established for the MEPS using the method of known groups. The test has discriminated between (1) adolescents in residential treatment and normal controls (Spivack & Levine, 1963); (2) preadolescents in residential treatment and normal controls (Shure & Spivack, 1972a); (3) adults in outpatient psychiatric care and normal controls (Platt & Spivack, 1972a); (4) known premorbid groups within a psychiatric population (Platt & Spivack, 1972b); and (5) groups rated on social adjustment within a residential treatment center for preadolescents (Larcen *et al.*, 1972).

Platt and Spivack (1973) have also reported a factor analytic study with MEPS and other problem-solving measures with an adult population. Their study suggests a multidimensional framework for problem solving and supports the convergent validity of the MEPS with other measures of this construct.

Shure, Spivack, and Jaeger (1971) have developed a problem-solving measure for preschool-aged children in which explicit directions (". . . to think of as many different ways to . . .") are used to assess the number of different alternative solutions that a child can generate. Using this measure, Spivack and Shure (1974) have been able to discriminate between groups of children rated on adjustment with Head Start programs.

Nelson (1970) reported a unique attempt to measure problem-solving behaviors by means of a behavioral criterion. Eleventh grade students were asked in this task to assist a hypothetical problem solver. The procedure involved using a series of slides to solve the problem: some slides defined the problem, others offered alternative solutions, and still others possible outcomes or consequences for the solutions. Nelson then observed the number of slides considered by the students and the duration of each consideration. He provided only six slides in each category, however, and his results may indicate a strong ceiling effect, since many of the subjects considered all of the slides available prior to making their decision. He also found a very strong relationship between the number of solution and outcome slides considered, which he concluded was due to the similarity of the two problem-solving strategies.

The above review indicates the empirical and methodological difficulties with measurement procedures in social problem solving. Scoring criteria and interrater reliability are absent in most work, and questionably complex and cumbersome in others. None of the reported measures have demonstrated internal consistency or item equivalence reliability, leading one to question whether the test items are measuring the same construct. None of the studies have used behaviorally measured problem-solving behaviors as referents independent of the measure to establish predictive or construct validity. Only one device, the Means–Ends Problem-Solving Measure by Spivack and Levine (1963), has demonstrated validity by the method of known groups and some relationships with independent measures of adjustment. Such validation methodology presents other problems for inferences about behavior generality, however, since it assumes that the "essence" of the known groups (that is, adjustment) accounts for the differences in verbally measured problem-solving behavior.

This review highlights the quite difficult tasks involved in the generation of a measure of social problem-solving skills. However, several considerations seem important at this point in the development of such a measure: (1) it should be methodologically sound vis-à-vis reliability, (2) it should include the major components of the problem-solving model while maintaining parsimonious scoring criteria, and (3) it should be imbedded within a network of related performances and behaviors that contribute to its construct validity.

Issues in the Training of Problem-Solving Skills

Strategies for the training of problem-solving skills appropriate for interpersonal situations are not well developed. The earliest effort to modify real-life problem-solving behaviors is reported in the study by Morton (1955) described above. Using TAT protocols, Morton attempted to train adult clients who were being seen in short-term psychotherapy in problem-solving strategies. He predicted that such training in problem solving would result in better adjustment. Using the Rotter Incomplete Sentence Blank (Rotter & Rafferty, 1950) as an outcome measure of adjustment, he found that the trained clients improved in their adjustment scores, but no assessment of problem-solving skills was reported.

A report by Giebink, Stover, and Fahl (1968) included a modification program for six boys in a residential treatment setting. Specifically, they sought to increase the number of alternative solutions given to four frustrating situations commonly found in such settings. Training consisted of the repeated playing of a specially devised board game in which winning was contingent on using all possible solutions when landing on "frustration squares." Since dice were used, each of the six boys had equal chances of winning and receiving reinforcements, and exposure to the alternative solutions was predicted to result in increased use of these solutions as rated by staff in the residential setting. The results were encouraging but limited by the size of the sample, the specificity of the problems used, and possible measurement bias on the part of the staff rating the child's progress.

In the study by Lundsteen (1970) mentioned before, an attempt was made to include abstract reasoning skills within a language arts curriculum for fifth graders. A detailed report of the techniques used is in preparation. The results indicated improvement for some of the trained groups on several of the problem-solving measures she developed. However, the abstract nature of the skills trained, the complex criteria used for scoring these devices, and lack of any reported curriculum design make interpretation of this program difficult.

Nelson (1970) reported an intervention designed to modify the problem-solving behaviors of a selected subsample of eleventh graders. Those students indicating need for or interest in receiving problem-solving training were randomly assigned to one of eight groups. The intervention was presented in four media: video, audio, instructional booklet, and lecture format. The first three of these media were all based on a script of a student model attempting to solve the problem of what to do with his summer vacation. His generation of alternatives and consideration of potential outcomes were explicitly displayed. Since the script did not vary in content, the author ran six groups across the three media. In half of these, he stopped the script and asked whether another alternative should be considered, reinforcing affirmative responses. Those in an additional lecture group were simply instructed to consider alternatives and outcomes in solving their problems. Finally, students in a control group were told they would receive help in social problem solving, but then proceeded to solve statistical problems. He then observed all participants in a hypothetical problem situation. His results indicated (1) no differences across media, (2) no differences between the lecture and control groups, (3) a nonsignificant tendency to consider more alternative solutions and outcomes than controls manifested in those groups receiving modeling and modeling with reinforcement, and (4) a significant media by reinforcement interaction, which indicated that the modeling with reinforcement condition was the most effective. Interpretation difficulties may be attributed to three factors: the ceiling effect reported earlier for the outcome measure, the nature of the control group manipulation, and possibly, the limited nature of his half-hour training session.

Shure and Spivack (1972b) have researched a problem-solving intervention within the context of prevention for preschoolers. The intervention focused on urban preschoolers in a Head Start Program, and training consisted of 20-minute sessions daily for a period of ten weeks. More recently, the authors have published the training procedures and script used to work with small groups of children (Spivack & Shure, 1974). The training sequence focused on two major areas, development of prerequisite language skills and increasing the interpersonal skills involved in problem solving. The teachers reinforced responses to the script that were considered part of the problem-solving process, such as new solutions and consideration of outcomes. The children were tested before and after the program on a preschooler assessment device (Shure *et al.*, 1971) and on teacher-completed behavior-rating forms. Their results indicated a significant improvement on verbal problem solving for those children who were trained. They also reported that fewer aberrant behaviors were reported by the teachers and their aides in the experimental classrooms. Also, the children whose behaviors were rated more favorably following treatment indicated greater improvement on problem solving. These data have been replicated within their program over a four-year period, and preliminary evidence supports the maintenance of these skills a year later in kindergarten.

Several conclusions follow from this review of the reports on the modification and enhancement of problem-solving behavior. Foremost is the consistent emphasis on the generation of alternative solutions and consideration of possible consequences as the primary component behaviors within the problem-solving process. Also, the appropriateness of modeling procedures in the learning of this complex set of social behaviors and the importance of reinforcing these component behaviors in order to improve problem-solving strategies is highlighted. While long-term interventions tend to produce more significant changes, recent data (Stone, Hinds, & Schmidt, 1975) indicate that problem-solving skills can be taught in a brief period of time. The data reported by Spivack and Shure (1974) with four-year-olds further support the selection of problem solving as a relevant intermediate criteria in a program of prevention with young children.

Problem-Solving Training: A Strategy for Primary Prevention

We are well equipped now to design a strategy for primary prevention in the elementary school based on problem-solving training. One goal of the project to be described in subsequent chapters was to train children in independent problem-solving skills. Preliminary evidence indicates that these skills may be a relevant intermediate criterion in a program of primary prevention. Two major questions remain. One, what techniques, if any, are effective in the modification of problem-solving behaviors in the elementary school? Two, does training in problem-solving skills result in the long-term reduction of behavior disorders in the elementary school population? This subproject will address itself to the first question.

The method of implementing social problem-solving training is through the development of a specific curriculum to be taught by teachers in the classroom. The focus on curriculum follows Levine and Graziano's (1972) observation that "the ideal of primary prevention is most closely approximated through devising curricula and teaching methods which can be broadly implemented, which maximize individual development and minimize the dysfunctional aspects of schools [p. 559]." Social problem solving seems to be an excellent content for such a curricula. As mentioned in Chapter 1, it was carefully chosen to fit in well with on-going school functions while offering a powerful, enhancement-oriented approach. The development of such a curriculum meant devising a set of class exercises with specific skill objectives based on the theoretical model of problem solving advanced by D'Zurilla and Goldfried (1971). The actual training package is presented in the Appendix and discussed in more detail in Chapter 6. The method of training is focused on modeling and reinforcement procedures that could be used in the classroom.

A complete battery of assessment techniques was developed to measure the effectiveness of this program, including behavioral measures of problem solving and specific techniques to assess the impact of training on each component skill. These measures and the actual implementation of the program in the classroom are described in Chapter 6. The qualitative and quantitative results of this project are presented in Chapter 7. Finally, the school system as a whole was observed in order to assess the broader impact of this phase of the intervention. The effects of the social problem-solving program from this perspective are presented in the last chapter.

4

Secondary Prevention: A Companion Program for Socially Isolated Children

The second approach in this intervention is aimed at the development of a functional, ongoing secondary prevention program in the schools. This aspect of prevention includes two components: (1) the early identification of potential problems in groups of high-risk children, and (2) a growth-enhancing intervention aimed at reducing these problems before they become more visible and severe.

The concept of secondary prevention assumes that the problems of an emotionally maladjusted adult often begin early in life and may be noticeable in the child's personality and behavior. In secondary prevention we try to identify children who are only beginning to manifest adjustment difficulties but who are a high risk to develop greater problems as they grow older. We assume that if such youngsters can be identified early enough, the opportunity exists to help them in the most efficient and economical fashion.

Essential to the concept of secondary prevention is the assumption that maladjustment seen in childhood will persist into later life. Some maintain, however, that childhood disorders may be ephemeral, and hence argue that early identification is a waste of effort (Allinsmith & Goethals, 1962). Others, while not going as far, see the quick appearance and disappearance of behavior problems in preadolescent children as common (Glidewell, 1968; Levitt, 1971).

The bulk of the evidence, however, does suggest that there are long-term negative consequences of early adjustment problems. Robins (1966) found that children seen in mental health clinics were significantly more maladjusted over a 30-year follow-up period than demographically comparable controls. Retrospective studies have shown that adults classified as schizophrenic had significantly greater pathology in childhood than controls (Bower, Shellhamer, & Dailey, 1960; Watt, Stolurow, Lubensky, & McClelland, 1970) and that adult neurotic behavior can be accurately forecast from nursery school records (Westman, Rice,

& Bermann, 1967). Several studies have shown that identified "problem" children are still inferior on adjustment and achievement indices from three to six years later (Feldhusen, Thurston, & Benning, 1970; Stennett, 1966; Zax, Cowen, Rappaport, Beach, & Laird, 1968).

A recent 11–13-year follow-up study of children identified as having manifest or incipient maladjustment showed that such children appeared in disproportionately high frequencies in a community-wide psychiatric register (Cowen *et al.,* 1973). However, it could not be concluded that all early problems lead to later ones, as only 19% of the identified "vulnerable" children showed up in the register. What this study seems to demonstrate is that, while a screening procedure may identify many children who outgrow their problems, it picks up a large number of those who do develop psychiatric difficulties.

As discussed in Chapter 1, programs in the elementary school offer an almost ideal opportunity for reaching the greatest number of children in the important stages of their early development (Zax & Cowen, 1972). Once emotionally vulnerable children are identified in this setting, the crucial question becomes what type of intervention can best deal with these problems. Traditionally, the more seriously disturbed children are referred to mental health clinics, where they typically must face long waiting lists, high costs, and often ineffective treatment. Many of those needing help thus do not receive it (Smith, 1969).

In the past decade several basic approaches have evolved in the area of secondary preventive interventions in the schools. Consultation by professionals to school personnel about mental health problems in general, as well as case-oriented consultation, is a common approach which has not produced many well-controlled evaluations (Cutler, 1961; Gordon, Berkowitz, & Cacace, 1964; Iscoe, Pierce-Jones, Friedman, & McGehearty, 1967). A second method, involving direct crisis intervention with the families of the screened children, also has lacked rigorous evaluation procedures (Newton & Brown, 1967; Brownbridge & VanVleet, 1969). A third approach, concentrating on the education of parents and teachers of problem children about child behavior and mental health, has had some positive (Hereford, 1963) and some less encouraging (Gildea, Glidewell, & Kantor, 1967) results. In summary, there is little clear evidence for the effectiveness of any of these three types of intervention. Much of the literature in this area is purely descriptive and does not provide any framework for scientifically evaluating success. Of those studies that do attempt to assess outcome, all have serious methodological problems. Among the more common shortcomings are lack of control groups, reliance on the ratings of teachers who are aware of the purposes of a program, and a general lack of any specific measurement of behavior change.

One type of secondary preventive intervention that has been growing rapidly is the use of nonprofessionals as companions to emotionally maladjusted children. There are several advantages to this approach. In a time of shortage of professional personnel, many nonprofessionals can be supervised by a single mental health professional. Economically, of course, it is far less expensive than traditional therapy. Such programs also allow the problem child to get much more individual attention than in any of the aforementioned preventive interventions or in traditional mental health services. Perhaps most importantly, the use of nonprofessionals taps into a large, enthusiastic, and potentially talented pool of human resources. The following section will trace the history of nonprofessional companion programs, serving both mental patients and children.

History of Nonprofessional Companion Programs

The first companionship program was the Cambridge–Somerville Youth Study which began in 1938 (Powers & Witmer, 1951). Six hundred fifty preadolescent delinquent boys were divided into control and experimental groups, with the experimental boys being paired with adult male counselors. The average relationship lasted five years. Outcome, primarily measured by frequency of contact with the courts, was not found to be different for the two groups, as both showed gains.

The first program involving the use of college students as companions to hospitalized mental patients began at Boston's Metropolitan Hospital in the early 1950s, and involved over 2000 Harvard and Radcliffe students over the ensuing decade (Umbarger, Dalsimer, Morrison, & Breggin, 1962). This idea was then introduced at Connecticut Valley Hospital where eight colleges have been involved (Holzberg, Knapp, & Turner, 1967). The research emphasis in this latter program has centered primarily on changes in the students themselves.

The first major research on outcome in the mental hospital setting was done by Poser (1966) who found that coeds working as group therapists produced more positive changes in hospitalized schizophrenics on several criteria than did the professional staff. Although approximately 600 such companion programs have been reported (Goodman, 1972), the only extensive evaluation of an entire program was done recently by Rappaport *et al.* (1971).

The number of companionship programs serving children is just as large as the mental hospital programs. The populations serving as companions have been diverse, including housewives (Stern, Nummedal, & Brussell, 1971; Zax, Cowen, Izzo, Madonia, Merenda, & Trost, 1966; Nichtern, Donahue, O'Shea, Marans, Curtis, & Brady, 1964), senior citizens (Cowen, Leibowitz, & Leibowitz, 1968), and high-school students (McWilliams & Finkel, 1973), as well as college students. The most well-known companionship program must surely be that administered by the Big Brothers of America, a national institution of scattered agencies pairing fatherless boys with adult males. The relationships are quite unstructured, and no research evaluations could be found of a Big Brother program. Similar programs to Big Brothers exist across the nation, but because they are primarily service-oriented, they do not appear in the literature.

The few programs that do find their way into the literature generally present little or no empirical outcome information but rather are primarily descriptive in nature. Mitchell (1966) described a program using students from three Vermont colleges who worked with 4–15-year-old children for up to three or four years. The project was not evaluated in terms of outcome. Patterson and Patterson (1967) briefly describe a program in which college students were paired with children who were being seen in an outpatient clinic; again, no evaluation was reported. Brennan (1967), in a very similar program, found that the use of college students as a supplement to the regular services of a child guidance clinic lowered attrition rates considerably. Davison (1966) trained undergraduates as social reinforcers for autistic children at a private day care center. His evaluation found the impact of the program to be nonsignificant.

In order to derive the utmost efficiency in utilizing our mental health resources, it is crucial that different types of interventions be critically evaluated. The use of nonprofessionals as companions, first to delinquents, then to mental patients, and finally to school children, has been a very popular approach in the last decade. Although most programs have not assessed outcomes with a great deal of methodological vigor, a small number of research studies do exist. The next section of this chapter will focus critically on research-evaluating companion programs that are secondary preventive interventions—that is, programs working with children who show manifest or incipient emotional problems but who still can attend a normal school. This will exclude research such as Davison's (1966) study, which involved autistic children, and the report by Nichtern *et al.* (1964), which encompassed schizophrenic, organically impaired, and other seriously disturbed children. The latter programs would come under the classification of tertiary prevention, which deals with already existing serious problems.

Research on Companion Programs

One of the first studies using nonprofessional companions in the schools was that of Zax *et al.* (1966). A group of housewives was selected on the basis of positive recommendations from "reliable" community leaders. Training was didactic, involving formal knowledge of mental hygiene, personality development, and adjustment problems in children. In addition, on-the-job training occurred as the companions discussed the children with whom they were working in meetings with advisors. The outcome of the study was evaluated on the basis of ratings made by the companions and teachers as to whether the child had improved.

Another study (Cowen, Dorr, Trost, & Izzo, 1972) attempted to do follow-up evaluations on children who had been involved in an expanded version of the Zax *et al.* (1966) housewife program. Thirty-six mothers were interviewed an average of 20 months after their child's last contact with a companion. After the interview, the mother and the interviewer each rated the child's improvement, and generally favorable results were found.

Smith (1969) also selected his housewife companions through "reliable" community sources. The only training involved was discussions about the particular needs of the children to which they were assigned. It is not clear exactly what the companions did with the children or whether they had any specific goals. Smith merely mentions that the majority of time was spent in talking and carrying out academic tasks. Four outcome measures were used: teacher behavior-rating scales, projective tests, school performance, and IQ. No positive changes were obtained when the 37 treated children were compared to a matched control group. The only favorable results were that the teachers and principals involved liked the program and expressed interest in implementing it again. It should be noted that the control group was matched for social class and IQ, but not for age or severity of behavior problem.

Stern *et al.* (1971) used three adult females as companions for a total of five children. Training and methods were not described. Evaluation of the program's effectiveness was made uninterpretable when the control children became "contaminated" through play interactions with the volunteers and the experimental children. In addition, several children were removed from the control group entirely when their behavior became very disruptive during the course of the program.

Cowen *et al.* (1968) used retired people in their study, choosing them on the basis of a global exclusionary screening process of those who volunteered. Intellectual discussions as well as on-the-job meetings constituted the training. Unfortunately, little of what went on in the relationships is reported. The outcome criteria of teacher and companion ratings of improvement in adjustment reflected positive gains.

One of the first research evaluations of the use of college students as companions was done by Cowen, Zax, and Laird (1966). Seventeen "enthusiastic" undergraduates were selected and given no formal training other than a brief discussion about the philosophy and objectives of the program. Pretreatment and postprogram ratings on a behavior-rating scale completed by teachers failed to discriminate the experimental children from a control group. The authors suggested that the lack of results may have been due to the brevity of the program, which spanned two months, and to the lack of a careful screening process in the selection of the companions. Another study (Cowen, Carlisle, & Kaufman, 1969) investigated a similar program conducted over a five-month period. Teacher and companion ratings of the amount of improvement both indicated significant progress by the children.

Perhaps the most extensive evaluation of a nonprofessional companion program has been undertaken by Goodman (1972). In his study, 88 fifth- and sixth-grade boys were paired with undergraduate males. The companions were carefully selected from 179 applicants through a method called the Group Assessment of Interpersonal Traits (GAIT), which Goodman developed in order to assess an individual's capacity to serve in a helping role. This is the most extensive selection process found in the literature, concentrating on choosing companions with positive qualities. Training for the companions had two aspects. First, all of the companions went through a four-hour orientation meeting where it was stressed that the relationships should be kept at a one-to-one level, without the presence of others. Practice in "empathy and openness" was given through the use of a programmed instruction course on interpersonal relations. In addition, half of the companions participated in weekly group training in interpersonal relations. However, individual contact between the companions and the project staff was not mandatory after the orientation (although reports of visitations had to be filled out); only one-half of the companions had as much as an hour of consultation with a professional with regard to the relationship with their child.

Goodman carefully selected the companions and emphasized a client-centered, unstructured, one-to-one approach in the relationships. Such an approach depends on the interpersonal qualities of the companions as the treatment modality, as opposed to specific training in how to deal with the children. The success of this project was evaluated through the repeated administration of an adjective checklist and behavior-rating scale to the parents, and a sociometric device consisting of 26 behavioral referents, for which both teachers and peers had to nominate children fitting the descriptions. Thus, potentially biased ratings by the companions themselves were avoided as an important outcome measure in this study. Results showed, however, that there were no differences between the 88 experimental and 74 control children. In fact, parents considered the experimental participants to have become more unmannerly, while the control youngsters became slightly more docile. The main positive results were found in retrospective descriptions by the parents, where improvements in the presenting problems were noted.

Recently, McWilliams and Finkel (1973) used underachieving high school students, selected by guidance counselors, as companions to shy, withdrawn children. Repeated teacher-determined behavior ratings of experimental and control children revealed significantly more improvement in the experimental group, while companion ratings of improvement indicated positive changes in the experimental children. Once more, however, we know little about what was done with the children, and the outcome assessment did not involve any specific observational measures.

Selection procedures for these studies ranged from gross negative screening of volunteers (Cowen *et al.,* 1968) to sophisticated evaluation of therapeutic talent (Goodman, 1972). There is no evidence of differential results from these approaches. The studies cited all seem to have involved fairly minimal training, relying on the interpersonal qualities of the nonprofessionals. The actual interventions with the children either were not described in detail or were intentionally unstructured (Goodman, 1972).

Most of the research also does not consider that maladjustment covers a wide range of problems which may require differential interventions. McWilliams and Finkel (1973) worked with a specific population of withdrawn children; they did not, however, state how their intervention was specifically oriented to such difficulties. Smith (1969) and Goodman (1972) did post hoc analyses which examine their programs' effects on different subgroups. Again, however, little attention is given as to how the processes of their interventions relate to the different problems among their subjects.

Behavioral Approaches in Secondary Prevention

As mentioned in Chapter 1, one of the underlying orientations of this book is the integration of a behavioral approach with the community perspective. One of the most fruitful areas of this merger is in secondary prevention programs using nonprofessionals. The adoption of the behavioral approach is useful for the community interventionist because it offers a specific format for training the nonprofessional. Training can be organized in precise behavioral steps. Specific behaviors can be targeted and outcomes can be objectively and independently assessed.

On the other hand, Reppucci and Saunders (1974) note that one of the major problems of implementing behavioral programs is the limited amount of professional personnel available to deliver and/or assess the impact of the behavioral techniques. Nonprofessionals, however, are readily abundant, eager, and available to serve in such roles. It is our belief that nonprofessional groups trained in behavioral analysis would be an excellent adjunct to the mental health team in the schools and would be especially useful in secondary prevention efforts.

Two relatively recent studies document the utility of such an integration in practice. Fo and O'Donnell (1974) found that school attendance was increased when adult companions from the community were trained to use contingency management techniques. Using such procedures, children who were rewarded with social and/or material reinforcement for attending school decreased significantly in truancy. This was not the case for children seen by the same companions in a noncontingent "relationship" interaction or for the control group, which received no treatment. Subsequent implementation of contingencies in the relationship condition was, however, successful in increasing school attendance. Another group of six children with a variety of difficulties (for example, fighting, not completing home or school chores) also showed a significant reduction of such problems in the contingent conditions.

Patterson (1974) reported a study with a twelve-month follow-up showing improvement of boys with conduct problems in both home-based and classroom-centered programs. Parents were used as change agents in the home and trained behavior analysts were employed in the classroom. Patterson (1974) concluded his study recommending an extension of such research interventions by other investigators. He also reported that he is currently training nonprofessionals as change agents in similar projects at the Oregon Research Institute.

Behavior Change of Socially Withdrawn Children

In order to maximize the efficiency of programs of secondary prevention in the schools, it is important to consider what types of behaviors would be most likely to predict future maladjustment and what problem behaviors are likely to be outgrown as the child matures. Present methods of identifying maladjusted children give little apparent consideration to classifying different types of difficulties with this criterion in mind. Usually, teachers are relied upon either to refer "problem" children or to fill out behavior checklists that are then used as screening devices. Historically, the attention of teachers has been most readily drawn to the aggressive, acting-out child. The behavior pattern of the withdrawn, socially isolated child is frequently ignored, because it does not actively cause any trouble for the teacher.

As long as 45 years ago, studies have shown that while teachers consider behaviors that interfere with classroom management to be most important, mental health professionals see behaviors such as unsociability, fearfulness, and withdrawal to be more crucial to future adjustment (Louttit, 1936). In a similar fashion, Bach and Wyden (1968) pointed out that Lee Harvey Oswald, Sirhan Sirhan, and James Earl Ray were all withdrawn, aloof, and secretive as children. Studies showing schizophrenic personality types to be introverted, shut in, and withdrawn (Watt *et al.,* 1970) also support the importance of an increased emphasis on social isolation. A contrasting view, however, is offered by Clarizio (1969), who concludes that children with severe acting-out, aggressive behavior are more likely to manifest significant later adjustment problems than shy, withdrawn children who, he feels, may outgrow their early difficulties.

The needs of the socially isolated child have not received much attention in most mental health programs. Exceptions have been the previously mentioned McWilliams and Finkel (1973) study, which concentrated on such a population, and the Goodman (1972) intervention, which found that the companion program was more effective for quiet, withdrawn children. Lorion, Cowen, and Caldwell (1974) have also concluded that the Primary Mental Health Project intervention has been most effective with "shy–anxious children" and relatively less successful with children described as acting-out or having learning problems. It appears, therefore, that socially isolated children may be the ideal target for a behaviorally based secondary prevention project in the schools.

Most interventions with such children using the behavioral approach have appeared as case studies in the behavior modification literature. Four studies (Allen, Hart, Buell, Harris, & Wolf, 1964; Harris, Johnston, Kelley, & Wolf, 1964; Hart, Reynolds, Baer, Brawley, & Harris, 1968; Kirby & Toler, 1970) have shown that contingent social reinforcement for cooperative social interactions increased such behavior in noncooperative, socially isolated preschoolers. Another study (Buell, Stottard, Harris, & Baer, 1968) demonstrated that the contingent reinforcement of outdoor play in an isolated preschooler led to collateral social development. Clement and his associates (Clement & Milne, 1967; Clement, Roberts, & Lantz, 1970) have used social and tangible reinforcers in a group play situation to increase the social behavior of withdrawn second- through fourth-grade boys. Unfortunately, most of these studies deal with only single subjects and do not present follow-up data pertaining to the permanence of behavior change.

O'Connor (1969) has demonstrated that symbolic modeling films can also increase the social behavior of isolated preschoolers. In a later study (O'Connor, 1972), it was found that treatments involving shaping (that is, reinforcing successive approximations of a desired behavior), symbolic modeling, and a combination of the two all increased social interactions; however, at a follow-up the group receiving only shaping had returned to their initial level of functioning. This shaping intervention was a poor one in that methods to insure the maintenance of behavior change (such as intermittent schedules of reinforcement) were totally neglected. An interesting compromise is found in a study using a technique called "modeling with guided participation" (Ross *et al.*, 1971). This approach used a college student as a live model to a socially withdrawn six-year-old; implicit in the intervention seems to be social reinforcement for appropriate behaviors. The results, obtained from independent behavioral ratings, provided a quite convincing demonstration of the efficacy of this procedure.

It therefore can be seen that experimentally validated methods of intervention do exist that can be employed with children who are socially isolated and deficient in social skills. The technique employed by Ross *et al.* (1971) seems particularly promising. Perhaps most important, these behavior modification studies have reliably employed objective behavioral rating systems that provide a clear-cut set of outcome criteria that differ from the verbal-report assessments used in many studies.

The Current Project

The current comprehensive mental health program includes an attempt at a rigorous evaluation of a secondary preventive intervention involving the use of college students as companions to children identified as likely to develop emotional adjustment difficulties. Several facets make this project different from previous research. First, the target population has a specified problem—these children are deficient in social skills, which presumably increases their social isolation. Such a population has frequently been neglected by mental health resources in the schools.

Secondly, the companions are given intensive training in the use of social reinforcement and modeling techniques. Weekly meetings insure that specific goals are formulated for each child, and that the interventions are proceeding satisfactorily toward these goals. Such an approach is quite different from the unstructured, unspecified relational interactions found in most programs. This training and supervision is in addition to the selection of socially skilled companions.

Most importantly, objective behavioral criteria are employed for the selection of the children and for evaluation of the outcome of the study. The selection of such criteria is made simple by the specification of a particular target population with which to deal. The main behavioral criterion is the frequency of social interactions with other children during free play, as assessed by a group of trained independent observers. Thus teacher nominations of social isolates can be validated, experimental and control groups are matchable, and program effectiveness is evaluated through the use of an independent behavioral assessment technique. Within this phase of the program, we operationally defined children who do not interact with their peers as deficient in social skills. An increase in social interactions would indicate an increase in social skills, which is assumed to imply a more positive prognosis for future emotional adjustment.

A detailed description of the procedure of the intervention is found in Chapter 6. The specific questions to be considered by this aspect of the study may be stated as the following:

1. Are teacher referrals of socially isolated children valid? Do nominated children differ from "normal" youngsters on behavioral, self-reported, and peer-rated criteria?
2. Is the program effective? Do experimental children show greater positive change in their social behaviors than control children, and what is the nature, consistency and stability of these changes? A complimentary question is whether the groups differ on secondary measures of change such as sociometric nominations by peers, behavior ratings by teachers, self-reported self-esteem, and companion ratings.
3. What is the relationship between the behaviorally measured change and the other indices of improvement, in particular the frequently used teacher ratings and companion ratings?
4. Are process differences, such as the type of activities the companions engage in, highly correlated with behavior change?
5. Does participation in the program affect the companions' attitudes toward themselves, their careers, children, and elementary schools?
6. Can such a program be maintained in the school system?

Answers to the first five questions are provided in Chapter 8; the wider impact of the program on the school is discussed in Chapter 10.

5

Behavior Analysis and Tertiary Prevention: Teacher Training in Classroom Management

Most educators are clearly aware of their responsibilities for aiding and educating even those pupils who are behaviorally disruptive or are lacking vital study skills. Elementary school personnel are primarily committed to ensuring the most optimal academic education for their students, and thus they wish to reduce the distraction that problematic children cause to both their teachers and the other students engaged in the learning process. Teachers quickly lose their efficiency and effectiveness as instructors if they must continually interrupt lessons to discipline disruptive children and regain the attention of other distracted pupils. Administrators and teachers also recognize to varying degrees a certain amount of responsibility for the social and personal development of individual pupils. When a pupil emits severe disruptive behaviors in the classroom, his or her potential for future academic success, peer adjustment, and personal adjustment to society suffers.

One vitally important question for educators, then, is how to best remediate academic and behavior problems. Until the 1950s, children who became identified as disruptive were ordinarily referred to an outpatient child guidance clinic, or, if the problem was severe enough, to a residential treatment center (Goodwin, 1970; Mordock & Phillips, 1971). The place for treatment was seen to be outside of the school, and the primary psychological responsibility of the schools was, at most, to be a diagnostic assessment and referral service. More recently, an increasing number of attempts have been made to treat at least those children having less severe problems within the school system itself. Treatment is ordinarily provided by specialized counselors and consultants hired by the system (Hops, 1971).

Dealing with the problem behaviors of elementary school pupils within their school has a number of advantages. First, since teachers have easier access to the source of treatment when it is within the school system, they would not have to wait until the child's problem behaviors became more severe before referral could be made. Second, by being able to intervene earlier with the developing problem, the school's behavior change agent will have a better chance to quickly and completely remediate the difficulty (Lovitt, 1970). This issue was discussed at length in the previous chapter. Third, treatment of a child using the school's counseling or consulting services is less stigmatizing to the child than referral to an outside agency. Although classmates may still be aware of differential treatment, the intervention is occurring in the school environment rather than at a clinic which is recognized as a place where "the troublemakers" and "deviants" of the community are taken. This minimization of stigma may be even more important for future teachers of the child who refer to his or her record. Fourth, the child can potentially be treated more frequently by the change agent because the latter is in close proximity to the child during the school day. More teaching trials lead to quicker learning. A final advantage is that in-school treatment is generally less expensive for the school system, the child's family, and the community. These points are all consonant with the emphasis of community psychology on tertiary prevention of an individual's currently existing problems by quick amelioration of these problems within his customary environment (Cowen, 1967).

Treatment Models within the School System

In the previous discussion, within-school interventions for behavior problems have been contrasted to outside referrals, and this may have suggested that all within-school treatment programs are highly similar. This is not the case. A major source of difference is whether the treatment of a child is directly implemented by (1) a psychological counselor such as the school psychologist or the social worker or (2) the teachers themselves with the aid of a consultant. In the former case, the mental health professional works directly with the child, usually in his or her office at the school, and only occasionally in the actual classroom environment. In the latter case, the professional only indirectly effects changes in the problem child's behavior by first directly counseling the teacher to change his or her own behavior. By manipulating the child's classroom environment through the planned systematic alteration of the teacher's reactions toward the child, the consultant expects to reduce the child's problem behaviors and foster appropriate academic study behaviors in the classroom situation. In the context of traditional psychotherapy, the consultant can be viewed as treating the teacher rather than the child.

Consultation to such community care givers as elementary school teachers is expressly called for as one of the five essential services provided by the Community Mental Health Centers Act of 1963 (Cook, 1970), and is therefore of major concern to community psychologists. Caplan (1963) has outlined four types of mental health consultation, of which two are especially relevant for aiding elementary school teachers working with problem pupils. The first form, client-centered case consultation, involves a consultant who counsels an individual consultee (teacher) to help find the most effective treatment for a specific client (child). The consultant's primary duty is to diagnose the client's problem and suggest a suitable treatment. The consultant is only secondarily interested in increasing the consultee's competence to handle this class of problems in the future. In contrast, consultee-centered case consultation is primarily designed to improve the consultee's working competence and knowledge of how to deal generally with clients having certain problems, even though the consultant–consultee contact may have originally occurred because of a specific problem client. The consultant relationship with the consultee is usually on a one-to-one basis, as in the client-centered consultation.

Caplan (1963) believes that the essential aspects for both types of consultation are that the consultee will come to deal more effectively with his or her problem, and that it is only the consultee who has direct control of the treatment of the client. However, the preventive effects of consultation do not accrue to the consultee, but rather to the client. Not only is it hoped that the problems of the client will be quickly ameliorated, thus preventing potentially more damage to that individual, but also future clients of the consultee with similar problems will receive the benefits of the consultee's increased competence (Caplan, 1963; Cook, 1970). The second consultation model, however, has the more significant preventive effects because of its stronger emphasis on training the consultee.

Kelly (1971) has stated more specifically that in order to show experimentally the preventive aspect of consultation, the "radiating effects" on the clients must be measured, as well as immediate behavioral changes emitted by the consultee. Since Kelly states that an intervention can be considered effective only if the consultee produces change in many significant others, the preventive effects should not be limited to just the treatment relationship between the teacher–consultee and the severe problem child. In the classroom there should also be evidence of behavior changes in the less severe problem children and normal children who were not specifically treated by the teacher but who did experience the radiating effects of general improvement in teacher behavior due to the consultation program.

Extending Kelly's concepts several steps further to the trilevel prevention schema stated by Cowen (1967), tertiary prevention can be demonstrated if the behaviors of the most severe problem children are improved, secondary prevention can be shown if those children with study skill deficits or less severely disruptive behaviors are improved, and primary prevention would be evidenced if the whole class came to behave more effectively and appropriately in the classroom situation.

Consultation strategies with elementary school teachers have recently been used in a number of research projects that were designed to demonstrate the therapeutic efficacy of various behavior change techniques derived from the operant conditioning research of Skinner (1953). Behavioral analysts use a functional diagnostic approach that focuses on the immediate environment to determine which situations elicit problems and which environmental consequences, including the reactions of significant others, maintain the behavior. The major assumption is that most behaviors are learned and are therefore potentially changeable, since new behaviors can be learned to replace the original problematic ones. Behaviors are learned because they lead to satisfying consequences or reinforcements for the individual. A person's immediate environment is manipulated to develop new desirable behaviors and to eliminate inappropriate ones by arrangement of differential consequences.

Since behavior analysts typically assume that a specific behavior is maintained by its situational consequences, their insistence on the necessity of treating the child in the classroom to change problem behaviors that occur in this setting is understandable. This therapeutic orientation is at variance with the majority of traditional evocative psychotherapeutic approaches, most of which require extensive testing and interviews to determine the status of internal attitudes, feelings, and beliefs, and personal family history. These latter therapies are based on the premise that an individual's behavior will not change until his or her attitudes and beliefs have, and therefore therapy should consist of verbal encounters designed to uncover the patient's internally determined perceptions. The optimal environment in which to achieve this change would be a counselor's office rather than a teacher's classroom. While a teacher could carry out a behavioral treatment project on a disruptive child relatively easily during the teaching of class, engagement in a verbal, personality-change treatment with such a child would be extremely impractical. One limitation of evocative approaches is the problem of transferring behavior changes that occur in the therapeutic setting into the classroom.

Not only is it possible to engage in behavior analysis in a classroom, it is highly desirable to do so. The school situation is a natural implementation point for behavioral change projects because of the significant amount of contact time that teachers have with their pupils. Because the teacher maintains an authoritative role in the classroom, the teacher has the power to control the behavioral consequences of many student activities. In recent years, behavior analysts have determined how to do this quite effectively and systematically.

Since relatively little theoretical background is required to use behavior change techniques successfully, the teacher can be quickly and efficiently trained. A number of studies have demonstrated that a teacher actually can influence the incidence of problematic classroom behaviors by increasing or decreasing the attention and social reinforcement that he or she gives contingently to specific student behaviors (Becker, Madsen, Arnold, & Thomas, 1967; Hall, Lund, & Jackson, 1968; Madsen, Becker, & Thomas, 1968; Thomas *et al.,* 1968). The best approach for training teachers in behavior change skills involves an extensive, on-going consultative process, in which the consultant can monitor and reinforce the consultee's progress (Goodwin, 1970; Grieger, Mordock, & Breyer, 1970).

Conceptually, it is not a far jump to see a marriage of convenience between behavioral analysis and community psychology as a useful strategy in tertiary prevention. The mutual use of consultation as a training procedure to help teachers deal with disruptive pupils provides a strong basis for this rapproachment. The effective technology of behavior analysis provides an excellent tool to implement a mental health philosophy of early prevention of behavioral disorders. While behavior analysis has frequently been shown to aid severely disruptive children, thus providing tertiary prevention, there are indications that teachers utilizing such behavioral techniques as token economies can even increase the academic achievement and appropriate behavior of normal children (Bushel, Wrobel, & Michaelis, 1968; Glynn, 1970; Lovitt, Guppy, & Blattner, 1969; Packard, 1970), implying their effectiveness in primary and secondary prevention.

In summarizing the advantages of this behavioral-analytic consultation model over direct treatment by a within-school counselor, it is evident that several gains of in-school treatment over out-of-school treatment are maximized under the consultation model. Specifically, in accord with the advantages discussed previously, (1) the child could get treatment even earlier in the developmental chain of his or her problem, (2) the child will be less stigmatized since he or she will not be withdrawn from the classroom for regular counseling sessions, and (3) the child will be available for treatment for a much greater period of time. Other advantages that accrue from consultation are: (4) training transfer, which allows the teacher to become more reinforcing to an increasing number of students and provides the skills to carry out future behavior change projects, and (5) the positive benefits that derive from early and accurate diagnosis and effective treatment based on empirical evaluation.

In formulating a specific behavioral description of the child's problem, an accurate analysis can be made of the causes and the exact nature of the problem, the situations in which the problem is most likely to occur, as well as continuing assessments of behavioral changes throughout the course of treatment. Intervention will presumably have a greater likelihood of changing a pupil's inappropriate behaviors when the treatment involves actually working through problem situations in the real environment and manipulating environmental pressures on the child, rather than just discussing the problem with the child in a therapy room. Direct changes can be made in the environment in which the problem occurs by varying the behaviors of teachers and peers or specific characteristics of the classroom and class format. The behavioral changes that occur in treatment within the school are likely to persist once therapy is terminated. Behavioral regressions or complications that may arise can also be readily identified and dealt with quickly.

Individual and Group Modes of Consultation

If it is agreed that behavioral-analytic consultation is a desirable approach for treating and preventing behavioral disorders, the next step for mental health professionals and educators is to explore various methods of implementing consultation programs. The two basic modes of delivering consultant services that have developed are workshop consultation (Mordock & Phillips, 1971; Zimmerman, Zimmerman, Rider, Smith, & Dinn, 1971) and individual consultation, with the difference between the two being the number of consultees who are trained at a given time.

In individually oriented delivery modes, the consultant advises teachers on a one-to-one basis about general reinforcement theory and principles and how to set up specific behavior change projects. The published examples of this consultation have followed both the client-centered and consultee-centered approaches outlined by Caplan (1963). Many research studies show that this format enables consultants to train teachers effectively in special classes (Brown, Montgomery, & Barclay, 1969; Hops, 1971), or in regular elementary classes (Breyer, Calchera, & Cann, 1971; Buys, 1972; Cossairt, Hall, & Hopkins, 1973; Hall, Panyan, Rabon, & Broden, 1968) to use social, tangible, and activity reinforcers to change the problem behaviors of their elementary school pupils. The behavioral improvement of the students in all of these studies was objectively rated by observers, and, in several cases (Breyer, Calchera, & Cann, 1971; Hall, Panyan, Rabon, & Broden, 1968), increases in the teachers' social reinforcement rate was also observed.

The second mode of consultation is potentially a more efficient and practical model for school systems to employ. Here the consultant trains a number of teachers at one time using a multisession workshop format. The consultant presents various behavioral change principles to the teachers, and they attempt to mold these into techniques that capitalize on the strengths of those individuals with problematic behaviors, in the manner of Caplan's (1963) description of consultee-centered case consultation. This approach is differentiated from those that have used the context of traditional graduate level behavior change courses to train teachers effectively in practical applications of behavior analysis (Hall, Fox, Willard, Goldsmith, Emerson, Owen, Davis, & Porcia, 1971; MacDonald & Gallimore, 1972). The latter, although having been shown to produce significant teacher and pupil behavior change, extend beyond the constraints of ordinary school-sponsored in-service training by requiring more teacher time, effort, and money, and by taking place outside the confines of the school itself.

Workshop programs, in addition to their increased efficiency, embody several other distinct advantages. Individual social reinforcement is provided by the consultant to specific teachers who acquire the behavior change skills, and, in addition, extra individual and group reinforcements are available from the other participating teachers. Teachers in such programs can also model their attempts to use the social reinforcement techniques on both the consultant and those teachers in the workshop who have been the most effective behavior change agents. A final advantage is that the teachers can potentially form a fairly permanent, self-sufficient group in which they will habitually consult one another concerning problems in implementing subsequent behavior change techniques. For these advantages to occur, teacher-initiated interactions should be stressed and the workshop sessions should be discussion oriented and highly involving rather than lecture dominated.

In relation to individual consultation, the workshop format also has some potential disadvantages. The consultees lack the individual attention of the consultant, and they thus may find it more difficult to rectify misunderstandings about the principles that are presented. In addition, there is less time and sometimes more reluctance to focus on individual problem children during the consultation.

The effectiveness of the workshop approach in producing pupil behavior changes has not yet been adequately demonstrated. Four recent studies have evaluated teachers' abilities as behavior change agents after undergoing a series of behavior modification workshops, but three of these have presented merely descriptive results.

Kennedy and Seidman (1972) conducted a four-session contingency management workshop in conjunction with a related human relations workshop. The 90-minute sessions were a combination of lecture and discussion, and although contingency contracting was the major emphasis, shaping and social reinforcement were also discussed. In all, several hundred teachers from 14 elementary schools attended the series of workshops when they were given in each school. The reported results were of a highly subjective nature, consisting of the author's judgements that the teachers had become more positive in their behavior and that they had requested more workshops on behavior modification.

Gile, Neth, & Shack (1972) presented eight 50-minute workshop sessions to 11 teachers who taught kindergarten through fourth grade. Their comprehensive workshop program covered observational procedures and major behavior modification techniques. Several pretreatment and postintervention questionnaires were administered, and an increase in knowledge of behavior modification principles was found after workshop training. Improvement on formulation of corrective strategies for hypothetical behavior problems was also noted. The teachers reported using behavioral techniques more frequently after the program.

Andrews (1970) reported on four weekly workshops with eleven teachers who instructed kindergarten through fourth-grade children. Observation techniques, as well as reinforcement, extinction, and counterconditioning procedures were discussed. The article described several of the teacher-prepared observation reports of pupil behavior, all of which showed dramatic improvement of target pupil behavior. The results of a program evaluation questionnaire showed that the teachers recommended the workshops to others and that they felt ten of the eleven target children showed at least some improvement.

While these three studies appeared to have detailed and well-planned information delivery components and reported signs of effectiveness, there were several obvious flaws in their experimental methodology and evaluation efforts that could serve to confound conclusions. The primary problem was the lack of actual behavioral evidence obtained by unobtrusive observers of the claimed changes in teacher and pupil behavior. The self-report measures that were used were constructed by the various authors, and no reliability or validity data were available. Teachers could have either deliberately or inadvertently biased their reports in order to please the experimenters. The major flaw in the experimental design was the absence of teacher and pupil control groups.

These shortcomings were avoided by Madsen, Madsen, Saudargas, Hammond, Smith, and Edgar (1970) in their evaluation of a two-week summer workshop which included weekly small-group sessions during the following year. This workshop was directed at training 28 kindergarten through sixth-grade teachers in more systematic formulations of classroom rules as well as reinforcement and extinction procedures. Using a time-sampling observational technique, undergraduate raters recorded the classroom behavior not only of the workshop teachers and their pupils, but also of 32 untrained control teachers and their pupils. As an indication of the effectiveness of the workshop, workshop teachers exhibited twice as many approval behaviors to appropriate student behaviors as did control teachers, and the disruptive students of the workshop teachers exhibited less than one-half the percentage of inappropriate behaviors shown by problem students in control classes.

However, the Madsen *et al.* (1970) study still had several methodological difficulties. The experimenters presented only the average ratings in workshop and control teachers' classrooms that were made over the semester following the workshop. There was no indication that the postworkshop differences were caused by the workshops rather than being representative of initial differences between the experimental and control teachers. In addition, the experimental teachers were shown exactly what the dependent measures of in-class observation were meant to assess as a result of feedback from the consultants during the weekly small-group sessions after the workshop. They thus could have temporarily altered their behavior in a desirable way much more easily than could have the control teachers.

Research Goals of the Behavioral Analysis Program

Although consultee-centered behavioral-analytic consultation in a workshop format appears to be an advantageous method of dealing with disruptive and academically deficient elementary school students, the previous literature review suggests that the effectiveness of this intervention has not yet been adequately demonstrated. Therefore, the fundamental purpose of this phase of the present investigation is to determine whether such workshops will lead to positive changes in the behavior of teachers and pupils. There are four subhypotheses to be examined here.

The first prediction is that certain classroom behaviors of the workshop teachers should change from pretest levels as a result of the workshop and that these changes should be maintained during a follow-up period. Specifically, compared with a group of untreated control teachers, the workshop teachers will become (1) more verbally reinforcing and (2) more accurate in their estimates of the on-task behavior of their students. The latter prediction was made because teachers were taught precise observational skills in the workshop and hence should be more realistically aware of the disruptive behavior of specific children. Teacher awareness of actual student behaviors is a vital prerequisite for the teacher becoming an effective behavior change agent (Hall, 1971b).

Secondly, the appropriate classroom behavior of those disruptive and academically deficient target students who are specifically treated by the workshop teachers will increase during treatment from the baseline level, and this increase will be maintained over follow-up. The behavior of these target children will be examined in relation to matched children in the control teachers' classes. In addition, three types of inappropriate behavior classified as aggressive, disruptive, and passive will be observed to determine changes in the performance of target children.

Thirdly, appropriate classroom behavior of the untargeted disruptive pupils and the nondisruptive pupils in workshop teachers' classes will also improve during the intervention period, in relation to similar children in control classes. Again, the experimental children will be continually rated on the three types of inappropriate behavior to see if there are decreases. This hypothesis results from Kelly's (1971) previously noted prediction that "radiating effects" should emanate from the teacher–consultee to many of the significant others in his or her educational life-space, and also from the expectation that teachers will generalize their use of reinforcement to all children (Sulzer & Mayer, 1972).

Finally, workshop teacher ratings of their pupils on a problem behavior checklist should improve from pretest to posttest, whereas the ratings by control teachers will not.

While the principal area investigated by this phase of the intervention is the behavioral efficacy of the workshops, three secondary goals also exist. The first of these is to discover some general correlates of highly disruptive behavior and to assess the nonbehavioral changes that occur with children who are the subjects of behavior change efforts. Although there are many studies reporting the behavioral changes resulting from behavior modification attempts with children, very few studies have reported psychometrically measured attitudinal changes of the children. Two exceptions are Ward and Baker's (1968) study which found that a reduction of classroom disruptive behavior of several children did not produce changes on an intelligence test or the Draw-A-Person Test, although these were not particularly appropriate dependent measures for this purpose, and the research of Buys (1972) who found that an increase in treated childrens' appropriate behavior was correlated with a greater belief by the children that their teacher liked them and with more favorable attitudes toward their teacher and school.

Some behavioral-analytic researchers are reluctant to assess any behaviors that are not observable because of the possibility of inaccurate or biased responding. However, children do not just learn discrete stimulus–response behavior patterns whereby they would respond in a different way to every different stimulus in the environment. Rather, children react with a certain amount of consistency across different stimuli and situations, and this consistency cannot be attributed to simple stimulus generalization alone. Several researchers (Blackwood, 1970; Glynn, 1970; Packard, 1970) have hypothesized that children acquire consistent, desirable patterns of behavior as a result of the increased or internalized self-control gained from the successful management of their own behavior during behavior-change projects, but this assumption has not been empirically demonstrated. In addition, consistency of behavior across situations has been attributed to a person's expectancies that a particular behavior will achieve a highly valued reward (Rotter *et al.*, 1972), but no empirical attempt has applied this exploration to behavior change of children in classrooms.

To summarize, changes in the appropriate behavior of experimental students are expected to be accompanied by changes in the children's locus of control, expectancy for success, self esteem, acceptance by peers, and attitudes toward teacher and school. Correlates of disruptive behavior in general will also be investigated.

There is no research evidence at present to indicate what kind of teachers achieve maximal benefit from behavior change workshops. Another secondary goal is to differentiate those teachers who benefit most from the workshops from those who benefit least.

One important variable for the success of behavior change approaches in the classroom is the degree of organization that a teacher exhibits when planning and executing the class lessons (Abidin, 1971; Greiger *et al.*, 1970). The teacher must be conscientious and have at least average organizational ability. A teacher's expectancy that he or she would be able to change a student's behavior through the behavior change strategies can also affect the teacher's ability to implement those strategies, particularly if he or she has low expectancies for the success of the techniques (Abidin, 1972; O'Leary & Drabman, 1971). Thirdly, the degree to which children find a teacher's attention to be rewarding (that is, social reinforcement value) is suggested as a most important predictor for the effectiveness of the teacher's behavior modification attempts (Abidin, 1971; Buys, 1972; Greiger *et al.*, 1970; O'Leary & Drabman, 1971). Finally, the teachers' actual behavior during the workshops, including their attention and their number of yawns, questions asked, and questions answered, may serve as predictors for specific teacher effectiveness.

A final secondary goal is to examine some of the correlates of the change in teacher behavior as a result of workshop participation. Specifically, teachers will make more favorable global ratings of the target children and of the whole class, and their expectancies for being able to change students' behavior will increase. Attitudes about job satisfaction, teaching role, and the success of the workshops and their components will also be assessed. Because of the small number of teachers, these questions will be examined only at a broad descriptive level.

As with the previous two components of the overall program, the specific strategies of implementing this intervention are provided in Chapter 6. The outcomes relating to the hypotheses just discussed can be found in Chapter 9. The next chapter provides a guiding framework for establishing a collaborative experimental innovation within a school system.

Part III

FROM PRINCIPLES TO A PROGRAM: THE COLLABORATIVE INTERVENTION IN ACTION

6

Getting It All Together in the School

The first five chapters described the theoretical model and guiding assumptions of the school intervention as well as the specific rationale behind each of the three subcomponents of the overall project. This chapter presents the actual procedures used to convert the proposed program into reality. It illustrates the real-life operation of the intervention and our attempts to assess its impact.

Whereas Chapter 2 may be considered as a blueprint for implementing and assessing comprehensive mental health interventions in school settings, the present chapter describes a finished product which incorporates many of the themes presented earlier. Our gradual entry into the school is first described, followed by our development of a viable structure of volunteers and an adequate and comprehensive program of evaluation. Finally, the structure of each component within the overall project and the specific assessment techniques used to evaluate its effectiveness are discussed. Despite the interlocking nature of these components, each level of intervention was designed as a complete and self-sufficient unit.

Obtaining Access to the School

The Connecticut town in which the project was conducted has a picturesque New England atmosphere. A large white church, a small town meeting house, and the public school which housed the intervention occupy three sides of a finely manicured village green. These buildings are flanked by stately homes, several of which date back to the founding of the town in 1715. The population of slightly over 9000 is almost totally white and predominantly Protestant in religious outlook.

The sense of history and initial impression of quaint tranquility one receives upon entering the town is somewhat illusory. Completion of a nearby interstate highway and the rapid growth of a major state university located about ten miles away has led to increased suburbanization in this formerly rural area. The socioeconomic backgrounds of the residents vary greatly. Farming is still a widely practiced occupation, although an even larger number of white-collar and professionally employed persons have moved into the community during the past decade.

School enrollment has risen at an average annual rate of 3% since 1970; at the time the project was initiated, it stood at 2134 students in the elementary grades and 663 in high school. Pupils in kindergarten through the eighth grade were housed in three separate buildings that formed a large educational park. The host school, which contained 483 third- and fourth-grade students, was built in 1908 and was enlarged in 1947 and 1953. Students in the project school were arbitrarily assigned to 19 homerooms as part of a new individualized educational system the school was introducing. All children and 17 of the 19 female teachers were included in some aspect of the various programs that were conducted.

Coincident with the beginning of the project, school personnel changed from an eclectic, traditional approach to an Individually Guided Education (IGE) program format. IGE allows each child to complete specific lesson packages in arithmetic and reading skills at his or her own pace. The implementation of IGE resulted in extra work plus some administrative and role confusion for the teaching staff. The school system was thus undergoing certain stresses resulting from these rather dramatic educational alterations concurrent with our implementation.

Because of the IGE program, the school was divided into four teaching units. Each of the units was composed of four or five teachers. Daily unit meetings were held to coordinate the teachers' academic activities. Within each unit, the pupils went to different classrooms for different subjects. Third and fourth graders were frequently present in the same classroom. In contrast to most elementary schools, a particular student was not usually with the same specific teacher throughout the day.

The access for this consultation program into the school system was greatly aided by the previous connections between this system and the faculty and the graduate students of the department of psychology at the University of Connecticut. For the last three years, some diagnostic and psychotherapeutic services had been provided to the school system at no cost by graduate students in supervised practicum courses. In addition, a psychology graduate student had conducted a service-oriented master's thesis the preceding year at the school. In his informal contacts with various teachers, he noted frequent inquiries about how to deal with particularly disruptive pupils.

One month before the end of the school year, which preceded the target date for beginning the intervention, the school principal and superintendent of instruction agreed to support a proposal for the project. The proposal had been drafted by three graduate students in conjunction with two faculty advisors. This proposal was also instrumental in helping to obtain a grant from the

University of Connecticut Research Foundation to cover purchases of evaluation materials. Although the use of volunteers made for a low-budget enterprise that was offered without cost to the school, a fiscal report estimating probable cost of identical services from outside agencies was prepared. The budget served to excite important school administrators about the program and was useful in helping them justify the program at community and board of education meetings.

During the summer, the *active* cooperation of the principal was obtained during a series of planning meetings. The principal was regarded as a member of the consulting staff, and his suggestions on how the program might best be implemented within the actual constraints of the daily school operation were sought and utilized. His interest generated enthusiasm among the teachers and was a critical factor in helping launch the program.

A meeting between the five-member consultation team, the principal, and all of the teachers was held just prior to the resumption of classes for the year. A detailed explanation of the project was presented, and the advantages and costs of each program from the point of view of the children, teachers, and consultants were clarified. Based upon the suggestions of the principal, a service-oriented approach was adopted. Following this general presentation, the consultants met with the teachers in small groups so that the latter would be less inhibited about asking questions and voicing their concerns. As a further inducement for teacher participation, any staff member who volunteered was offered the option of receiving three graduate level academic course credits.

As a result of this meeting, four teachers from one particular unit agreed to participate in the problem-solving workshops, six teachers signed up for the behavior-training program, and seven additional teachers consented to allow observers into their classrooms. These seven teachers comprised a control group against which the efficacy of the behavior modification workshops was compared. All 19 teachers agreed to nominate socially withdrawn children as candidates for the companionship program, which was conducted outside of the classroom. Figure 6.1 summarizes the overall design of the project in relation to the four units of the target school.

Developing a Volunteer Organization

The graduate student and faculty consultants met weekly during the spring and summer prior to the initiation of the program to plan the intervention strategies in detail. Discussion with the principal yielded vital information regarding the number of children who might possibly benefit from the programs and these data allowed an accurate estimate of volunteer manpower needs to be made. Potential volunteers were recruited from undergraduate psychology courses.

The use of volunteers was planned carefully so as to avoid unnecessary duplication of effort and to insure the efficient and complete collection of large amounts of information. In order to accomplish these aims, the hierarchical

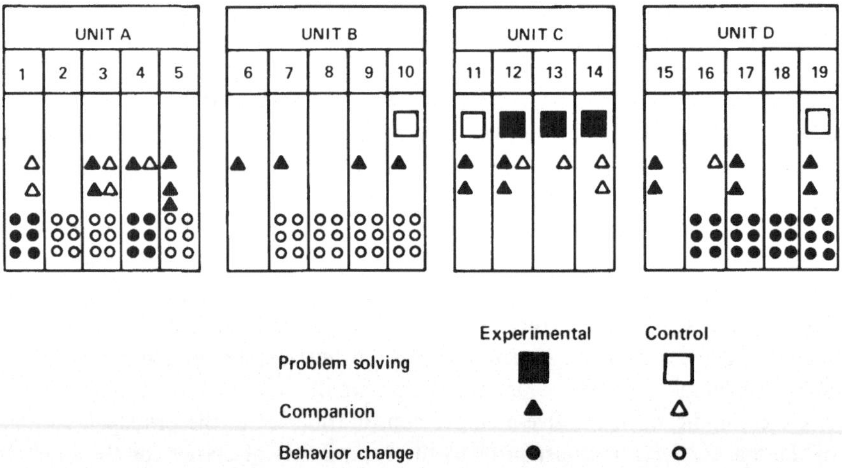

FIG. 6.1 Overall design of the intervention within classrooms.

organizational framework shown in Fig. 6.2 was employed. Two faculty advisors assumed overall administrative responsibility for all programs. Each of the three graduate students designed and evaluated a particular intervention within the overall project and was responsible for contacting and screening applicants and organizing them into teams. Weekly planning meetings involving faculty advisors, graduate students, and undergraduate supervisors were held until major conceptual and practical problems were resolved.

Undergraduate supervisors were drawn from the larger pool of student volunteers on the basis of having demonstrated (1) well-developed administrative and interpersonal skills, (2) a sense of responsibility, and (3) a strong commitment to the success of the program. These individuals performed a variety of functions including: assisting the graduate students in training observers, serving as test administrators and companions, working out scheduling conflicts, informing students of weekly assignments, and coordinating collection of the evaluation measures. The three undergraduates who assisted in implementing the behavior change workshops also occasionally served in various supervisory capacities. All undergraduates who participated received academic credit in a course called "Field Study in Psychology" over a two-semester time span. The criteria for selecting volunteers differed for each program, as did the tasks for which they were trained.

Problem-Solving Intervention

Eight volunteers were selected on the basis of an interview with the graduate student who was in charge of this program. These participants were trained to administer a battery of verbal report measures to the students involved in this intervention package. Several of the measures necessitated individual one-to-one

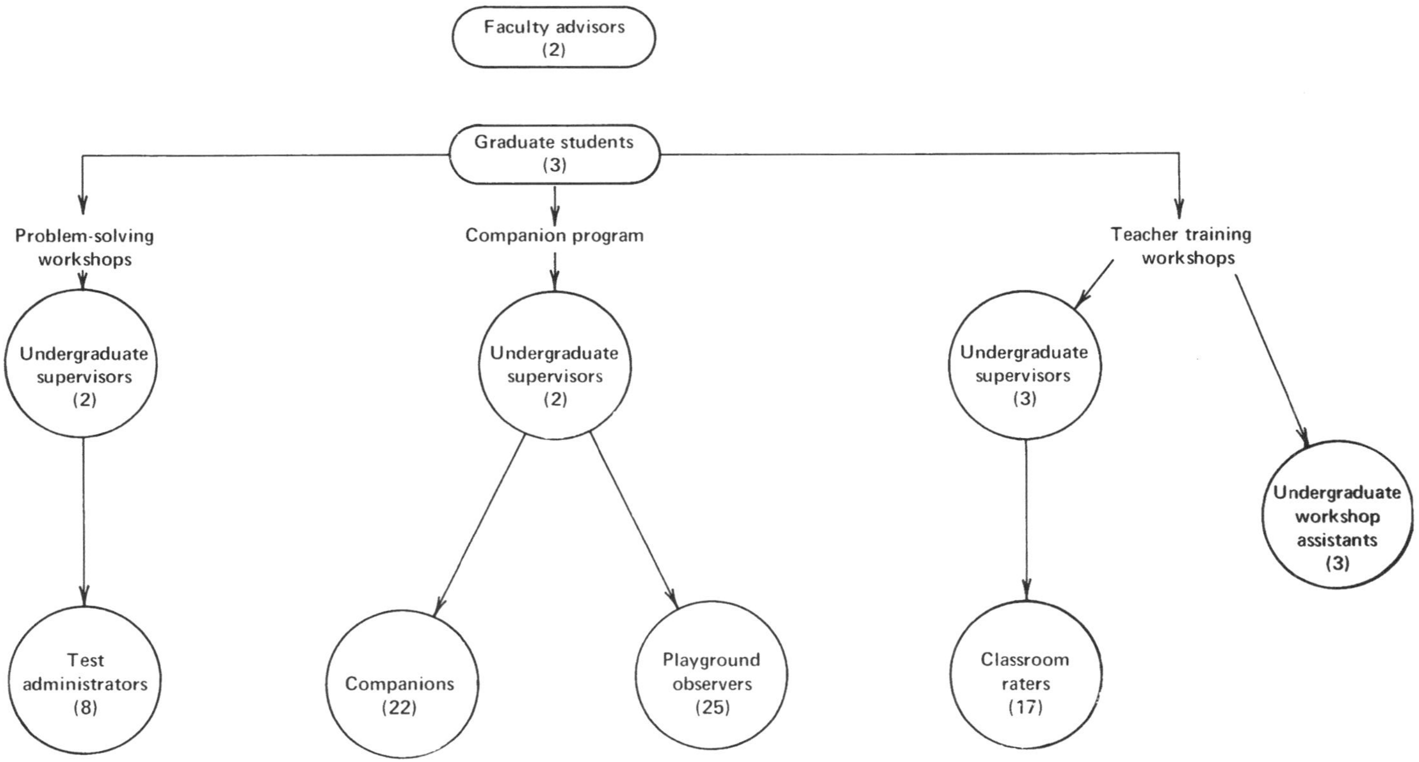

FIG. 6.2 Organizational structure of the intervention program.

testing formats, while others were administered in groups. One undergraduate supervisor coordinated the schedules of the test administrators with classroom activities so as to minimize disruptions in the school. The other assisted the teachers in the use of the problem-solving material in the classroom.

Companionship Program

This level of intervention necessitated the use of two independent groups of volunteers; one set was selected and trained to interact with the target children, while the other was used to observe playground interactions between the targets and other children during recess and lunch periods.

Approximately 80 students who expressed interest in the project were seen in semistructured interviews by two of the graduate student consultants in the preceding spring. They were given a rating along a five-point scale, determined by their apparent motivation and level of social skills. Academic schedules were obtained for the top half of the applicants the following fall. The 22 undergraduates with the highest interview ratings and compatible class schedules with sufficient free time were selected. An attempt was made to have equal numbers of males and females; however, the small number of male applicants yielded only eight who met both the interview and scheduling criteria. Remaining volunteers were considered for positions in the behavior change workshop program.

The quality of these eight males and 14 females was quite high. A good number of them had some type of experience working with children in summer camps, recreation programs, and so on. Sixteen of the 22 indicated at the beginning of the project that their career goals included some type of professional work with children. The grade point average of the companions was 3.3 out of a possible 4.0. Seventeen were seniors, the remaining five being juniors. Their ages were commensurate with their academic level (20–22 years old), with the exception of one 26-year-old male who had worked in a children's institution before entering college. The companions majored in several areas including psychology, child development, rehabilitation, and education.

Companions were generally assigned to children of the same sex. Since there were ten isolate boys and only eight male companions, two of the female companions who felt most comfortable interacting with boys were assigned to males. Otherwise, the assignments to the 20 children were made randomly. Two of the female companions were randomly selected to serve as "rovers." Instead of being assigned to a particular child, they assisted in working with several of the children. This served the dual purpose of providing extra attention for several of the more severely disturbed children and assuring that two trained, experienced people would be available should there be any unforseen attrition in the companion population, which fortunately did not occur.

Twenty-five undergraduates served as observers for the project at various times during the year. They were trained to use a behavioral rating system (described below) on the playground itself; this not only facilitated quick learning of the system, but also allowed reactive effects of observation to dissipate before data were collected. An observer would be assigned one child per recess period, and would rate that child for 15 minutes, or 60 15-second intervals. To minimize their obtrusiveness, the observers did the rating from as great a distance as was possible without sacrificing reliability.

Behavior Change Workshops

This phase of the program required the use of observers to monitor the behavior of teachers and specifically designated pupils in the classroom. In addition, three highly trained undergraduates assisted the consultant in conducting the behavior-training workshops and made unobtrusive ratings of teacher behavior during these sessions, which were subsequently related to indices of teacher effectiveness. From those undergraduates who proved to be acceptable at the previously described initial interview, an additional 14 were selected to be classroom raters. These individuals were again contacted during the first week of the following semester and arrangements for their training were made. Like the companions, these students were selected on the basis of criteria reflecting competence, enthusiasm, and social skill. Special consideration was given to selecting participants who would have minimal interaction difficulties with teachers and students in the classroom.

Five meetings were held with these raters to train them in how to utilize the Behavioral Observation Schedule for Pupils and Teachers (Breyer & Calchera, 1971). Data relating to this measure will be examined in a subsequent section. Role-played and videotaped classroom interactions provided the basis for the training, which continued until an acceptable level of reliability (80%) was attained between pairs of observers. The raters entered the classroom as early as possible in the school year to allow the students and teachers to become familiar with them and thus reduce potential disruptive effects due to their presence.

The observers were instructed not to interact with the students, and proper school protocol was stressed. Specific provisions were made to preclude the teachers' receiving either feedback or advice about their own behavior or that of their students. Throughout the year, the raters were kept blind as to which classes were experimental and which were control, and also as to the exact nature of the intervention. Reliability assessments for each rater were made twice during the year by having two raters observe the same class at one time.

Except for vacations, the raters were scheduled to observe their classes twice a week for the duration of the school year. The actual number of observations was less than this because of inclement weather, sickness, and occasional transportation difficulties. Transportation to the school and weekly data collection were supervised by two advanced undergraduates. Although a determined attempt was made to keep raters in specific classrooms for the entire year, scheduling problems in the spring semester caused two of the raters to switch assignments.

In addition, several raters could not readjust their schedules to the new semester, and training sessions for three new raters were held in the last two weeks of January before they were introduced into their classrooms.

Evaluation Measures and Experimental Design Considerations

As we stated previously, a primary goal of community interventions is the demonstration that the treatment programs are the true cause of any reported improvements in the functioning of the target population. In Chapter 2, we proposed that this goal is more likely to be attained if the consultant employs multiple channels of measurement and uses untreated control groups to assess the operation of factors that represent plausible alternative explanations of the obtained outcomes. All three levels of intervention met both these criteria in an attempt to produce clearly interpretable results.

Table 6.1 contains a list of all the evaluative measures used to assess the efficacy of the program. The channel of measurement through which each assessment device operated is also specified. Behavioral rating included two aspects: global ratings involved assessment of general characteristics of the targeted students by their peers or teachers; specific ratings were obtained by counting the frequencies of (or time-sampling) discrete behaviors. The five measures contained in the first column were administered to every child in the school both prior to and following the project; these were used to ascertain whether the interventions produced general changes in the self-perceptions and observable functioning of the students. These assessment devices are described in more detail below.

Self-esteem inventory. This scale is a self-report measure of self-esteem developed by Coopersmith (1967). It can be group administered and yields subscales for four factors (general–self, social–self, home–parents, and school–academic) as well as a total score over the 56 items. The child is asked to rate each item as "like me" or "unlike me," thus yielding a dichotomous decision on each item. A total score is derived by summing those items which reflect positive self-esteem.

Locus of control. This construct was first elaborated by Rotter (1966) who developed a scale to assess the degree to which people believed important outcomes in their lives were due to their efforts or to factors over which they have little control. Individuals who attributed their successes to hard work, effort, persistence, and so on, and their failures to the absence of these characteristics are described as having an "internal" locus of control. Those who attribute successes and failures to luck, fate, chance, and so on are designated as being "external." Nowicki and Strickland (1973) recently developed a 40-item measure of this construct, which is designed for use with children and is particularly amenable to group administration. This self-report measure employs a dichotomous format whereby children answer either "yes" or "no" sentences

TABLE 6.1
Evaluation Measures Used in the Multilevel Intervention

Target subjects			
All students	Problem-solving workshops	Companion program	Behavior change workshops
Self-esteem inventory (VR)[a]	Problem-Solving Measure (VR)	Behavioral ratings of peer interactions (BR-S)	Pupil perception of teacher (VR)
Locus of control (VR)	Structured Real-Life Problem Situation (BR-S)	Companion rating (BR-G)	Workshop efficacy questionnaire (VR)
Level of aspiration (VR)	In-Class Assessments (VR)	Companion attitudes (VR)	Principal ratings (BR-G)
Sociometric (BR-G)	Peabody Picture Intelligence Test (VR)		Teacher behavior in class (BR-S)
Walker PBIC (BR-G)	Attitude Questionnaire (VR)		Student behavior in class (BR-S)
			Teacher behavior in workshops (BR-S)

[a] Channels of measurement are denoted as (VR) verbal report, (BR) behavioral rating, either (G) global or (S) specific.

such as, "Do you believe most problems will solve themselves if you just don't fool with them?"

Level of Aspiration. The level of aspiration technique (Rotter, 1954) examines the effect of success and failure on the explicitly set goals of a subject. The way a testee solves this task provides a basis for inferences about self-confidence, self-esteem, and defensive reactions concerning need for success and fear of failure. An aspiration task suitable for group administration was given before and after the intervention. In this task the participant attempts to match letters to symbols in a specific time period (it is similar to the digit–symbol test in the Wechsler Adult Intelligence Scale); thirteen different trials are given, each with a different key. After each trial, the subject must estimate how many items he will complete on the next trial.

This particular task has been used previously only with adults. Its use here is thus largely of an exploratory nature. Several types of data are generated from this technique: a mean difference score between estimates and previous achievement, number of times the estimate is shifted from the previous estimate, number of unusual shifts (shifting the estimate down after a success and up after a failure to meet the previous estimate), and, most importantly, nine basic classes of response determined on the basis of their psychological significance and involving the combined use of these objective indices (Rotter, 1954).

Sociometric. A modification of the Ohio Social Acceptance Scale (Rucker, 1967) was used as the sociometric device. Each child rated all of the other children in the homeroom on a scale of 1–5, with 1 being "one of my very best friends" and 5 being "I don't care for that person," both prior to the program and after its termination. Each of the five categories has a detailed description of the perceived level of friendship between the rater and other students in the class. This particular sociometric was considered superior to the type where only a few children are nominated for particular categories, or a forced-ranking procedure. The reasoning was that a child could become better liked and accepted by his classmates yet might not replace the limited number of children nominated for specific categories. This measure yielded two sources of information. The first involved averaging the ratings that all other students directed toward a particular student. The second rating involved how a particular student rated his peers as opposed to being rated by them. This second measure simply involved averaging the ratings each student assigned to his or her peers.

Teacher ratings (Walker PBIC). Language arts teachers of the experimental and control children were asked to fill out a behavior-rating scale before and after the program. An attempt was made to minimize expectancy effects due to knowledge of which children were in the program, in several ways. First, the teachers had to fill out the scales on their entire language arts classes in the fall and on at least ten children in the spring; the children relevant to the project were embedded in those larger numbers, and the teachers were not told which project these ratings were for. Secondly, teachers were never informed of the names of the control children in the project. Thirdly, the language arts teacher, who saw the children for several hours each day, filled out the scale rather than the homeroom teacher, who had made the original referral of the child.

A modification of the Walker Problem Behavior Identification Checklist (Walker, 1970) was used. This scale consists of 50 items which yield a total score as well as scores for five subscales–acting out, withdrawal, distractibility, disturbed peer relations, and immaturity. The modification was the use of Likert-type responses ranging from "never" to "always" rather than simple dichotomous (yes/no) responses. A Likert format is used in the Devereux Child Behavior Scale (Spivack & Spotts, 1965) and seemed more appropriate here since a dichotomous format might be insensitive to changes in the maladaptive behaviors under study.

These five assessment devices were used either to evaluate specific outcomes of the experimental procedures or to provide additional explanatory information relating to the processes and outcomes of the project. The remainder of this chapter is devoted to describing the procedures used in the three specific levels of the total intervention. The evaluative measures that were unique to a specific program are described in detail within the context of that particular level.

PROBLEM-SOLVING PROGRAM

Nine of the teachers in the school indicated interest in the problem-solving program at the general meeting during which the overall project was described. To control for voluntarism, the six participating teachers were selected from this interested group. The student sample consisted of 150 children from these six classrooms; the pupils had an average age of 9.0 years.

Four of the six teachers, and two teachers' aides, attended workshops designed to teach problem-solving skills. For organizational purposes, these four teachers all belonged to the same unit. Three classes within this unit comprised the experimental group (E), as the children received training in problem-solving skills. One additional class in the unit (C_1) served as a group to control for the nonspecific impact of teacher attendance of the workshops, as this teacher attended the workshop but did not use the techniques in her classroom. The remaining two classrooms in separate units (C_2) provided pupils who served as untreated control subjects; neither the teachers nor the students received any training in problem solving.

The curriculum was based on the theoretical framework of D'Zurilla and Goldfried (1971) and focused on the particular component behaviors involved in the problem-solving process. An outline of the curriculum is presented in Table 6.2. The problem-solving lessons were divided into four components preceded

TABLE 6.2
Problem-Solving Curriculum

I. Divergent thinking. A. Brainstorming B. Alternate uses C. Alternate consequences	IV. Consideration of consequences A. Videotape model B. Small-group shaping C. Follow-up exercises D. In-class assessment
II. Problem identification A. Definition of problem and goal B. Small-group shaping C. Follow-up exercises D. In-class assessment	V. Elaboration of solutions generated A. Videotape model B. Small-group shaping C. Follow-up exercises D. In-class assessment
III. Generation of alternative solutions A. Videotape model B. Small-group shaping C. Follow-up exercises D. In-class assessment	VI. Integration of problem-solving behaviors A. Video model B. Follow-up exercise C. Role play and behavioral rehearsal of problem-solving behaviors.

by general exercises in divergent thinking and concluded by practice sessions in implementation. The format for training each component behavior consisted of four stages: (1) modeling of the particular problem-solving behavior via videotape, (2) small-group exercises in which the teacher shaped the particular behavior, (3) follow-up exercises in which the children practiced the behavior, and (4) in-classroom assessment of that behavior. The specific exercises to be used with the children in the classroom were codeveloped with the teachers in the workshops.

Four videotapes were developed to model the specific problem-solving behaviors to be learned. These videotapes focused on the major components of the problem-solving process. Faculty children of approximately the same age as the viewers acted as the models in these videotapes. These actors were given a particular social problem and they then modeled a specific problem-solving behavior (for example, looking for alternative solutions). The model was reinforced by peers and adults in the videotape for engaging in these problem-solving behaviors.

As a result of the work reported by Nelson (1970), the modeling tapes were used in conjunction with external social reinforcement. At certain points in the presentation of the videotape, the teacher stopped the tape and elicited suggestions from the class as to what the model should do prior to the model taking action in the film. Responses indicating use of the particular problem-solving behavior being trained were praised by the teacher.

Following the modeling session, the teacher worked with small groups of five or six children, shaping the desired behavior. The small group would focus on a problem, and the teacher would praise each child for demonstrating appropriate problem-solving behaviors. In subsequent sessions, the small groups would practice the problem-solving behaviors on sets of typical problems. Both teachers and students provided input in generating the problems for these follow-up sessions.

Development of Problem-Solving Assessment Devices

Table 6.3 summarizes the measures developed to assess the effectiveness of the problem-solving program.

The major outcome measure for the study was a modified version of the MEPS developed by Shure and Spivack (1972a). This problem-solving measure (PSM) differed in two major ways from the MEPS. First, since assessment of the generality of problem-solving strategies was of interest, it was decided not to give the same set of stories pre- and posttreatment. Thus, two sets of five stories having similar themes were developed. Some of the stories from the original MEPS were included in the two sets. Secondly, scoring criteria for the MEPS

TABLE 6.3
Measures Developed to Assess Effectiveness of Problem Solving

- I. Outcome measures
  - A. Problem-solving measure (PSM)
    1. Number of alternative solutions
    2. Number of elaborations
    3. Number of obstacles
    4. Number of problems correctly identified
  - B. Structured real-life problem situation
    1. Number of alternative solutions generated
- II. In-class measures
  - A. In-class measure-problem identification (ICM-ID)
    1. Number of problems correctly identified
  - B. In-class measure-alternate solutions (ICM-ALT)
    1. Number of solutions generated
    2. Number of solutions sampled from set
  - C. In-class measure-consequences (ICM-CON)
    1. Number of consequences generated
    2. Percentage of solutions selected that are effective
  - D. In-class measure-elaboration (ICM-ELAB)
    1. Number of steps given to solution

were modified to reflect the specific component behaviors being trained. The total score on the PSM consisted of three parts: the total number of alternative solutions generated, the number of specific steps elaborated to implement the solutions, and the potential obstacles generated that limit the effectiveness of a solution or elaboration. The PSM was also scored for the number of problems that were not correctly identified. Details concerning the administration of this measure are provided in the next section of the chapter.

A Structured Real-Life Problem Situation (SRLPS) was developed so that an assessment of problem-solving performance could be systematically observed outside of the classroom situation. The simulated problem selected for this interaction was the following: On approaching the testing room, the student was told that it was occupied and that it could not be used, although the experimenter really wanted to play the story-telling games with the pupil. The child was then asked by the experimenter to help solve this problem. The interaction was taped, and every effort was made to insure realism in the encounter. The tape was scored for the number of solutions each child generated to the simulated problem.

Finally, a series of modular In-Class Assessment Measures (ICMs) was developed. These measures were designed to be used by the teacher and served primarily to provide the teacher with useful feedback concerning the effectiveness of the training while the program was still in progress. Each of the measures was designed to assess the specific problem-solving skill being taught in the training sequence. Since the children completed these measures in class, they were usually very short and required a minimum of writing on the part of the child. They were presented in the form of quizzes or games.

Problem Solving in Action

Table 6.4 outlines the time sequence for this aspect of the study. There were essentially three facets to the procedure: assessment, in-service workshops, and classroom training.

Assessment

To control for a possible interaction between taking the PSM and receiving training in problem solving, a modification of the Solomon (1949) Four-Group Design was employed. In addition to using experimental and control groups, this design provided that half of the children in each group be assessed both before and after the program, while the remaining pupils in each group receive the posttreatment assessment only. To control for attrition, twelve children from each class were randomly selected to be pretested. Ten children from each class were randomly assigned to the posttest-only group. The students were then randomly assigned to one of five male experimenters, who tested each child individually outside the classroom in one of three rooms provided by the school. These assistants would orally present each of the five stories to the child and ask

TABLE 6.4
General Design of Procedures and Assessment Information for Problem-Solving Program

Time period	Experimental procedures	Data collected
September	Contact teachers	
	Train experimenters	
October	Pretreatment assessment	
	Individual testing	Problem-solving measure (PSM)
	Group testing	Locus of control
		Sociometric
		Self-esteem
		Level of aspiration
	Teacher ratings	Walker
November	Intervention initiated	
	Problem-solving workshops	
	Problem-solving training	In-class measures (ICM)
March	Posttreatment assessment	SRLPS
	Individual testing	PSM
April	Group testing	Locus of control
		Sociometric
		Self-esteem
		Level of aspiration
	Teacher ratings	Walker
		Peabody IQ
May	Debriefing	Teacher feedback

the child to tell him "what happens in between." For example, in one story the student was told:

> Al had just moved into the neighborhood. He didn't know anyone and felt very lonely. The story ends with Al having many good friends and feeling at home in the neighborhood. What happens in between Al's moving in and feeling lonely, and when he ends up with many good friends?

Testing time for each child was approximately 30 minutes. The experimenters were not connected in any way with the problem-solving training and were blind with respect to scoring criteria and experimental grouping.

During the posttest period, a subsample of those children in the posttesting-only group were randomly selected to be given the SRLPS. Because of space and recording limitations, only one experimenter was trained to administer the SRLPS procedure.

The four ICMs were administered by teachers in the three experimental and one control (C_1) classrooms, following standardized instructions. Each measure was given after the completion of a unit of problem-solving training. These were later scored by an undergraduate aide who worked in the school. After the final assessment period was completed, the C_2 classes were administered the ICMs. This was done to ensure that the PSM scores of the C_2 classes would not be affected by taking the ICMs.

Two additional measures were used to assess the impact of the problem-solving program. Both scales were administered to all of the students before and after the program and are briefly described below.

Peabody picture vocabulary test. This is a standardized verbal intelligence test developed by Dunn (1965). This measure was administered by the teachers at the end of the school year. Verbal IQ was selected as a possible controling factor affecting problem-solving performance. The Peabody was selected because of its reported standardization via group administration and its relatively high validity as an IQ measure of this type.

Attitude questionnaire. This measure consisted of eight questions dealing with attitudes and expectancies concerning school, making friends, and use of alternate solutions. It was included to assess self-reported changes by use of a seven-point Likert format to such items as "I can (can't) think of lots of ways of getting the teacher's attention."

In-Service Workshops

Four teachers and three aides attended 18 weekly, one-hour workshops in problem-solving conducted by one of the graduate student consultants. One of the aides was a university volunteer who spent two full days per week in the elementary school. She became integrated within the staff at the school and worked primarily with the teachers in the experimental group.

Workshops were scheduled within school hours, during time designated for curriculum development and planning. A workbook presenting the basic skills necessary in problem solving and possible techniques for facilitating these skills was developed by the consultants. Three types of activity took place in the workshops: (1) training teachers in the problem-solving curriculum and techniques (that is, reinforcement procedures, modeling, and role playing skills), (2) codevelopment of the specific in-class exercises and tasks to train the children in these skills, and (3) feedback and evaluation of the success of activities used in the classroom. It was expected that through the co-development of the actual exercises used with the children, the teachers would have stronger feelings of program ownership.

Classroom Training in Problem Solving

Two 30-minute periods were scheduled each week for problem-solving training in the classroom. The four teachers and three aides worked in teams in the three experimental classes. This system provided for two trainers in each classroom for most exercises, which was especially helpful when the teachers were working with the children in small groups. This also allowed for one control teacher to use the workshop materials in one of her colleagues' classrooms, but not her own. Training began in early November and continued through the middle of March. With vacations, inclement weather, and scheduling conflicts, a total of 24 exercises were completed in the 18-week period.

The first few days of training consisted of warm-up exercises in divergent thinking and brainstorming. This was followed by training in problem identification, generation of alternative solutions, consideration of consequences, and elaboration of solutions. Finally, the children were trained to integrate these problem-solving behaviors and actually experiment in implementing them via role-playing and behavioral rehearsal techiques.

COMPANIONSHIP PROGRAM

The overall experimental design of this program is presented in Table 6.5. The procedures in this level of intervention involved four components: (1) selection of target children, (2) training of companions, (3) implementing real-life interactions between companions and children, and (4) conducting behavioral observations of peer interactions.

Selection of Children

The 19 classroom teachers were asked to nominate the three most withdrawn, socially isolated children in their homerooms. These did not necessarily have to be quiet children, but rather children who had few friends and few social interactions with other children, and who seemed generally deficient in their social skills. These nominations were obtained during the last week in September, about three weeks after the school year had begun. This procedure yielded the names of 52 children. Nominations of 30 children who did not show these social deficits were also obtained from the teachers.

A behavioral validation of these referrals was then conducted. A group of trained observers assessed the frequency of social interactions of each of these children at recess using the rating system described below. These baseline rating sessions continued for a total of five weeks. In addition to the isolated children, ten children from the 30 nominated by the teachers as "normal" were randomly

TABLE 6.5
General Design of Procedure and Assessment for the Companionship Program

Time period	Procedure	Types of data collected
September	Train companions Train behavioral observers	Companion attitudes
October	Teacher nominations Selection of target children Baseline evaluation	Recess behavior ratings Teacher ratings of problem behaviors Sociometric peer ratings Self-esteem inventory Locus of control Level of aspiration
November	Initiation of companion intervention	Companion process ratings
December-March	Intervention continues	
April	Evaluation of program effectiveness	Same measures as used in October Companion ratings of behavior change

selected and rated during baseline, in order to set norms for social behaviors in this age group. If the behavior of a child designated by the teacher as "withdrawn" actually approximated that of the "normal" group, the child was eliminated from consideration.

The original research design called for experimental and control groups of 20 isolated children each. The behavioral validation, however, determined that only 30 children could be clearly defined as such. These 30 children were then separated into an experimental group of 20 and a control group of ten, matched on their rates of social interactions. Each group contained half boys and half girls.

Training of Companions

A series of six 90-minute workshops was conducted prior to any companion contact with the children. These meetings included lectures by one of the graduate student consultants on traditional and innovative mental health interventions, principles of a behavioral approach, and the promotion and evaluation of behavior change. Round-table discussions considered the different types of problem behaviors that might arise and how to deal with them. Role playing was used extensively as the companions practiced social reinforcement, modeling, and dealing with specific problem situations.

A behavioral approach was stressed during the training. In particular, techniques of social reinforcement and modeling were explored. Each companion was required to read *New Tools For Changing Behavior* (Deibert & Harmon, 1970), a book on behavior analysis, as well as several technical articles involving social reinforcement and modeling interventions with socially isolated children. It was made clear, however, that the techniques involved could only be employed after the companion had developed a warm relationship with the child and had thus attained a role of some importance.

Each companion spent two sessions at the school in the first week in November observing his or her assigned child during recess and lunch. The companions were then required to write a functional analysis of the child's social behavior, describing the potential controlling reinforcers, environmental factors, initial goals, and so on. This exercise was assigned to give the companion some idea of the child's problems before any personal involvement began. In addition, it encouraged the companions to think in terms of specific problematic behaviors and remediation strategies.

Once the program was initiated, weekly group meetings were held during which the progress of particular cases was discussed along with suggestions for new strategies of helping behavior. In this way, each companion was continually contributing ideas to the other companions while presenting his own case approximately every second or third week. In addition, the companions were required to submit a report form for each session they spent with the child. These reports included specific goals for the session as well as descriptions of the activities of the child. This procedure encouraged the companions to maintain a concrete task orientation.

A good deal of time was spent near the end of the program discussing strategies for the maintenance of the behavior changes. These methods included a gradual decrease in individual attention to the child in question, with social reinforcement becoming more intermittent, arriving after recess began so that the child could not depend on the companion to organize activities, and eventually reducing the number of sessions to once a week before termination. It was emphasized from the beginning that the ideal ending of the relationship would be the companion standing off to the side watching the child happily interact with his peers.

Sessions with the Children

Each of the prospective participants' parents was sent a brief letter describing the program and requesting permission for their child's involvement. The parents of one girl objected to her participation in the program, and she was switched to the control group before the intervention began.

Instead of formally introducing the companions to the children, thereby risking stigma from the child's peers, the companions unobtrusively began the program by talking to the child on the playground as well as to other children in the vicinity. The companions explained that they were learning about children as part of their work in college. By expressing particular interest and affection for the child to which they were assigned, the companions were all able to develop good relationships with the children.

The meetings occurred twice weekly during the child's lunch and recess periods. The initial sessions took place during the second week in November; the time of the final session was individualized, depending on the child's reaction to the upcoming termination and on whether the companion felt a great deal would be gained by continuing for a few additional sessions. Termination dates thus ranged from March 20 to April 24. As a result of vacations, child absences, and the like, the number of sessions spent with the children ranged from 17 to 28, the average being 22.

The emphasis in this intervention was on fostering social interactions between the target child and his peers and improving the general climate of the play area; one-to-one interactions between companion and child, stressed in many previous studies, were not that important here. The companions praised positive peer interactions, good manners, conversation between children, and other types of approach behaviors to peers. They also modeled the proper form of such behaviors. In addition to concentrating on the target children, however, the companions tried to effect changes in the child's peers, particularly with regard to their behaviors toward the child in question. Thus, the companions tried to change both the target child's own behavior and his wider social environment.

Modeling Film

Research has indicated that modeling films may change the behavior of isolated nursery school children, both independent of or in conjunction with social reinforcement (O'Connor, 1969, 1972). It was therefore decided to make an age-appropriate film as an adjunct to the present intervention.

The film included six separate scenes, three involving girls and three boys. Each scene presented a social problem where a child had to find a strategy for making friends. For example, a boy is rejected when he tries to barge into a group of other boys playing a board game; when he asks nicely and waits his turn, he is then accepted and has a good time. Another scene shows a little girl by herself; she decides to organize a game, and makes several friends in the process.

The 15-minute film was shown to 18 of the 20 experimental children during two days in February. The other two children were absent, and a reshowing could not be arranged. Each child saw the film during recess along with his companion and two or three friends he selected. The companions used the film as a focus for discussions during the ensuing sessions, particularly when examples from the movie became relevant to a specific real-life situation.

Behavioral and Attitudinal Evaluations

Several studies with socially isolated nursery school children have suggested the possibility of using the rate of social interactions during free play as an outcome measure (for example, O'Connor, 1969; Ross *et al.,* 1971). The consultants operationally defined children who did not interact with their peers as deficient in social skills. An increase in the intermediate criterion of social interactions would be presumptive of an improvement in social skills, and this measure was considered to be an excellent outcome index of the project.

The rating system employed was a combination of several interaction measures, modified for a playground full of eight- to ten-year olds. Briefly, every 15 seconds a child's behavior was coded in four different ways:

1. *Type of Interaction*–Is the child interacting with his or her peers? If so, the interaction is coded as either cooperative play, verbal interaction, touching, or physical proximity. These were considered to be a hierarchy; therefore only one could be coded at a particular interval.
2. *Number of Peers*–If the child is involved in an interaction, is it with one other child, two others, or more than two (group)?
3. *Consequences*–Is the reaction of the child's peers to interaction positive, negative, or neutral?
4. *Initiations*–Did the child initiate an interaction during that particular interval?

It should also be noted that a social interaction was defined as any behavior directed toward another child, which involved a reciprocal quality. Neither parallel play nor solitary verbalizations qualified. Thus, a scorable interaction necessitated not only the output of the subject but some indication of recognition from another child. Each of the 30 "isolated" children, as well as the ten "normal" children, was rated for ten separate sessions during a baseline period which spanned the entire month of October. During the few times that the children had indoor recess, rating was still done as long as the child's class was allowed to interact freely; if the children were assigned activities by the teacher, however, rating was not conducted.

A midpoint evaluation took place in late January, after the companion program had been operating for three months. This consisted of two rating sessions on each of 20 experimental and ten control children. Ratings were conducted on days when there were no companions on the playground during a particular recess. Posttest rating began in late March and involved ten rating sessions for each of the 40 children. Because of the imminent end of the university semester, this posttest rating began before all of the companions had completed their interventions, although rating was always done on days when the companion was not present. For the experimental children, then, a minimum of four rating sessions and a maximum of ten took place after the companion had terminated the intervention; the average was eight sessions after the completed intervention. Since the posttest spanned five weeks, a large percentage of the observations were conducted weeks after the program had ended.

In addition to the behavioral evaluation of peer interaction, the effectiveness of this intervention was also assessed from the viewpoint of the companions through two additional measures.

Companion ratings. After the program ended, companions rated the change in their child on items taken from the Child Behavior-Change Scale (McWilliams & Finkel, 1973). These items are similar to those commonly used as the sole or major measure of outcome in previous companion projects. Seven-point Likert scales were employed by the companions to estimate the change shown by each participating child on 14 items such as "angry," "cooperative," "restless," "frightened," and "attentive." Seven of the objectives had negative valences, while the other seven tapped socially desired attributes.

Companion attitudes. A semantic differential scale measuring attitudes toward eight categories related to the present project was given to the companions before and after the program. This scale was also given to a group of undergraduates in a psychology course, matched to the companions by sex and age, before the program began. The use of the companion control group allowed for a comparison of initial attitudes and has potential utility for the selection of future companions in subsequent projects of this type.

BEHAVIOR CHANGE PROGRAM

The general experimental design of this level of intervention is presented in Table 6.6. Basically, this program contained three components: selection of participating and control teachers as well as disruptive students for inclusion, training of teachers in the use of behavioral control procedures, and evaluation of the intervention.

Selection of Teachers

Seven of the 15 teachers in the three units not involved in the problem-solving program volunteered for participation in the behavior-change workshops. As indicated in Fig. 6.1, two of these were from Unit A, one from Unit B, and four from Unit D. Seven untreated control teachers were selected from Units A and B. Only one nonparticipating teacher was not selected to be in the control

TABLE 6.6
General Design of Procedures and Assessment for the Behavior Modification Program

	Procedure	Data collected
September	Train behavioral observers	
October	Pretreatment assessment	Classroom behavior ratings Teacher ratings of problem behaviors Sociometric Self-esteem Locus of control Level of aspiration Pupil attitudes
November	Initiation of teacher workshops	Teacher attitudes and expectancies Workshop behavior ratings
	Selection of problematic pupils by teachers	
December	Initiation of teacher assessment of "rated pupils"	
February	Initiation of behavior change projects by teachers	
April	Posttreatment assessment	Same measures as used in October and November Principal ratings of teachers
May	Debriefing	Teacher feedback

group. Because she was a member of the unit that already had four participants, it was felt that her pupils could be greatly affected by being in the classrooms of the other four workshop teachers throughout the day. The teacher from Unit B was later dropped from the statistical analysis of the effects of the workshops as a result of her failure to attend seven of the ten workshop meetings, including the last four in a row, and her failure to turn in required behavior change reports on her pupils. The average previous teaching experience of the remaining six experimental teachers was 6.1 years, with a range of 3–10 years. The average previous teaching experience at this school for the same six teachers was 4.5 years, with a range of 3–7 years.

Selection and Grouping of Children

The 151 students of the six volunteer workshop teachers served as the total sample of treated experimental students for this program, while the 182 students of the seven control teachers comprised the total control sample. These experimental and control children were in the language arts classes of the Unit A teachers and the math classes of the Unit B and Unit D teachers. These specific classes were chosen after coordinating the class schedules of the three Units and the available rating times of the undergraduate observers. The total experimental sample was comprised of 80 male and 71 female pupils. Of these, 75 were third graders and 76 were fourth graders. The mean age for this sample was 9.4 years. The total control sample included 89 male and 93 female students, of whom 84 were third graders and 98 were fourth graders.

These total samples of workshop and control classes were broken down into various groups for experimental purposes, and these divisions are summarized in Fig. 6.3. After two months of classes, the six workshop and seven control teachers were requested to nominate the six most disruptive and/or study-skill

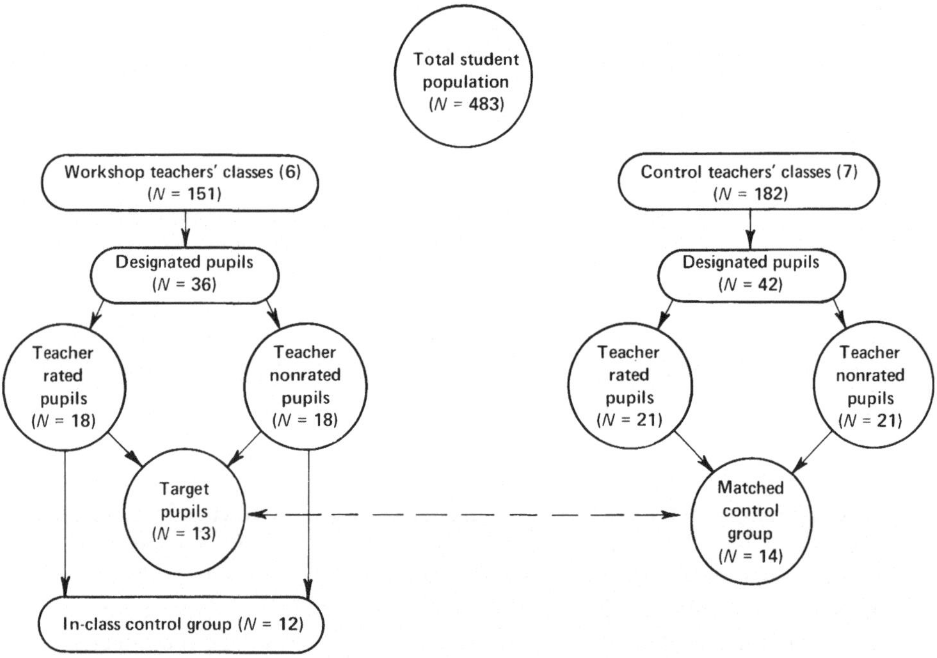

FIG. 6.3 Division of student population into experimental groups..

deficient children in their respective classes, and to rank order them on the strength and frequency of their problematic behaviors. In Fig. 6.3, these are the children referred to as the "designated pupils."

Teachers often had difficulties listing more than three or four severely to moderately disruptive pupils and usually had to fill out their lists with children showing less severe or less frequent problem behaviors. When some of these children were transferred out of their classes between semesters, they were replaced by the next most disruptive children in their class. The 36 pupils designated by the workshop teachers consisted of 25 boys and 11 girls, of whom 17 were third graders and 19 were fourth graders. The 42 pupils designated by the control teachers were 26 boys and 16 girls, with 21 being in third grade and 21 in fourth grade.

The consultants randomly chose three pupils from each teacher's list of six designated disruptive students. These students comprise the "Teacher-Rated Pupils," as shown on Fig. 6.3. At a later date, the teachers were asked to estimate the appropriate behavior level of these rated pupils. Of the 18 teacher-rated pupils in the experimental classes, 12 were boys and 6 were girls, while the 21 similarly designated students in control classrooms consisted of 13 boys and 8 girls. This grouping was included to allow assessment of behavioral improvement caused by heightening the attention the teachers paid to these "rated" pupils.

In mid-January, the six workshop teachers were requested to select the target children with whom they wished to carry out their behavior change projects. The target students came from the list of designated disruptive pupils that each had prepared and could be either teacher-rated or nonrated (refer to Fig. 6.3). Each workshop teacher had two target students, except for one teacher who had three. These 13 target children consisted of seven boys and six girls. Six of these were third graders and seven were fourth graders.

Once the workshop teachers had selected their target children, the experimenter selected two designated students who had been rated most closely to the targets by the teacher to form a control group within the experimental classes, known as the "in-class control group." Since the teachers generally selected the most disruptive children in their classes as target children, the in-class control children were expected to represent less of a behavior problem to the teachers and therefore were not expected to be a rigorously matched control group. They came from both the teacher-rated and nonrated groups. The 12-member in-class control group included 10 boys and 2 girls, of whom 6 were third graders and 6 were fourth graders.

After the workshop teachers had decided upon their target children, a more rigorously matched control group was formed by taking two pupils from each of the control teachers' lists of disruptive pupils, regradless of whether they were teacher-rated or not. The average level of appropriate classroom behavior of this group was matched to within a few percentage points to the mean level displayed by the target children. This group consisted of 12 boys and 2 girls. Nine were third graders and 5 were fourth graders. This somewhat complex design allowed an evaluation of the potential radiation of training effects from the target children to the other groups.

Format of the Workshops

Between early November and late March, ten 90-minute behavior modification workshop sessions were held at the school shortly after the dismissal of pupils. In addition to the six workshop teachers and the consultant, the meetings were attended by the school's guidance counselor, three undergraduate assistants, and, on two occasions, by an additional consultant.

The required readings for the sessions were *Modifying Classroom Behavior* by Buckley and Walker (1970) and two short modules by Hall (1971a, b); these books were supplied to the teachers at the first meeting. The subject matter of the workshops was prepared by coordinating these readings with the research reports of other workshops, journal articles evaluating behavior change procedures, and comprehensive behavior modification texts such as those prepared by Bandura (1969), Homme (1970), and Sulzer and Mayer (1972). The topics discussed at each session are briefly outlined below.

In Session 1, traditional methods of dealing with problem pupils were reviewed, and the basic elements of an applied behavioral approach were introduced. Ethical issues were also thoroughly discussed. Session 2 presented five different methods for observing behavior in order to facilitate awareness of the actual occurrence of problem behaviors. Session 3 was devoted to learning how to describe and target specific behaviors that a teacher might wish to change. Session 4 consisted of a review of the observational projects that the teachers had developed for specific pupils, as well as a presentation of methods to summarize observational data. Session 5 occurred after a one-month break because of school vacations and was devoted to discussing how behaviors are maintained. Delineation and the effective use of social, activity, and material reinforcements were discussed. Session 6 presented methods for developing new behaviors through modeling, shaping, and chaining. Procedures involving small-scale token economies, contingency contracts, and the Premack principle were also reviewed. Session 7 presented methods for decreasing the frequency and intensity of problematic behaviors. These methods included extinction, punishment, time-out, response-cost, and stimulus change. Session 8, which occurred several weeks later, was devoted to reviewing the teachers' proposals for using the change techniques on specific problem behaviors of their pupils. Both Sessions 9 and 10 occurred after a lapse of several weeks and were designed to review the progress of teachers' efforts in modifying the behavior of their target children. Teacher discussion of the required alterations in each other's modification projects was encouraged. A questionnaire assessing teacher attitudes and reactions to the workshops was administered at the end of Session 10.

In general, the workshop sessions had similar formats. During the first part of each session, the material covered during the previous session was reviewed, with emphasis on obtaining feedback about the teachers' use of techniques or principles mentioned in former sessions. The second part of each session consisted of the exposition of new subject matter by the consultant. The final part of each session was spent discussing how the principles that were presented could be applied. This was done by encouraging general, free format discussion by the entire group, and also small group discussion of exercises designed to explicate the principles by their use in hypothetical situations. Each small group consisted of several teachers and one of the three undergraduate assistant consultants. These assistants played a major part in the preparation of the practice exercises.

The workshop requirements for the teachers were outlined during the first session. In order to benefit from the meetings, the teachers were advised to (1) design applications of the principles presented in the workshops to fit at least two target problem children in their classrooms, (2) apply consistently the techniques they developed, and (3) keep records of their progress, and, at the completion of the workshops, (4) prepare a behavior change report for each of their target children. All the teachers were offered the opportunity to earn three graduate credits at the University of Connecticut for their attendance and for their completion of the reports in a more rigorous fashion. One teacher accepted the opportunity, and she worked with three rather than just two target children.

Evaluation of the Program

Several specific measures were used to assess the efficacy of this particular program, in addition to the five scales which were administered to all the students in the school. As Table 6.1 indicates, these measures tapped verbal report and both specific and global behavioral assessment channels from the perspective of students and teachers. These measures are described below.

Pupil perceptions of teacher. A self-constructed battery of attitude questions to assess a pupil's attitudes and perceptions of teacher and school using a Likert-type format was devised. These items are included in an eight-item Teacher Attitude Scale and an eight-item School Attitude Questionnaire. The first questionnaire involved having students rate items such as "My teacher goes too fast for me," "My teacher is happy," and "I like to talk to my teacher" on a three point scale of "always," "sometimes," or "never."

By averaging the total scores achieved by each of a teacher's pupils on this scale, an overall figure that represents her presumed social reinforcement value to the class was obtained.

The School Attitude Scale required responses to bipolar items along seven-point dimensions. Items included, "I really like school . . . I really hate school," "Lots of kids play with me . . . hardly any kids play with me," and so on.

Workshop efficacy questionnaire. The attitudes of the workshop teacher toward her job and her students and her expectancies for being able to induce behavior changes in her pupils were assessed at the first and last workshop session by way of the Preworkshop Questionnaire and the Postworkshop Questionnaire. The pretreatment form contained eight questions to which the teachers responded by checking one of six possible categories of agreement or disagreement. The items tapped teachers' views of their ability to change student behavior and their willingness to use systematic change efforts and behavior modification procedures. The posttreatment form contained these same eight items and an additional twelve questions that assessed teacher attitudes toward the workshop format (such as, "were workshops too long?" "too simplistic?" and so on) as well as their perception of how successful they had been in modifying student behavior. The teachers also turned in written reports of their behavior change projects at this meeting.

Principal ratings. The school principal was asked during June to rate the organizational ability of the workshop and control teachers, using a five-point Likert Scale. This global impression was to be made after consideration of a teacher's consistency in interacting with her children, directiveness of teaching style, energy and enthusiasm while teaching, and thoroughness in planning and conducting classroom lessons. The principal was requested to reply as frankly as possible and to base his current evaluation on the teachers' behavior from the beginning of the school year.

Classroom behavior of teachers and students. From the fourth week of October until the fourth week of April, undergraduate observers were present once or twice weekly for 40-minute periods in the workshop and control teachers' classrooms to observe the behavior of the pupils and teachers. The measure utilized for this purpose was the Behavioral Observation Schedule for Pupils and Teachers (BOSPT, Breyer & Calchera, 1971). The BOSPT provided a time-sampling method of observation (Hall, Lund, & Jackson, 1968), in which the raters sat at one side of the classroom observing six different pupils in a row for six ten-second rating intervals, then the teacher for three successive intervals, and finally they recommenced this six-intervals-on-pupils, three-intervals-on-teacher cycle.

Observations of pupil behavior were classified by the raters into one of four categories for each interval. These categories were (1) on-task behavior when the pupil was performing appropriately, (2) passive off-task behavior when the pupil was behaving inappropriately but not disturbing the teacher or any other pupil (for example, staring into space, looking out the window, placing head on desk, and so on), (3) disruptive off-task behavior, when the pupil was disturbing someone else (for example, tapping pens or pencils, scraping feet along the floor), and (4) aggressive off-task behavior when the pupil behaved aggressively (for example, hitting or pushing another child).

The raters employed twelve categories to rate teachers' behavior. Only five of these behavior categories were likely to be affected by the workshops and hence were the only ones examined in this investigation. The examined categories included: (1) *reward,* representing verbal praise for a student, (2) *feedback,* which is a briefer form of reward, (3) *prohibition,* representing significant verbal displeasure with a pupil, (4) *correction,* which is a more moderate form of prohibition, and (5) *attention,* representing listening to, maintaining eye contact with, or orienting toward a student. The first two categories may be described as positive teaching behaviors, while the second two have negative connotations of aversiveness.

The period from October 23 to November 30 served as the baseline period for total classroom ratings, and the total classroom ratings between March 26 and April 26 served as the follow-up period. In regard to the ratings of "designated pupil" behavior, the baseline period extended from November 30 to February 8, the date of implementation of the behavior change projects; the treatment period went from February 9 to March 23, which was the date of the final review workshop, and the follow-up period went from March 26 to April 26. Referring to the ratings of teacher behavior, the baseline period extended from October 23 to November 30, the date of the first didactic workshop; the workshop period extended from December 1 to March 23, and the follow-up period went from March 26 to April 26.

Throughout the period from November 30 to April 26, the classroom teachers were asked on ten occasions to give an estimate of the on-task behavior of the three "teacher-rated pupils" in each ones' respective class, at the same time that the undergraduate observer was monitoring this behavior. Comparisons between the teacher estimates and the observer ratings were then made.

Ratings of teacher behavior in workshop. The teachers' behaviors during the first seven workshops were also systematically observed during the lecture portions of these sessions. One of the undergraduate assistants used the four previously mentioned pupil behavior categories of the BOSPT to observe the on- and off-task behavior of the teachers on a time-sampled basis. The two other undergraduate assistants observed the frequency of each teacher's yawns, questions asked, questions answered, and statements made. On the basis of their observation, the two assistants also made global ratings of the interest and enthusiasm of individual teachers at each session.

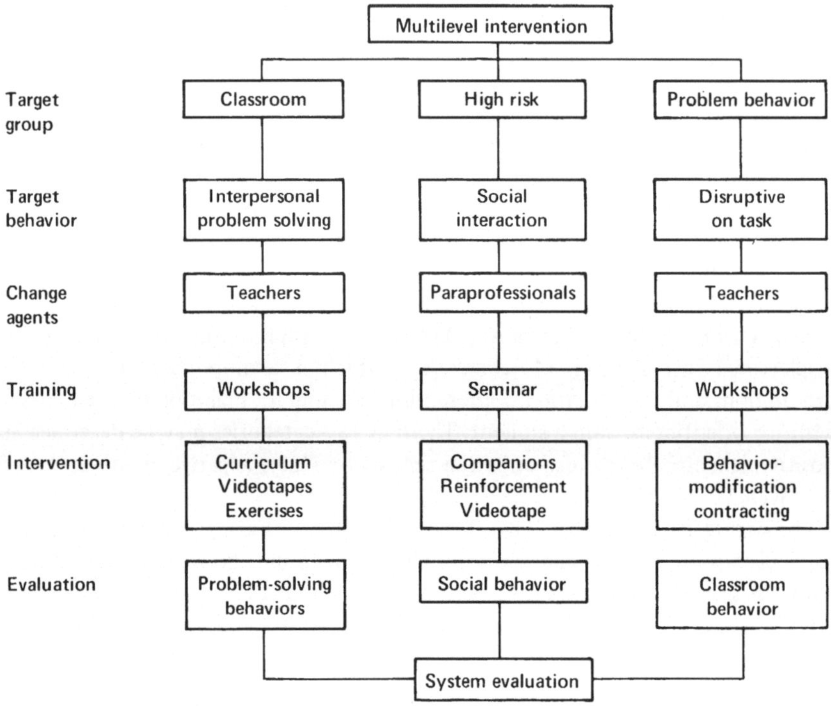

FIG. 6.4 Summary scheme of the multilevel intervention.

Summary of the Multilevel Intervention

Figure 6.4 summarizes the overall design of the multilevel intervention. The next three chapters describe the major results of each of the three levels of the study. These are followed by a final chapter outlining the effects of the programs on the school system as a whole, the strengths and weaknesses of this intervention, and our estimates of the potential future of this form of community intervention.

7

Enhancing Social Coping Skills: The Creative Problem Solver

The purpose of this chapter is to examine the results of the problem-solving training program in more detail. As noted in the preceding chapters, the evaluation of the effects of this program includes not only the specific assessment of the children's problem solving but also the impact and feasibility of the program on the school system as well.

Training and Assessment Procedure: Some Examples

The meaning and implications of the problem-solving intervention will be enriched by first providing a more tangible description of what happened in a typical problem-solving training session and also the kinds of changes in particular children that are reflected by the overall results. Hopefully, this kind of anecdotal information will help concretize the abstractions involved in the group summaries which follow.

Chapter 6 presented the method of training in problem solving, and the Appendix outlines in detail the content of the videotapes and exercises used in the classroom. Typically, a section in the training program would begin with a videotaped story of a peer model attempting to solve a problem. These tapes were structured so that the story line could be interrupted at various decision points, and the teacher could elicit discussion and suggestions from the children. The teachers were enthusiastic about this technique. They commented that the children's attentiveness to the videoscreen was exceptional and that even typically disruptive children were attentive and interested in the content of the stories. The teachers also particularly enjoyed the opportunity to stop the tape every few minutes to get the children involved in the problem-solving process. These pauses were helpful for two reasons. First, they increased student participation in what otherwise would be a normally passive activity (that is, watching television), and secondly, it also kept the segments moving quickly enough for those children with short attention spans to maintain their interest.

For example, in the first tape dealing with the generation of alternative solutions, the story is about an eight-year-old girl who has lost her lunch money at school. After the initial scenes in which she asks her friends and teacher for help, the tape is stopped and the children in the class are asked what they think she should do next. The teacher encourages the children to suggest that the actress think of alternative solutions to her problem and praises them for their attempts. The teacher may also elicit some possible solutions at this time. The tape is then resumed, and the heroine models consideration of additional solutions. Later in the story, she is still unsuccessful in solving her problem and quite discouraged. The tape is stopped and the children are asked if they think that the actress should give up since the problem appears unsolvable. Again, the teacher encourages responses that indicate that the actress should persist and elicits additional potential solutions from the children. The modeling story ends with the child working with her friends, generating alternative solutions, and successfully solving her problem. As the screen fades with the picture of a smiling, happy youngster who has solved her problem, the narrator reviews the steps she went through and emphasizes that she was successful because she looked for alternative solutions to her problem.

In subsequent classroom exercises the teacher had the students form small groups of four or five children each. One child served as the secretary for the group. Each group would take a problem from a list they had generated earlier. The goal of the group would be to brainstorm as many solutions as possible to the selected problem. The teacher's role was to circulate, along with her classroom aide, to each of the groups to help the children stay on task and to encourage the quieter children to think of alternatives too. Teachers reported that the children worked well in these groups and looked forward to these "problem-solving classes." Interest level was consistently high, and distractions were generally kept at a minimum. Often the groups would give a report to the larger class at the end of a 20-minute period. Use of these small groups permitted participation by a greater number of children and allowed for the better problem solvers in each group to model for other children. Often, the teacher offered a prize to the group with the most solutions or the most original solution to a problem. These gamelike guidelines further increased the children's interest in the activity. An example of a problem used during these sessions would be a child on the playground wanting to participate in a game with the sides even.

Some children are better problem solvers than others, as they already approach problems with flexible and successful strategies. As a preventive program, the goal of the problem-solving training was to increase the skills of the children as a group. However, analysis of the group data gains a more concrete perspective if the reader can directly observe the changes in particular children.

Our goal in the problem-solving training program should probably be restated. Given a problem situation, we wanted a child to be able to identify the situation as a problem and work toward reaching the goal. We also wished to have evidence that alternative solutions were considered, the apparent limitations and obstacles cited, and the necessary steps developed to implement the solution. Keep these goals in mind as you read the child's reaction to the story stimulus prior to and after training.

Story stimulus pretraining: Joyce had just moved into the neighborhood. She didn't know anyone and felt very lonely. The story ends with Joyce having many good friends and feeling at home in the neighborhood. What happens in between Joyce's moving in and feeling lonely, and when she ends up with many good friends?

Lisa's response[1]*:* Joyce just moved into the city and she felt lonely because she missed all her friends and didn't have anything to do. She kept on thinking what to do and how to make new friends, because it was her first time moving and she didn't know how to make new friends. So she stayed in all day and helped her mother fixing up the house and helping her father fixing up the car—giving him the tools. Then the next day she thought how to make friends and she made friends. The next day she made even more than five friends. Then she played with one of her friends and had a good time.

While the story line reflects that this child wants to think of ways to make friends, she does not produce any specific steps to reach the goal. All of a sudden she has friends.

Story stimulus posttraining: One day Amy was standing around with some other kids, when one of the kids said something real nasty to Amy. Amy got real mad. She got so mad she wanted to get even with the other girl. The story ends with Amy happy because she and the other kid were friends. What happens in between one of the kids saying something real nasty to Amy and when she is very happy because she and the other kid were friends.

Lisa's response: Out on the playground she saw some girls playing jump rope, and she asked them if she could play, and they said no. She went over to the steps and thought how she could make friends to be able to play with them. She thought of one good solution, that she could set up a hopscotch game. Then she went over there to ask if they would like to play. She took out four balls and used cracks in the sidewalk for the game. One of her friends, who was nasty, won the game. When the whistle blew, they lined up, and she sat with her friend at lunch, and they were friends again.

[1] The names of the children have been changed to maintain confidentiality.

This story reflects a greater degree of solution generation. Here the child has elaborated specific steps to reach her goal of reestablishing friendship with the other girl. The following child shows rather dramatic change on the same PSM story as a result of training.

Carol before: She is very sad. She don't got any friends.

Carol after: Amy invited her to a party. And they went out to the movies together. They ate dinner together. So then she said, "Let's be friends." Amy took the other girl on a vacation.

The next two children represent more moderate changes in problem solving. Their stories are based on the same stems with male characters (Al and George.)

Bill before: He feels sad because he didn't have any friends and he was lonesome. And then he was walking down the street, and he met a friend coming down the street and then went over to his house.

Bill after: He went home first. And then he came back to the kid and asked him if he wanted to be friends. The kid said no. So George went back home. A few days later, George went back to the kid once more and asked him if he wanted to be friends. And the kid said yes.

Eric before: He lives next door to this boy. He goes bike riding with him. They have a bike race but Al hit a sharp curb and got hurt badly. But his mother was at work so his friend's mother took him to the hospital. Al came back from the hospital with crutches. And they became friends.

Eric after: George went home and told his mother who said, "Don't do anything with him." So George went over and played baseball with the kids, and the other boy who was nasty came over to play, but the other kids pushed him away. But George said, "What kind of friends are you if you don't want him to play?" So George decided to quit also and went with the other kid to George's house. His mother gave them a game to play and they became friends.

In all of the above stories, the children take a more active role in problem solution and, in general, consider more than one solution to the given problem after training. These children's performances are typical of many in the training classrooms.

Reliability of the Problem-Solving Assessment Measures

The goal of the problem-solving program was to enhance the child's ability to apply a set of problem-solving skills and strategies to a variety of problematic social and interpersonal situations. As noted in Chapter 6, two assessment procedures were developed to predict problem-solving behaviors in the generalized situation. The Problem-Solving Measure (PSM) was designed to sample a variety of problem situations. The Structured Real-Life Problem Situation provided an opportunity to observe problem-solving behavior within the context of a standardized situation.

Two of the three methods of reliability computation mentioned in Chapter 2 were employed in this phase of the program. To determine interrater reliability, two undergraduates were trained to score sample protocols in accord with a carefully specified scoring manual. Each rater then independently scored 20 PSM protocols selected at random from the entire sample. Their ratings were highly correlated for total score, $r = .85$, as well as for alternative solutions, $r = .75$, elaborations, $r = .75$, and obstacles scores, $r = .90$. Their percentage of agreement for those stories on which the child had correctly identified the problem was 95%. The internal consistency form of reliability of the PSM depends on the degree to which each of the stories contribute to the total score after removing the contribution of each particular score to the total. The results of these computations were correlations ranging from .47 to .64, with a median correlation of .55 being found. This analysis supports the cohesiveness of this measure and indicates its utility for assessment.

Analysis of Program Effectiveness

Pretest scores on the PSM are presented in Table 7.1. An analysis of variance of these scores indicated that there were no significant differences between the classrooms at pretest. This preliminary analysis rules out the alternative conclusion that any improvements found as a result of the program were due to a systematic distribution of prior skill in problem solving across the experimental conditions.

The postintervention PSM scores are also presented in Table 7.1. When an analysis of variance was computed for the total number of problem-solving behaviors scored for each story, the difference between experimental and control children was significant, $F(1, 117) = 15.86$, $p < .001$. Analyses of each of the component scores indicated that trained children generated significantly more alternative solutions, $F(1, 117) = 21.80$, $p < .001$, and elaborations to these solutions, $F(1, 117) = 9.03$, $p < .01$, but did not consider more obstacles to these solutions, $F(1, 117) = 1.81$. Thus, it is clear that problem-solving training did indeed produce reliable increases in the intermediate criteria being investigated (see Fig. 7.1).

In order to determine whether these significant differences were due to improvement on the part of trained participants, scores for those children in the experimental and control groups who were assessed on the PSM both before and after the intervention were examined. The degree of improvement for both groups was evaluated by means of repeated measurements analysis of variance.

TABLE 7.1
Means on Problem-Solving Measure for Experimental and Control Groups[a]

	Experimental				Control			
	Group I (*N*=31)		Group II (*N*=25)	Groups I & II (*N*=56)	Group I (*N*=33)		Group II (*N*=30)	Groups I & II (*N*=63)
	Pre	Post	Post only	Post	Pre	Post	Post only	Post
Alternatives	8.0	11.0	10.9	10.9	7.9	8.1	8.5	8.3
Elaborations	2.0	4.5	4.9	4.7	2.3	3.6	3.4	3.5
Obstacles	1.3	2.1	2.6	2.3	1.3	1.2	2.1	1.8
Total score	11.3	17.6	18.5	17.9	11.4	12.9	14.0	13.6

[a]The testing sequence from which the means were derived was based on the Solomon Four-Group Design mentioned in Chapter 6.

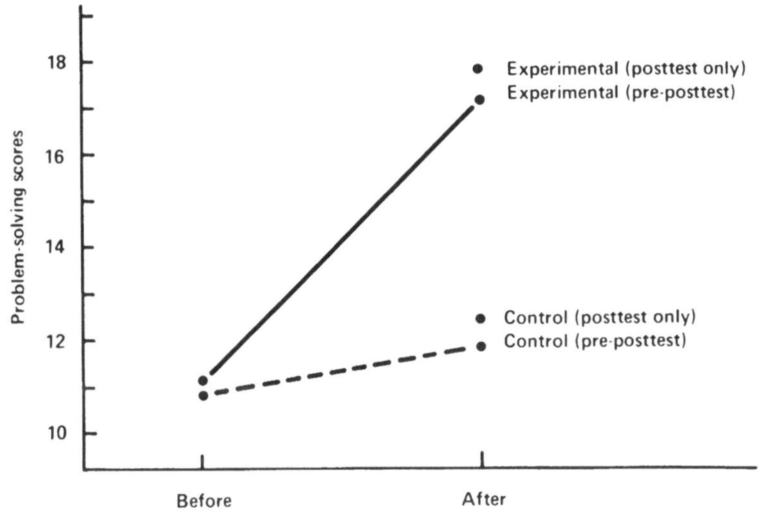

FIG. 7.1 Mean problem-solving scores achieved by the experimental and control children.

The results of these analyses demonstrated a significant improvement in total score performance for the trained children when they were compared to the control children, $F(1, 62) = 13.26$, $p < .001$. Further repeated measurement analyses on component scores showed that trained children demonstrated significantly more improvement than controls on alternative solutions, $F(1, 62 = 13.90$, $p < .001$, and tended to show greater improvement on the number of steps or elaborations generated for each solution $F(1, 62) = 3.27$, $p < .10$. There was no significant training effect on the number of obstacles cited to solutions, $F(1, 62) = 2.28$.

Identification of problem components. Inspection of Table 7.2 indicates that the number of children who correctly identified all problem components before the intervention was characteristically high. Chi square analysis of the raw

TABLE 7.2
Percentage of Children Who Correctly Identified Problems on the Problem-Solving Measure

	Experimental		Control	
Number of problems identified	Pre	Post	Pre	Post
5	80	96	84	74
4	13	4	10	19
3	7	0	6	3

frequency data indicated that these performances at pretest were comparable for both experimental and control groups. $\chi^2(2) = .28$. However, analysis of postintervention performances indicated that training resulted in a greater number of subjects generating a solution to all five problems, $\chi^2(2) = 8.78, p < .05$.

In summary, these data indicate that the Problem-Solving Measure is a fairly reliable instrument and that the experimental and control groups were initially comparable on this measure. The effectiveness of training was supported by increased frequency of the problem-solving strategies at postintervention. Specifically, trained children performed significantly better on the PSM total score, generated significantly more alternative solutions, and provided more elaborations or steps to these solutions at posttreatment. Further, these differences were a result of significant improvement from pre- to postintervention. Also, training resulted in more experimental children identifying a greater number of problems on the PSM. However, training did not result in children considering more obstacles to the solutions generated.

Generalization of Training to a "Real-Life" Situation

The number of alternative solutions generated to a problem situation were also observed in the Structured Real-Life Problem Situation. The results presented in Table 7.3 indicate that responses to the problem fell into three categories: the child generated (1) no solution, (2) one solution, or (3) two or more alternate solutions. Forty-seven percent of all subjects did not generate a solution in the situation. A chi square analysis indicates that this tendency not to respond was not significantly different between the experimental and control groups, $\chi^2(1) = .33$. A 2 X 2 table combining the number of children who generated none or only one solution compared with the number generating two alternate solutions was derived. Fisher's Exact Probability Test (Siegel, 1956) indicated that significantly more experimental children generated more than one solution to the problem presented in the Structured Real-Life Problem, $p < .05$. This result suggests that the experimental training had generalized applicability in an interpersonal problematic situation.

TABLE 7.3
Number of Children Who Generated Solutions in the Structured Real-Life Problem Situation

Number of solutions	Experimental	Control
None	7	5
One	3	5
Two	6	0

The percentage of children who failed to respond with a solution in the Structured Problem Situation places some limitation on these preliminary findings concerning training generalization. However, this low response rate must be considered within the framework of the contrived situation. From the child's viewpoint the situation might be considered a problem primarily for the adult experimenter to solve. This suggests that the children in the "no response" category were not necessarily poor problem solvers but that they did not perceive the problem as one that necessitated their participation.

Extraneous Influences on Intervention Outcomes

The results indicating that the program was effective were examined to rule out logical alternatives that might account for such findings. Of specific interest were the following four issues: (1) that the effects were due to differential teacher effectiveness, (2) that training was differentially effective for children of different ages or sex, (3) that the measurement procedures, particularly the PSM, interacted with the training procedures, and (4) that intellectual or verbal aptitude factors affected the impact of training in problem solving.

Differential teacher effectiveness. The first possible alternative to the results was that only particular teachers could produce the effects described previously and that perhaps one or two teachers accounted for the observed training outcomes. An analysis of variance with classes nested within experimental condition permits assessment of the effects of particular teachers within the treatment groups. This analysis was performed on PSM total score data as well as on each of the component scores. These analyses all indicated similar training effects for posttreatment differences and for improvement following the intervention. More importantly, these analyses indicated that there were no differences between teachers within the experimental groups in their ability to implement the training program.

Sex and age influences on problem-solving outcome. Two separate one-way analyses of variance indicated no significant sex differences on PSM performance either prior to or following participation. A further analysis of variance was employed to determine if there was any interaction between the child's sex and improvement on the PSM. The results of this analysis led to the conclusion that children of both sexes can profit equally from problem-solving training.

Analysis of variance of pretreatment PSM scores by the grade of the child indicate that fourth graders did significantly better than third graders, $F(1, 68) = 5.57$, $p < .02$. These differences were not present at posttreatment assessment of PSM performance. Further, there was no interaction between the grade of the child and subsequent improvement of PSM performance.

Finally, when the age of the child is correlated with his PSM performance at pretreatment or at posttreatment, the resulting coefficients are low and nonsignificant. Likewise, correlation of the child's age and improvement in PSM performance approaches zero. While children in the fourth grade as a group may perform higher on the PSM at pretreatment, these differences are eliminated over the school year. Training also appears equally effective for children of different ages or grades.

Pretesting as a factor in intervention outcome. Use of the Solomon Four-Group Design mentioned in Chapter 6 permitted analysis of repeated assessment on the PSM as well as possible interactions between taking the pretest and receiving training. Analysis indicated that taking the PSM twice did not affect posttreatment performance on the measure. In fact, inspection of Table 7.1 suggests that those children tested twice on the PSM in both experimental and control groups performed slightly lower at posttreatment. Further analysis indicates that there were no sensitizing effects for those children who were pretested and received training.

Intellectual and verbal aptitude influences on outcome. Since the PSM relies on assessment of problem-solving strategies through the verbal-report channel, the results needed thorough examination to assess the effects of verbal fluency and verbal aptitude on PSM performance. Correlations between the number of words generated by a child and total PSM score at pretreatment, $r(63) = .68, p < .001$, and at posttreatment, $r(118) = .58, p < .001$, were both significant. However, when the experimental and control groups were compared on the number of words generated on the PSM at pretreatment and at posttreatment, there were no significant differences. In fact, the control children as a group used more words at posttreatment than the experimentals. Thus, while there is some relationship between the verbosity of a child and his or her PSM score, this relationship does not account for the differences in PSM scores between experimental and control groups.

The relationship between verbal intelligence as measured by the Peabody Picture Vocabulary Test and performance on the PSM were also investigated. Correlations were computed between scores of verbal aptitude and PSM scores at pretreatment, $r(63) = .27, p < .05$, at posttreatment, $r = .04$, and with improvement on the PSM, $r = -.08$. These correlations indicated that (1) there was a low but significant relationship between intelligence and problem solving before participation, (2) training apparently attenuated this relationship, and (3) verbal aptitude scores did not predict improvement in problem-solving performance.

In-Class Measurement of Problem Solving

A series of In-Class Measures (ICMs) were developed to provide the teachers with feedback concerning the various components of the problem-solving training package. These measures also permitted limited assessment of the effectiveness of each step of the training procedure. They also provided feedback on problem identification, alternative solution generation, elaborations, consequences cited to solutions, and percentage of effective solutions selected by children in both experimental and in one control classroom.

The results from these ICMs suggest that the most effective steps of the training program were those which dealt with problem identification and generation of alternative solutions. This suggestion is further strengthened by the outcome data on the effectiveness of training on PSM performances reported earlier. Training in the generation of elaborations and the consideration of potential consequences were not as effective, and this was also supported, in general, by the PSM data. However, while the children did not cite more consequences or obstacles to potential solutions when presented with a series of solutions, the trained children picked a higher percentage of effective strategies when compared with control children on the ICM.

Measuring Problem Solving as a Psychological Construct

The construct of problem solving is a complex one. The major device used to measure this construct (PSM) contained components that were designed to evaluate various aspects of the construct. As reported in Chapters 3 and 6, the PSM was adapted from the MEPS (Shure & Spivack, 1972a), which was originally validated by the method of known groups. The data generated by this study provides some additional preliminary assessment of validity for this measure. The construct validity of the PSM depends, in part, on the convergence of the component behaviors of problem solving that it measures. Correlations between the various subscales should be of intermediate strength since these components are presumably measuring related but not identical behaviors. The intercorrelations between these three components (alternative solutions, elaborations, and obstacles) were computed for both forms of the PSM. The correlations for the pretest form of the PSM ranged from a generally low but positive .20 to .34, indicating a tendency for the component problem-solving behaviors to be interrelated. The posttest form is based on a larger sample and a greater dispersion of scores for each of the components. These correlations ranged from .46 to .55 and were all statistically significant. These data lend some support to the convergent validity of the PSM, and they suggest that this measure adequately taps three of the many possible component parts of the problem-solving process.

Further analysis of the construct validity of the PSM draws upon its concurrent relationship with other referents of problem-solving behavior. Children were grouped by their performance on the "Structured Problem Situation" and compared on their scores on the "alternative solutions" component of the PSM. Analysis of variance indicated that those children generating two solutions in the contrived situation performed significantly higher on the PSM alternative solutions than those who produced no response or only one solution, $F(2, 23) =$

6.47, $p < .01$. This finding lends further concurrent support to the validity of the PSM.

Correlations were also computed between the component and total scores of the final PSM and the parallel performances on the ICMs. The correlations between each ICM and the posttest PSM it parallels were significant or tended toward significance in three of six cases. The alternative solutions of the ICM correlated .16, $p = .10$, with the alternative solutions component of the PSM. The ICM of consequences generated to a solution correlated .19, $p = .05$, with the obstacles component of the PSM. And the percent effective solutions chosen on the ICM correlated .19, $p = .05$, with the obstacles component. Also, correlations between total score on the PSM and the ICM scores were low but significant in the same three cases. Three legitimate method differences contributed to these characteristically low correlations: (1) the format and scoring of the PSM and ICM were completely different, (2) there was a 1–3-month time lapse between administration of particular ICM and the posttreatment PSM, during which there was additional training, and (3) teachers administered the ICMs to groups of students in the classroom, while unfamiliar male experimenters administered the PSM individually outside the classroom.

These preliminary data lend support to the construct validity of the problem-solving measurement procedures and extend the previously limited validation procedures for measurements of this kind. These data support the positions of D'Zurilla & Goldfried (1971) and Nelson (1970) who have proposed that looking for alternatives, elaborating the steps necessary for execution, and considering possible consequences are an interrelated set of problem-solving behaviors. These data provide particularly important factual evidence in an area replete with speculation and mark a significant improvement over earlier attempts to measure social problem-solving skills.

Analysis of Secondary Outcome Measures

As indicated in Chapter 6, a series of additional measures was used in the study to assess secondary outcome as a function of the problem-solving training program. The inclusion of these measures was considered exploratory; of interest was whether there would be nonspecific generalization of training effects to other areas frequently viewed as important in school programs.

Six secondary outcome measures were administered to the children in the problem-solving intervention. These included group-administered measures of locus of control, self-esteem, level of aspiration, self-reported attitude, peer sociometric ratings, and teacher-completed ratings of classroom behaviors on the Modified Walker Problem Behavior Checklist. Changes on these measures are summarized in Table 7.4.

Locus of control. Pretreatment scores on the Nowicki and Strickland (1973) Locus of Control Measure correlated at low and nonsignificant levels with PSM

TABLE 7.4
Means of Secondary Outcome Measures before and after Treatment for the Experimental and Control Groups

	Experimental		Control	
Measure	Pre	Post	Pre	Post
Locus of control	16.70	14.70	16.50	16.60
Self-esteem	63.40	64.30	62.00	60.10
LOA *d* score	.95	−.07	.64	−.09
Expectancy 1	4.70	5.50	5.40	4.70
Expectancy 2	4.70	5.90	5.50	4.90
Sociometric	3.20	3.00	3.40	3.10
Walker	94.80	84.10	91.60	86.80

scores at pretreatment, $r = .17$, and posttreatment, $r(113) = .17, p < .10$. These correlations indicate that "internals" on this measure tended to do better on the measure than did "externals." However, when all children were divided at the median on this measure of locus of control, "internals" were found to perform significantly better on the PSM both before, $t(60) = 2.067, p < .05$, and after, $t(116) = 2.091, p < .05$, the program. One can conclude, then, that scores on the Locus of Control Measure are related to some slight degree with problem-solving performance. However, analysis of improvement of PSM performances indicated that there were no significant differences as a function of locus of control.

In contrast to this last finding, when experimental children are compared to control children there is a significant change toward "internality" on the Locus of Control Measure, $F(1, 109) = 13.51, p < .001$. Thus, the data reported earlier indicate that children on the internal end of the continuum demonstrated higher frequencies of the various problem-solving strategies. Apparently, "internal" children believe that the solution of a problem is contingent upon what they do, and they are more likely to persist in the generation of new strategies to solve a given problem situation. It is also significant that training in problem solving, which emphasized that problems could be solved and encouraged children to solve their own problems, resulted in significantly more frequent expression of "internal" statements on the Locus of Control Measure administered after participation in the program.

Expectancy questionnaire. Analysis of self-esteem and level of aspiration scores pre- and posttreatment for experimental and control groups indicated no significant differences on these variables as a function of problem-solving training. Of eight statements concerning expectancies about future school performance and social experience, two demonstrated significant change as a function of training in problem solving. Experimental children reported higher expectancies that many children will ask them to play on the playground ($F(1, 130) = 19.5, p < .001$) and higher expectations that when on the playground they will look for lots of ways to get friends ($F(1, 130) = 19.5, p < .001$). These results indicate that, as a result of training in problem solving, children will report greater expectancies that more children will play with them on the playground and that, given a lack of friends on the playground, they will look for alternative ways to get friends. There were no significant changes on any of the component or total scores of the Modified Walker Problem Behavior Checklist or peer sociometric ratings as a result of training.

Appraisal of the above data for the secondary outcome measures indicates that the gradient of effect for the problem-solving intervention is rather specific. Expectancies dealing with locus of reinforcement and specific problem-solving self-reported expectancies appear to change with treatment. However, other more generalized areas of functioning (that is, disruptive behavior, peer sociometrics, self-esteem, and level of aspiration) are not affected.

The lack of change for the teacher and peer ratings suggests several alternative hypotheses. The first is that these behaviors were not functionally related to those in the program. The second is that these broader and more generalized behaviors were slower to change, or that the time period between assessment was too brief. The third alternative is that some form of measurement artifact (that is, rater bias) may have been operating. Preliminary evidence (Larcen *et al.*, 1972; Shure & Spivack, 1972a) seem to rule out first alternative, since these studies have found a functional relationship between adult ratings of adjustment and problem-solving scores. The second alternative must be tested by additional long-term research. However, the present study contributes some data to support the third alternative.

Specifically, it is suggested that rater bias persists in the school setting as a function of a labeling process that is resistant to change, even when there are observable changes. First, there is support that both teachers and peers perform similar labeling procedures. Inspection of peer and teacher ratings indicates that these ratings are significantly correlated with each other, $r(133) = .30, p < .001$. Both ratings also showed little change over the six-month period from pre- to post- . This stability is supported by significant correlations between pretest and posttest ratings by peers, $r(133) = .41, p < .001$, and by teachers, $r(133) = .53, p < .001$. These data suggest that both teachers and peers label children in similar ways, and that these labels tend to remain rather stable over time. These findings are similar to those discussed in Chapters 8 and 9.

Impact of the Intervention on the School System

As part of the evaluation process for a community-based intervention such as this one, it is essential to consider the factors that influenced the impact of the training program on the school system. This assessment combines systematic observation of the system with the reactions and feedback from those agents in the organization responsible for implementing the project. As mentioned above, this information is crucial in designing interventions that are maximally effective and practical.

One primary impact of this intervention on the school system was that it provided a vehicle or process for the teacher to directly intervene in the social–psychological development of the children in the classroom. As a preventive program, its procedures were applicable to all children in the classroom setting, and its techniques were adaptable for inclusion in the ongoing educational curriculum. Five of the factors discussed in Chapter 2 contributed to the practicality and success of this intervention:

1. The school administration made a firm committment to the project, including the allocation of time for the implementation of the project within the curriculum and for the necessary in-service workshops during the regular class schedule.
2. Program objectives and time requirements were clearly specified prior to the implementation of the intervention.
3. Classroom techniques and exercises were developed cooperatively by the teachers and the consultants, providing flexibility and feasibility to the program, as well as promoting feelings of program ownership by the school system.
4. The specificity of the skills being trained facilitated their inclusion in the educational format.
5. Finally, the commitment of extremely competent undergraduates, serving as raters and as a teacher aide, provided the program with a liason and facilitated staff rapport with an "outside" intervention in the school system.

Teacher feedback consisted of both informal conversations and formal written evaluations. The informal feedback was consistently favorable and highlighted three areas. First, the teachers felt that the use of videotaped models in the problem-solving training was an especially suitable technique for children in this age range. The attention of the students was reported to be above average for each of the four tapes, and the teachers also found that stopping the tapes and eliciting discussion of alternative problem-solving strategies from the children an excellent instructional technique. Second, informal feedback supported the success of the role-playing exercises. The teachers emphasized the need for additional exercises of this nature to maximize each child's experience in implementing problem-solving strategies. Third, teachers reported several anecdotal examples of children actually implementing the training strategies when problematic situations arose in the classroom or on the playground throughout the year.

The teachers also commented on the strengths and weaknesses of the intervention within the context of a written evaluation. As a group, they felt that the preventive aspects of the program were successful in providing children with a specific set of skills that could be used in everyday life situations, contributing in a positive way to their mental health. Further, when asked if they would recommend such a program to teachers in other school systems, all answered in the affirmative.

The teachers delineated two drawbacks in the current program. First, they felt that the initiation of a new training curriculum and the codevelopment of the exercises necessitated a large time investment. They hoped that this initial commitment would not have to be repeated in subsequent uses of the already developed training materials. Secondly, they stated that the training procedures should be modified to include more exercises dealing with feedback designed to provide verification of the ultimate adaptiveness of generated alternative solutions. They encouraged further use of role-playing procedures to accomplish this. Their perceptions of program weaknesses were mirrored in the data obtained, which concerned the effectiveness of the obstacles and consequences measures.

Perhaps the clearest indication of the positive impact of this intervention on the school system was the decision of the teachers to include problem-solving training in their own curriculum for the following year and the desire of the administrators to extend this training into additional classrooms. These intentions were, in fact, operationalized, and the school personnel are currently conducting the program for the fourth consecutive year. This continued utilization after the completion of the project is of primary importance in assessing its feasibility.

Implications for Future Research

It appears that this level of intervention has effectively provided children with problem-solving skills that will enable them to better resolve everyday dilemmas. Successful implementation of these skills by the children in their daily lives bears directly on the preventive nature of this intervention. It is necessary to assess the long-term effects of interventions in problem solving in order to address its ultimate preventive effects. Do the skills acquired in the training program persist over time, and, more importantly, does training in these skills result in lowered incidence rates of subsequent indices of deviance and pathology? These questions represent a meaningful challenge for future research.

There are other important questions generated by this program of research. First, what aspects of the training procedures are most effective? Can training be condensed in time, or does a maximally efficacious program need to be longer? This intervention combined modeling, small-group discussion, and role-playing techniques. Future research is needed to assess the impact of each of these components. Second, more varied and better methods need to be developed to allow clear-cut behavioral assessment of problem-solving skills. New procedures should include developing a series of possible structured situations in which to observe problem-solving behavior, as well as naturalistic observation of these behaviors. Third, training procedures in problem solving should include more effective techniques to enhance implementation of the problem-solving strategies (for example, role playing and behavioral rehearsal).

Training should also provide additional emphasis on the adaptiveness of solutions (training children to consider many possible consequences prior to taking action) and the ability to process feedback (once having taken action). In an important first step in this direction, McClure (1975) has reported an almost exact replication of the major outcomes described in this chapter. He has expanded the curriculum to include additional exercises in testing the consequences of solutions and role playing of problem situations in order to improve opportunities for feedback. In addition, he provided a methodological improvement by utilizing videotape recording procedures to assess generalization of actual problem-solving behaviors to a real-life interpersonal situation. McClure found a positive relationship between the number of alternatives generated and ratings of their effectiveness. We are beginning to collect longitudinal data on the effects of training conducted over a four year span. We are also currently investigating the effects of an adapted version of the curriculum with second graders, and evaluating the impact of including parents in the training program.

These are only a few of the heuristic implications generated by this portion of the overall program; considerable research concerning the use of training in social problem solving as a preventive intervention in the school system remains to be done. We believe, however, that if children trained in these skills can more effectively cope with difficulties in their interpersonal environments, it seems well worth the effort.

8

Promoting Social Interactions: The Blooming of Wallflowers

Assessing the Representativeness of Teacher Referrals

The first question that we sought to answer in this subcomponent of the intervention was whether teacher referrals of socially isolated children were accurate representations of their naturally occurring interactions in a different setting. Of the 52 children nominated as such, 16 were eliminated from consideration when they interacted with peers more than 90% of the time for the first three baseline observation sessions. The other 36 children, along with the 10 normal control children, were rated for the entire 10-rating-session baseline period. Twenty-five of the 36 clearly had lower rates of social interaction than the normal controls. Of the 11 borderline cases, 5 had virtually all of their interactions with only one other child; these five completed the sample of 30 "isolates."

The isolates' baseline rate of social interactions (66.8%) was significantly different from the rate of 91%, $p < .001$, manifested by the nonisolated control children. In addition, when compared to the rest of the school population, these 30 isolates were significantly less popular with their peers, $p = .003$, had slightly lower self-esteem, $p < .07$, and were rated by their teachers as having more problem behaviors, $p = .006$. It was concluded that teacher nominations, combined with a quick behavioral screening process, was a useful method of identifying a sample of children deficient in social skills. A large number of those initially nominated, however, could be considered false identifications, as their behavior did not meet the minimum criterion set for social isolation. This was to be expected given the setting differences in which the two types of ratings were made. Furthermore, it was not clear how many socially deficient children in the school were not nominated by the teachers.

The Companionship Process

One of the shortcomings of many of the companion programs reported in the literature has been that they do not give any information as to the content or process of the intervention. In the current study, this deficiency was partially avoided by asking the companions to fill out reports of individual sessions, which included estimates of time engaged in various categories of activities.

An approximate comparison of the companionship process for the first and second halves of the intervention was made by dividing this process information into sessions before and after the long Christmas vacation, which was roughly the program midpoint. The most frequent activity throughout the intervention was talking, with organized physical play second and semiorganized play (throwing a ball around, building snowmen, and so on) third. There was a significant decrease in organized physical play from the first to second half of the intervention; in addition, the children involved spent significantly more time with other children present (in addition to the companion) during the second half of the program.

These findings, along with a trend toward an increase in semiorganized play, seem to indicate the following process: at first, a great deal of time was spent in formal games with large groups of children (tag, kickball, and so on), while a moderate amount of time was spent where either the companion talked alone with the child or the child wandered away by himself or herself. As the intervention progressed, the companions stressed more intensive but less formal activities (semiorganized play) where the child could build relationships with peers, resulting in more time spent with other children.

In addition to the session reports, the companions were asked to write a summary of their intervention at the program's end. The anecdotal information collected gives perhaps the best insight into the mechanisms for change that operated in this intervention. Following are three case histories, using the companions' own words.[1] These also serve to illustrate two additional points. First, they demonstrate that the companions had an excellent grasp of the behavioral techniques that they had been taught. Second, they help to show that the children involved were not necessarily shy but, rather, lacked certain social skills that led to their isolation from other children.

Marc: After doing some background reading and working through a few hypothetical situations in workshops, my initial contact was observing Marc from a distance. The first step in changing any behavior is careful and controlled observation of that behavior. It is to one's advantage to note what

[1] Thanks to Gene Fergione, Josie Mazzerella, and Ken Richard, the companions whose write-ups appear here. The names of the children have been changed to maintain confidentiality.

happens before and after each behavior occurs. In addition to this, I searched for what was rewarding for Marc. Until you know this you can't supply the appropriate reward for the appropriate behavior we wish to see a person performing.

Therefore, my initial impression of Marc was based on two 30-minute observations of his interaction (perhaps noninteraction would be a better word here) with his peers during his lunch and recess periods in mid-November. Marc was a small, cute but chubby little boy. His actions seemed to be explainable by shyness and politeness. His desk was isolated from the rest of the class; he had to turn around if he wanted to see the teacher or his classmates. The other kids rarely initiated activity with him, and when he endeavored to reach them, they seemed to either disregard him or to talk *at* him, not *to* him. He was used to wandering around aimlessly in the classroom and on the playground. Marc felt isolated and left out, as he was off by himself, periodically glancing at the others while they played their games of kickball, basketball, tag, and so on.

I also had the opportunity to talk to Marc's teacher. She said that Marc was very bright. In talking about the position of Marc's desk, she said it was there by his own choice. She said she knows Marc has problems, and she's glad the program can help.

My first real meeting with Marc was very frustrating. I walked over to him as he was getting ready to go outside for recess and said, "Hi." He looked at me, then looked away. When we got outside I asked him if he wanted to have a contest to see who could throw a ball the farthest. He said, "No, because you're not going to really try." I tried to get him to play football, but he said he didn't like to play. The others wanted me to play football with them, and they asked Marc to play but he refused. He said, "No, leave me alone." I asked him again to play but he said, "No, get away." I played football with the other boys; it was a promising session because I noticed Marc watching us from a distance.

My goals at this point were to get Marc to have more confidence in himself and to get him experienced in being involved with others in games during recess and lunch periods. Personality can change due to the influence of external social or behavioral forces acting on a person. Knowing the specific behaviors which Marc exhibited (wandering around by himself, afraid to give himself a chance, sitting apart from the rest of the class) I now had to go about changing them. The main things I used were attention and praise, which served as rewards for appropriate behaviors. Behaviors were also reduced in frequency by withholding attention.

On my fourth session I got Marc to play a game of tag. At that point I began reinforcing him for his good playing and interacting with others during recess or lunch. In subsequent days, whenever he made a hit in kickball or a good play in football, I gave him a lot of attention. On my fifth session, I played on Marc's team in football and tried hard to make him look good. Well, the final score was 6–0, and guess who scored the only touchdown? The kids all congratulated him, and after that day he often wanted to play football.

At about the seventh session I began to change gradually to a more intermittent schedule of reinforcement. In the beginning I had suggested games and appointed Marc captain, in addition to playing on his team to give him more confidence. Now I moved to letting the kids suggest their own games. Marc even offered to be captain several times! I ignored various behaviors which I did not want repeated, such as his lack of confidence in himself, his fighting, his arguing, and his lack of initiative. Sports are an important part of Marc's life; by getting him involved with the games, he has a sound basis for interacting with his peers.

By the sessions after Christmas vacation, I was trying to fade out of the picture, just letting Marc be one of the guys and thus more independent from me. I did try to vary the activities, getting Marc to interact more inside at lunch and in more intensive situations with fewer children around. By February I would come late on purpose and sometimes would disappear between lunch and recess to see what would happen. He continued to do well.

On my 17th visit, we went to see the modeling film on making friends. Marc was very impressed, as he clearly identified with the kids in the movie. When he saw a kid sharing, he said, "That's me, I've done that." When a kid in the film wasn't being nice, he said, "I've had that done to me."

On my twentieth and last session, in mid-March, Marc enjoyed playing even without any attention from me. We had a talk about how I wasn't going to be coming back anymore. He said he promised he was going to play with his friends even if I wasn't there.

Wendy: During lunch Wendy would speak with the other girls at her table. Her recess period, however, consisted of walking around the playground by herself, occasionally encountering one other girl briefly. Wendy was very reluctant to take part in group activities outdoors. This puzzled me, for she did have the physical ability and the girls did not purposely alienate her.

I concentrated at first on getting her to participate in group activities outdoors and to carry on conversations with others during lunch. The initial step was gaining her confidence. She had to believe that I was her friend.

All during lunch Wendy would talk to me, but when it came to playing outside her enthusiasm declined. Occasionally, I was able to get her to participate in group games, but once she conceded to take part, different obstacles would materialize. If it was not something specific that had displeased her, then it was that she had lost interest. If and when she took part in a game, she often would either physically leave or be mentally isolated (Wendy could physically be in a game, but mentally shut herself out). Once in a while she would return, whereupon I made a conscious effort to reinforce her behavior.

During this period, however, her verbal abilities did improve. I worked on this part of her social skills by first initiating topics of general interest. In the process I insisted that if someone spoke everyone should listen; everyone would be given the opportunity to speak if they extended this courtesy to others. From that time on every time Wendy started a conversation I made sure that no one interrupted her. In turn, when others spoke I directed her attention to me. To my surprise, before long Wendy was listening closely to the discussions of the group, adding interesting anecdotes, and starting topics herself.

Slowly Wendy began to show other improvement. She was participating in group activities nearly 70% of the time. She was also becoming quite friendly with one of the other boys in her class.

In the first few sessions after Christmas, however, Wendy was quite disruptive. She was more outwardly aggressive towards her acquaintances, drew away from group games, and instead spent her time distracting the boys. At this time I decided to change the methods of implementing my goals. I made Wendy understand that I did not condone her disruptive behavior. I ignored any aggressive encounters she initiated, reinforcing only socially appropriate actions.

In a few weeks, changes occurred in Wendy's behavior. She took part in more outdoor activities; playing with other children gradually encompassed more of the recess period. In fact, Wendy was leaving games I had started to join other activities that were in progress elsewhere.

In the last few sessions of the program I concentrated on reinforcing the children in Wendy's class who paid attention to her. I wanted to be sure that she had a few friends she could depend on after I left. In the playground I stayed on the sidelines rather than take an active part in the games Wendy was participating in. Before I left, Wendy was easily carrying on conversations with others and was getting involved in group activities on the playground without my intervention. Rarely was she seen wandering off by herself.

Steven: Steven was a small, eager, and active child. He was equipped with higher-than-average intelligence and a quick wit. Although when speaking to him individually he seemed happy and well adjusted, Steven was a problem child. His eagerness often manifested itself in aggression, both physical and verbal. In the classroom he was sassy and forever out of his seat. He was a ringleader, and central to almost every disturbance that arose. On the playground he seemed willing to play with the other children, but unfailingly would fight or simply run from group to group, never fully becoming involved. He seldom initiated any games.

A few observation periods were all that was needed to see the repetitiveness of his actions. Many of the reasons became apparent: Steven was overly eager to be accepted, to be liked; however, he did not have the vaguest notion of what others expected from him. He was without a role other than that of troublemaker. In the absence of acceptance he sought attention. The uncertainty of expected behavior, the insecurity of nonimmediate acceptance, the lack of knowledge of social skills—these were often too much for Steven to bear.

There were three possible reactions that the other children displayed toward Steven upon his entering a game. Rarely, they would accept his presence readily and acknowledge him, in which case Steven's insecurity was relieved and he would stay and play. More often, there was indifference to his presence. This being the case, he would make his bid for that second-best reinforcer, attention, generally by disrupting the ongoing game. The third possibility was rejection, to which Steve had two stereotypic responses depending on the viewed importance of the situation. If the situation was viewed as unimportant, Steven would simply run away to find another group of children. If important, his reaction was immediate physical aggression. Steve is a small but very strong child and a very apt fighter. If he fought, he generally won, thereby maintaining or increasing his own self-esteem and reducing the status and importance of those individuals who had rejected him. If he could not be accepted, at least he could overpower.

It became easy to get close to and manipulate Steven on the basis of his great desire for acceptance. I verbally rewarded him for correct behavior and ignored him when he misbehaved. Once in a while it became necessary to gently scold him. I modeled behaviors and, through illustration, taught him to initiate games. His natural knack for leadership was given a constructive direction and he became an integrative force upon the playground. Often I would take him off to the side and teach him game skills privately to increase his confidence and self-esteem.

The consequent acceptance and high regard given to him by the other children became rewarding in itself. Steven had never been rejected by the other children on any other basis than his own malevolent actions, so when he altered his behavior patterns, his acceptance was secured. It was not so much working with other children that was involved; rather, it was only necessary to teach Steven constructive ways to take the initiative. The modeling movie also helped with this.

For Steven, the program was a success. I can only hope that his newly learned behaviors will not become subject to extinction. The one thing I felt unable to alter significantly was Steven's temper. If there is anything that retards his progress, I suspect it will be this. We seemed to be making some gains with it, but I have some doubts as to the permanency of the changes in this area.

Interrater Reliability of the Behavioral Rating System

Interrater reliability was assessed during both rater training and the actual collection of data. Pairs of observers rated a child at the same time for a total of 47 recess sessions. Reliability figures were computed in two ways. For the interaction/no interaction, specific interaction category, and number of peer classifications, all of which were rated during every interval, the number of agreements was divided by the total number of intervals for each of the 47 rater pairings. Ratings of the affect (consequences) and initiation classifications, which occurred only during the relatively rare appearances of such behaviors, required a separate computational method. Reliability was calculated by dividing the number of ratings in each category where both raters agreed by the total of agreements and disagreements and then multiplying by 100 to obtain a percentage.

For the dichotomous interaction/no interaction rating, the mean percentage of agreement for the 47 sessions was 96%, with the median also equal to 96%. For the specific category of interaction, the mean and median agreements were both 84%. The mean percentage of agreement for the number of peers involved in the interaction was 85%, with a median of 90%. The affect ratings had only 22% agreement, whereas 47% agreement existed for initiations. The very low reliability for positive affect ratings, which were the most difficult to score, led to an elimination of that classification. Instead, only very obvious occurrences of negative affect, involving such behaviors as fighting and screaming, were coded. Subsequent reliability checks showed a 64% agreement in these negative affect observations. Ratings of affect and initiation thus proved to be fairly unreliable, and their use as outcome criteria did not appear to be justified. Consequently, these measures are not considered in the remainder of this chapter.

Overall Effectiveness of the Program

Behavioral observations of social interaction. The key question to be answered by the study was whether the intervention was effective by the evaluative criteria specified in Chapter 2. A summary of the behavioral data is shown in Table 8.1. The most important outcome criterion was the total rate of social interactions with peers. The experimental and isolate control groups were matched as closely as possible on their rates of social interaction. The postprogram evaluation indicated that 19 of 20 experimental children had improved, while only six of ten isolate controls did so. A Fisher exact probability test showed this difference between the groups to be highly significant, $p = .03$.

The mean rate of interaction for the experimental children improved from 66.3% to 84.7%, a difference of 18.4%. The isolate controls increased their interactions from 68.1% to 74.6%, an improvement of only 6.5% during the course of the program (see Fig. 8.1). An analysis of covariance was performed

TABLE 8.1
Means and Standard Deviations for Percentage of Time Spent by Experimental, Isolate Control, and Normal Control Children in Peer Interaction

		Experimental[a]		Isolate control[b]		Normal control[b]	
		Pre	Post	Pre	Post	Pre	Post
Rate of interactions	Mean	66.3	84.7	68.1	74.6	91.0	87.7
	S.D.	18.7	11.4	15.2	19.5	3.4	9.9
Cooperative play	Mean	33.4	55.0	32.7	50.4	59.6	67.6
	S.D.	14.1	18.9	18.6	24.6	17.8	18.5
Interaction with group of peers (> 2)	Mean	28.8	39.7	33.7	33.4	62.0	59.7
	S.D.	13.4	21.5	18.6	23.3	13.9	16.6

[a] N=20.
[b] N=10.

comparing the postprogram rates of interaction using initial rates as a covariate. Such an approach controls for individual preprogram differences. Results of this analysis indicate a strong trend in the predicted direction, $F(1, 27) = 3.24, p < .09$; that is, the program was effective in increasing the positive social behaviors of the experimental children to a higher rate than that of the untreated isolate controls.

Several important factors mitigated against an even more clear-cut demonstration of program effectiveness of the social interaction outcome criterion. First, a general ceiling effect on this measure effectively limited the amount of improve-

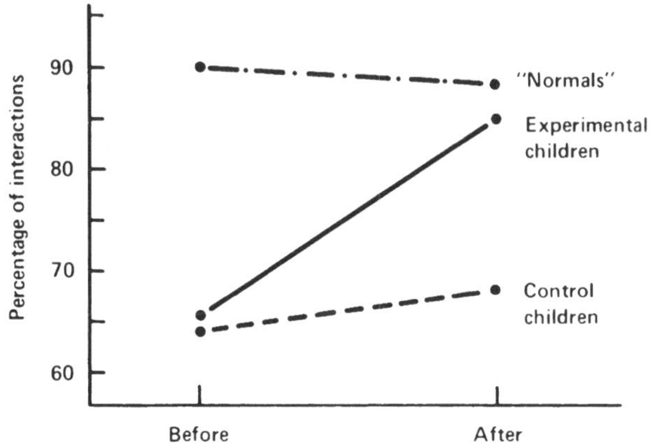

FIG. 8.1 Percentages of interactions observed for the experimental and control participants and nonisolated children.

ment the experimental group could show. The normal control group, which had a baseline interaction rate of 91%, interacted only 88% of the time during postprogram assessment. This would seem to indicate that natural conditions in the recess situation tended to limit the rate of interactions to approximately this level. Thus the increase by the experimental group to a rate of 84% closely approximates the limit of this highly variable measure. While 11 of the 20 experimental children had postprogram rates equal to the mean of the normal group, only 3 of 10 isolate controls reached this level. This indicates that differences between the groups might have been greater were it not for this ceiling effect.

The second factor influencing this outcome measure was the appearance on the playground of several male student teachers midway through the post-program assessment. These student teachers organized large group activities involving many of the children, thus changing the free-play situation of the recess period. The five rating sessions collected prior to their appearance showed that the experimental group was already interacting at a rate of 84%, while the isolate controls were only interacting 69% of the time. Thus it is quite possible that these teachers caused some spurious improvement in the final data of the isolate control group, while the experimental group had already demonstrated improvement.

Two additional mitigating factors existed. First, the companions' interventions included control children in several instances. These children were in the same classrooms as experimental children, and sometimes were unintentionally drawn into companion-initiated activities. It is likely that this resulted in at least some behavioral improvement in several of the isolate control children. Finally, the original teacher nominations were solicited too early in the school year. This resulted in the inclusion of several children in each group who were apparently only showing difficulty in adjusting to the new school setting. Teachers later mentioned that several children who ended up in the isolate control group should not have been nominated. While this problem should theoretically have affected each group equally, it produced further limitations on showing statistically significant group differences in this intervention that involved a relatively small number of participants. When these four practical limitations are considered, it is concluded that the results obtained on the main outcome criterion indicated that the intervention had a very significant impact on the social interactions of the children involved.

When the behavioral data were broken down into more specific rating categories, no significant differential improvement was shown between the experimental and isolate control groups, although differences were generally in the predicted direction. This lack of differentiation is not surprising in view of the fact that the group differences found on the total rate of interaction criterion were here divided along several dimensions. For example, it was predicted that experimental children would increase more in the amount of cooperative play shown, and in the amount of group play (interaction with more than two peers).

The data showed a 22% increase for experimentals in cooperative play, compared to an 18% increase for isolate controls. For group play, experimentals improved 11% while isolate controls did not improve. However, due to great variability within groups, differential change was not statistically significant in either case. In addition, both experimental and isolate control groups were still significantly different from the normal control group after the program on these and several other behavioral indices.

One final behavioral outcome was that the experimental children appeared to show more consistency in their behavior after the program than did members of the isolate control group. Data supporting this contention are presented in Table 8.2. Group means of the rate of social interaction were computed for each rating session. Variances of these means were then calculated for each assessment period (that is, pre- and postprogram), indicating the consistency of group behavior across sessions. Two F ratios, comparing experimental and isolate control group variability during the baseline and again during the postprogram assessment periods, were also computed. The baseline data indicated the normal group to be the most consistent. Postprogram data, however, showed that the experimental group had become the most consistent. Furthermore, the ratio of isolate control to experimental group variances increased greatly over time $F = 2.5$ to $F = 5.3$. This means that the experimental group had attained a fairly stable day-to-day behavior pattern after the program, while isolate controls showed very variable behavior both during baseline and postprogram assessments.

In summary, data collected through the behavioral performance channel indicated that children who were supplied with a companion manifested a

TABLE 8.2
Consistency of Social Interactions for Experimental, Isolate Control, and Normal Control Groups

	Baseline: Variance of ten rating session means	Postprogram Variance of ten rating session means
Experimental[a]	23.8	6.3
Isolate controls[b]	58.5	33.3
Normal control[b]	11.3	15.6
F ratio $\left(\frac{Var_{IC}}{Var_E}\right)$	2.5	5.3*

*$p < .01$; $df = 10, 10$.
[a]$N = 20$.
[b]$N = 10$.

significantly greater interaction rate with peers than did a matched sample of control children. Treated participants also shared more consistency in their observed interactions following intervention. More specifically defined categories of peer interaction, however, failed to reflect treatment effects, although anecdotal observations suggested that the experimental group tended to develop more stable friendships than those who received no systematic treatment.

Verbal Report and Global Assessment of the Intervention

Summary data from the teacher-rating, sociometric, and self-esteem measures for the experimental and isolate control groups are presented in Table 8.3.

The teacher ratings of the children's behavior showed that both groups received more negative scores after the intervention. Although the experimental group's scores changed the most in this direction, group differences in change over time were not significant. While such results would imply that all children demonstrated more problem behaviors as the year went on, a possible alternative explanation does exist. When the teachers made their preprogram ratings, they were considering behaviors that they had observed in the one month that they had known the children. At the beginning of the school year, teachers may have tended to give children the benefit of the doubt on some of the behaviors that had to be rated on a scale from "never occurs" to "always occurs." The postprogram instructions were to consider only the last several weeks of the child's behavior. It seems quite likely that to a large extent these instructions were either unclear or ignored, resulting in ratings that represented subjective summations of all negative behaviors over a long period of time. This alternative hypothesis is further documented by the teacher ratings of all children not

TABLE 8.3
Means and Standard Deviations of Verbal-Report and Global Behavioral Outcome Measures

		Experimental		Isolate control	
Measure		Pre	Post	Pre	Post
Teacher	Mean	89.9	105.2	106.4	111.7
behavior ratings[a]	S.D.	28.3	25.3	34.1	32.5
Sociometric	Mean	3.18	3.26	3.52	3.46
ratings by peers[b]	S.D.	.44	.42	.43	.46
Self-esteem	Mean	56.7	61.2	61.2	60.8
	S.D.	15.8	15.2	13.7	20.0

[a] High scores correspond to more frequent problem behaviors.
[b] High scores correspond to more negative ratings.

involved in a treatment program, which showed an increase in problem behaviors from a mean score of 84.0 to a mean of 90.3. In this way the scores of almost all children, both in this program and the behavior modification program, indicated a possibly spurious increase in problem behaviors. In addition, the teachers knew which children were in the experimental group, but were unaware of which children were in the isolate control group. This may have made the teachers more sensitive to any negative behaviors by experimental children throughout the year, resulting in slightly larger increases in negative ratings for these youngsters.

The sociometric ratings made by peers were essentially unchanged for either group after the program. Children were apparently put into categories that were fairly rigid over time. Hence even the expected result that all children would make a few more friends over the course of the school year was not supported by the data from this measure. It is possible that the choice of a sociometric measure in which children were given labels such as "very best friend" encouraged such categorization. Perhaps a better measure might have involved some behavioral statements such as "gets along with others"; the children could then have named the students to whom each statement applied.

Results from the self-esteem measure showed experimental children improving an average of 4.5 points, while isolate controls went down an average of .4. This difference in change over time was not statistically significant, however, due to high variability in scores on the measure.

Following McWilliams and Finkel (1973), scores from the companion ratings of improvement were derived by subtracting actual ratings for each adjective from the "no change" point. These difference scores for each item and *t* ratios for correlated means are shown in Table 8.4. Positive difference scores and *t* ratios indicate an increase in the behavior, and negative scores indicate a decrease. Companions perceived children as becoming significantly more warm, outgoing, cooperative, trusting, friendly, and attentive, while becoming less angry, withdrawn, sad, and moody. They also rated the children as significantly improved in terms of overall behavioral change. The one somewhat negative finding was that children were seen as more overactive.

In order to further investigate the relations between objectively assessed behavior change and the other outcome measures, a correlational analysis was undertaken. Change on each assessment device was correlated with total improvement in the rate of social interaction and a residual change score in the rate of interaction. This residual change statistic was used in order to control for initial within-group differences and effects due to statistical regression from pretreatment to posttreatment (Tucker, Damarin, & Messick, 1966). The Pearson Product Moment Correlations, shown in Table 8.5, were uniformly low and insignificant. Behavior change was thus not related to change on the nonbehavioral measures, a conclusion that could have been expected from the results already reported.

TABLE 8.4
Companion Ratings of Behavior Change

Behavior	N^a	Mean change[b]	S.D.	*t* value
Overall behavior	20	1.75	.55	14.22**
Angry	13	−1.30	.95	−4.95**
Calm	17	.59	1.66	1.47
Withdrawn	17	−2.12	.99	−8.75**
Warm	19	1.68	1.00	7.32**
Overactive	12	.58	.79	2.54*
Outgoing	20	1.80	.83	9.70**
Sad	12	−1.33	1.23	−3.74**
Cooperative	19	1.79	1.27	6.14**
Moody	18	−0.89	.83	−4.55**
Trusting	20	1.35	.88	6.86**
Restless	17	−0.18	1.29	−0.57
Friendly	19	1.95	.78	10.89**
Frightened	10	−1.20	1.03	−3.68**
Attentive	16	1.00	1.03	3.88**

*$p < .05$. **$p < .001$.
[a]*N* varies due to use of "never acts this way" category.
[b]Negative scores mean decreasing frequency of behavior.

TABLE 8.5
Correlations of Specific Behavioral Change
with Other Change Indices

	Gross improvement in rate of interactions	Residual change in rate of interactions
Improvement in teacher ratings	−.25	−.26
Improvement in sociometric ratings by peers	.03	−.24
Increase in self-esteem	.13	.31
Companion ratings of overall change	−.03	.28

Impact of the Intervention on Participating Groups

A most important innovation of the present companion program was the introduction of an objective behavioral assessment of program outcome. Support for the effectiveness of the intervention was obtained from the main behavioral criterion, the rate of social interactions during free play. This is the first empirically oriented companion program that has demonstrated such objective behavioral changes with postkindergarten-age social isolates in the schools. It shares the behavioral perspective with such studies as Fo and O'Donnell (1974) in a community program and the work of Patterson (1974) in the home and school environment.

The most consistent positive outcome in previous companion studies has come from ratings of change by the companions themselves (McWilliams & Finkel, 1973; Zax *et al.,* 1966). Such ratings were used in the present study to allow comparisons with previous research. Results were found to be significant and substantially higher than in previous studies, indicating more positive companion ratings than previously had been obtained. However, neither companion ratings of overall change nor companion ratings of specific adjective items correlated significantly with objectively assessed behavior change.

This lack of correspondence highlights the need for multiple channels of measurement as mentioned in Chapter 2. The differential findings may mean that more subtle improvements in the children's behavior were evident only in the specific relationships with the companion. It may also mean that the behavior-rating procedure was not sensitive to changes perceived by the companions. Finally, it is possible that companions overestimated the improvement in their student's behavior because of their personal investment in the child's performance. Nonconvergence on these measures indicates that only limited conclusions can be made on the basis of companion ratings alone, and more sophisticated measurement methodologies must be developed to assess the exact nature of the impact of a program such as this one.

The other measures used also did not demonstrate positive outcome from this program, and these were shown to be relatively independent of objective behavioral change. Almost all previous companion studies, however, have failed to obtain positive results from sociometric ratings (Goodman, 1972) or teacher ratings of specific behaviors (Goodman, 1972; Smith, 1969; Stern *et al.,* 1971). The only positive outcomes obtained from teacher ratings have involved measures that ask teachers to rate amount of change on a 1–7 scale or to rate the children on more general behavioral statements (for example, Cowen *et al.,* 1969; McWilliams & Finkel, 1973). Subjective statements by teachers to the authors, however, indicated satisfaction with the progress of the companion program, in contrast to their ratings of specific problem behaviors.

Several possible explanations exist for this dichotomy between specific behavioral and other outcome criteria. One possible interpretation is that the effects of the program have been limited to the playground situation and have not generalized. This conclusion could be supported by the lack of changes in self-esteem and teacher- and peer-rating measures. It is conceivable that these behavioral changes will never generalize to new situations and therefore are not particularly meaningful to the child's life.

Another possibility is that these behavioral changes have begun to generalize to new situations but have not been documented because of deficiencies in the teacher- and peer-rating measures. It has already been mentioned that problems existed in the teacher-rating measure, resulting in most children regardless of experimental group being rated as having more problems after the program. Furthermore, many teacher–child interactions are of a highly formal nature, and the children may not have had many opportunities to demonstrate some of their newly acquired skills.

The sociometric ratings by peers were very stable over the year for participants in all three intervention programs. One of the problems with this measure was that children were asked ro rate the peers in their homeroom. They spent little time during the day with these homeroom children, however, as their language arts and mathematics sections were with different groups of children. Thus the homeroom class may have included few children who came into contact with a participant at recess, where the behavior-change strategies were implemented. Furthermore, the contact of the homeroom children with a targeted child was minimal enough to make any initial, fairly rigid categorization of that student extremely difficult to change. Thus it is possible that behavioral changes had generalized, but were not documented by the relatively insensitive teacher and peer ratings.

Another explanation would be to contend that generalization had not yet, or had only recently, begun but would continue to take place after the program. A more optimistic position would be to claim that the behavioral changes found in this study indicate the beginning of a benign cycle. Before the present project took place, the isolate children had very poor social skills and therefore spent a great deal of time alone. This intervention concentrated on improving these social skills through modeling and social reinforcement. By the end of the program the experimental children were spending an increased amount of time interacting with other children. This behavioral result, the increased interactions, might be considered the beginning of the benign cycle. While a good deal of improvement in their social skills was made, these skills would, hopefully, continue to develop further over time as the child is constantly interacting with his or her peers. Such development could not take place if the child was still spending most of the time alone. Peer and teacher ratings, which are quite stable and are based on a great deal of past behavior, are probably quite insensitive to the types of changes produced by the intervention. Only the increasing development of social skills, with concomitant positive behaviors, over a long period of time can change such relatively categorical and perhaps stigmatizing peer and teacher ratings. In addition, the child's self-esteem should improve after an increased period of positive social experiences. Although the authors would prefer to accept this more optimistic alternative, our current data do not favor it over the other possibilities. A more definitive conclusion must be postponed until longer term evidence is available.

This project, being exploratory in nature, did not implement extensive procedures to assure the maintenance and further development of the improvements achieved. Teachers were not given any special training in this aspect of the study and, despite attempts to inform them of the progress of each relationship, they generally stayed aloof from this program. Attempts to maintain behavior changes were restricted to procedures internal to the intervention: increasingly intermittent reinforcement by the companions, less intense companion involvement, and less frequent visits.

For the limited scope of the present study, the results were quite encouraging. Particularly important was the demonstration that a program of this nature can be implemented effectively without a great strain on the resources of the school system. In accord with the suggestions for entering such a system, the project did deliver more than was initially promised. Interventions of the present size, or slightly smaller, are extremely practical and can be implemented by the school itself. A case in point is that this program has been continued up to the present.

One of the subsidiary questions this study sought to examine was whether nonprofessional college students could be trained to apply behaviorally oriented techniques. While the effectiveness of the companions' interventions was demonstrated by the behavioral data, anecdotal evidence indicated that behavioral strategies were applied efficaciously and innovatingly. Two examples of the use of contingency contracting will serve as illustrations. One little girl had made two friends, but the interactions of the three frequently included a good number of negative comments, both toward and from the target child. The companion, aware of the girls' affinity for playing jacks, set up a contract where a game of jacks at the end of recess was contingent upon an absence of negative verbal behaviors. Not only did this strategy produce rapid and dramatic changes, but when it was gradually discontinued, the absence of such negative behaviors continued in other situations.

The second example involved a little boy who was very afraid of physical activities and of other children, but who loved the library. His companion agreed to take the child, along with two peers of the child's choosing, to the school library on every other visit, where they explored books together. This was contingent, however, on the child's participation in some type of group game on the alternate visit. This contingency also showed positive results. Both of these innovative strategies were formulated by the companions independently and were discussed with the program consultant during the weekly workshops.

The effective application of behaviorally oriented strategies may indicate that it is not necessary to depend solely on the benefits of a "relationship" as a change mechanism. As mentioned in Chapter 4, Fo and O'Donnell (1974) found that a warm and positive relationship and noncontingent rewards were not sufficient to produce the desired behavior changes in their program. Further research is necessary to determine whether such effects are specifically due to the strategies employed or merely to general qualities of the companions and hence the relationships. In addition, no attempt was made to separate the effects of the modeling film from the direct contributions of the companions. The film was shown late in the program, not for any theoretical reason but because that was when production was completed. It appears to have functioned as an adjunct regarding maintenance of behavior change, consolidating many of the changes that the companions had already brought into being. However, research is necessary to evaluate separate effects of companions and a modeling film.

Changes in companion attitudes, shown in Table 8.6, supported several general impressions of the authors. Change was computed by subtracting differences on a semantic differential given before and after the project. Companions' attitudes toward behavior modification, already fairly high to begin with, improved significantly, probably because they found it to be effective. Companions' feelings about school principals became more positive, due to the considerable cooperation and sensitivity demonstrated by the principal in this particular setting. Their attitudes toward elementary school teachers became more negative, a result consistent with the sometimes adversary relationship that existed between the companions and several teachers. This relationship developed as a result of role conflicts, despite our attempts to follow the guidelines presented in Chapter 2. Companions resisted disciplinary roles, teachers thus felt threatened by the companions, and a lack of communication sometimes occurred. This was an unfortunate aspect of the study, one that occurred despite attempts to

TABLE 8.6
Attitude Changes Reported by Companions

Concept	Mean change	S.D.	*t* value
Elementary school	−6.18	16.1	−1.76*
Companion groups	1.86	13.1	0.65
Mental illness	−2.46	7.2	−1.57
School principal	6.32	14.9	1.95*
Withdrawn children	3.77	10.5	1.65
Behavior modification	5.95	13.2	2.02**
Myself	0.96	9.0	0.49
Elementary school teachers	−10.40	14.1	−3.37**

$^*p < .10$. $^{**}p < .05$.

encourage positive communication. In retrospect, more teacher preparation for this subprogram should have been made. Even though the bulk of the project was conducted outside of the classroom, the effects of the companion–student relationships may have been enhanced by more teacher–companion contact. Our major problem was in underestimating the disciplinary involvement of teachers during the childrens' playground and recess periods. Closer attendance to our own guidelines for intervention would have easily reduced or eliminated the difficulty. Future programs must continue to deal with these role problems in order to ensure complete cooperation from all concerned.

In summary, a behaviorally oriented companion program was efficiently implemented and was shown to be effective in demonstrating behavioral changes. These new positive social behaviors were, hopefully, only the beginning of a benign cycle that will continue to produce new improvements in social skills. This cycle should ideally result in changed peer and teacher perceptions of the child and, eventually, in adequate adjustment as the child reaches adolescence. With regard to these conclusions, two future research areas stand out as being crucial:

1. A long-term follow-up of the children involved in this or a similar study. Do the observed changes indeed result in better future adjustment beyond the intermediate criteria chosen in this study?
2. A comparison of the differential effects due to training the companions in behavioral techniques, as well as a comparison of the differential effects of a modeling film, companion program, and combination of the two.

It is our hope that programs similar to the present one will become widely implemented. For any person who saw the many sad faces on the experimental children in October and the happy faces in April, there can be no doubt as to the importance and utility of such projects.

9

Building Constructive Teacher–Child Relationships

The analysis of the third level of intervention involved examination of five separate issues. First, the initial compariability of the various experimental and control groups of pupils on the behavioral and self-report measures was assessed. Second, the reliability of all the assessment measures was examined to demonstrate their degree of stability. Third, the specific behavioral effects of the workshop intervention on teachers' classroom behavior is presented. Next, behavioral changes of all the experimental groups of pupils was examined. Finally, supplemental analyses were executed for the secondary issues involving predictor variables of teacher success as behavior change agents, nonbehavioral trait effects on pupils, and attitude changes of workshop teachers.

Comparability of Experimental Groups

To determine whether the various divisions of experimental and control pupils were initially equivalent on their behavioral, teacher-rating, and self-report scores during the baseline phase of the intervention, *t* tests and Mann–Whitney *U*-tests were computed. This preliminary analysis was necessary in order to insure that any subsequent differences between experimental groups could be attributed to program effects rather than to initial differences that were already present. The four examined comparisons of pupil groups were: (1) all pupils of workshop classes versus all pupils of control class, (2) designated pupils of workshop classes versus designated pupils of control classes, (3) target pupils versus matched control pupils, (4) target pupils versus in-class control pupils. The reader is referred to pages 106–108 for a discussion of how these groups were initially determined.

With regard to the behavioral ratings of the students on the four pupil categories of the Behavioral Observation Schedule for Pupils and Teachers

(BOSPT) (Breyer & Calchera, 1971), 12 *t* tests and 4 Mann–Whitney *U* tests were executed, with only one of these indicating a significant initial difference (workshop teachers' designated pupils having higher aggressive off-task scores than control teachers' designated pupils). Three significant differences out of 12 *t* tests were discovered on the teachers' ratings of pupil problem behaviors (Walker Problem Behavior Identification Checklist, 1970), which involved the total score and two subscales assessing acting-out and distractability. On the 11 pupil self-report test scores, 38 *t* tests were computed between pupil groups, with seven of these tests indicating significant initial differences. In all of the cases where significant initial differences were found between pupil groups on teachers' rating and self-report scores, the experimental children had more maladjusted scores than did the control children. Where initial differences were found, subsequent statistical analyses of program effects utilized analyses of covariance in order to control for the effects of initial differences. In summary, the experimental and control pupil groups were initially comparable on most measures, with congruence being particularly pronounced on the behavioral scores.

Besides examining the comparability between groups, it is also necessary to assure that there is comparability between individual classrooms within the workshop and control groups. If differences existed between classrooms, then later analyses of variance would have to utilize nested designs. Thirty-two chi square analyses were calculated, using the means for individual workshop and control classrooms separately on 16 behavioral and self-report student measures. The only finding was that control teachers manifested greater variability in their ratings of pupils on the total score of the problem behavior checklist.

To test for the initial comparability of the classroom behavior of the workshop teachers and control teachers, six Mann–Whitney *U*-tests were computed on the teacher categories of the BOSPT ratings. Significant differences between groups were found on the feedback category and on the summary category of reinforcement plus feedback. In addition, a tendency for differences was found on the reinforcement category. In all three of these cases, the means of the workshop teachers were lower than the means of the control teachers.

Reliability of the Measures

Interrater Reliability

As was observed in Chapter 2, to ensure that changes in dependent measures are due to the experimental intervention rather than to the basic instability of the measures, the realiability of the measures must be sufficiently high. The interrater reliabilities of the BOSPT ratings in each classroom were assessed twice, once during October and November, and again during March and April. The reliability was measured by having a pair of observers rate the behavior of teachers and their pupils over the same time period. Observers worked in pairs for this assessment. To calculate the reliability coefficient, the number of 10-second intervals in which there was agreement between the raters was divided by the total number of agreements plus disagreements. The interrater reliability for all the BOSPT teacher categories combined averaged 80.3% and ranged from 69% to 91% in the first assessment, while at the second assessment the mean reliability was 88.9%, with a range of 70%–100%. The mean reliability of the combined pupil categories at the first assessment was 92.8%, and at the second assessment was 94.6%. The ranges for these respective assessments were 86%–97% and 88%–98%. At the second assessment only, reliability for the specific pupil and teacher categories of the BOSPT were calculated with all the categories having interrater agreement of at least 75%. In general, the behavioral ratings appear to have adequate interrater reliability.

Test–Retest Reliability

For the teachers' behavioral ratings of pupils and the student verbal-report measures, reliability was assessed by correlating the pretreatment and posttreatment scores of the pupils in the workshop and control teachers' classes, who were not receiving treatment. Treated subjects and one control comparison group were not included because of their central importance in the investigation of the behavioral efficacy of the workshops, based on the hypothesis that the workshop intervention would produce significant behavioral change on the part of target pupils. The nine verbal-report measures had a median test–retest reliability coefficient of .36, with a range of .19–.45. The reliabilities for the Walker (1970) Problem Behavior Identification Checklist and its two subscales were higher, having a median of .67 and a range of .62–.71. However, the reliability coefficients in general indicate that the student self-report measures were not very stable.

Effects of Workshop Training on Teacher Behavior

The results of the observation of the classroom behavior of teachers who attended the behavior modification workshops, as measured by the BOSPT, can be broken down into three areas. First, tendencies for improvement on the combined positive verbal categories of reinforcement plus feedback were noted for the workshop teachers when they were compared to the control teachers at the workshop period by an analysis of covariance, $F(1, 10) = 2.54, p < .15$. No significant changes were found for these two combined categories at the follow-up period, or for either category examined individually. Referral to the means of these categories given in Table 9.1 indicates that the control teachers increased slightly on the reinforcement and feedback category from baseline to the workshop period, while the workshop teachers tripled their baseline level. By

TABLE 9.1
Means of BOSPT Rating Categories on Teachers during Baseline, Workshop, and Follow-Up Periods

	Workshop teachers			Control teachers		
Category (%)	Baseline	Workshop	Follow-up	Baseline	Workshop	Follow-up
Reinforcement	.1	1.1	1.0	.5	1.1	.7
Feedback	1.4	3.3	5.3	4.8	5.4	5.8
Prohibition	1.1	1.3	2.3	2.1	4.8	4.2
Correction	3.7	2.3	1.9	3.1	1.8	2.6
Attention	28.9	24.4	18.1	20.0	20.3	21.5
Reinforcement and feedback	1.5	4.4	6.3	5.3	6.5	6.5

follow-up, the initial differences in the verbal reinforcement levels of the two groups of teachers were nonexistent.

The most obvious conclusion is that while workshop teachers initially emitted few of these behaviors, the workshops helped them to increase their social reinforcement frequencies to bring them up to the level of the control teachers. This view implies that those teachers who volunteered for these workshops were actually most in need of the help, and the workshops served to correct their deficiencies. Of course, a statistical regression may have occurred here and perhaps acted to negate the conclusions that effective teacher change was due to workshop participation. However, since the control group did not regress to a point midway between the initial level of the two groups, but remained rather stable over time, this alternative hypothesis is weakened.

There are several explanations why only a tendency toward statistical significance was found for these data and may include (1) the small sample sizes of the teachers who were involved in the analysis and (2) the fact that half of the workshop teachers relied most heavily on activity or free-time reinforcements in their actual modification projects. The most important reason, though, is (3) that the workshops would not necessarily be expected to increase significantly the absolute frequency of social reinforcements but, rather, could just increase the contingent timing of the teachers' social reinforcements to appropriate pupil behaviors. Ward and Baker (1968) reported this for the teachers they trained in behavior modification techniques. Since this ability of teachers to reinforce positively only the appropriate behaviors of their pupils was not assessed in the present study, future research of behavior modification consultation should examine the contingency as well as the frequency of teacher verbal reinforcements.

The second area of teacher classroom behavior involved two categories of verbal punishment–prohibition and correction. No significant changes were found for these categories. In the workshops, positive reinforcement of appropriate pupil behaviors was encouraged more often than was punishment of inappropriate behaviors alone. This attempt to achieve a positive approach to behavior modification may account for the lack of an increase in teachers' punishing verbalizations.

In the third relevant area of classroom behavior, workshop teachers showed a marked decline in their nonverbal attention behaviors, $F(2, 22) = 3.69, p < .05$, bringing them at follow-up assessment to a level more similar to the control teachers. To the extent that a teacher's attention is a positive reinforcement to his or her pupils, the use of attention would be expected to increase as a result of the workshops. The basis for the decrease in teacher attention in this study appears to be due (1) to the increase in verbal reinforcement behaviors, and (2) to the broadness of the "attention" category on the BOSPT. Teachers apparently have a limited amount of time available for nonacademic, child management behaviors, and when there is an increase in one behavior in this class (that is, verbal reinforcement), others (that is, nonverbal attention) are likely to decrease. In regard to the second point, the attention category was a broad one that comprised 20% of the teachers' total behavior. By the nature of the BOSPT category definition of attention, it included some negative and neutral kinds of attending behavior as well as positive instances and was therefore an inadequate measure of nonverbal social reinforcement.

The ability of teachers to estimate and be aware of the behavior of their students was also evaluated. The ten occasions on which both observer ratings and teacher estimates were made of the percentage of appropriate behavior of each teacher's three "rated pupils" were collapsed into the three periods of (1) early workshops, consisting of the first four workshop sessions, which focused on observation techniques, (2) later workshops, consisting of the period including the last six sessions, and (3) follow-up. Absolute value difference scores between teachers' estimates and the observers' ratings were made for each period. These scores indicate discrepancies between teachers' and observers' estimates of pupil behavior, with low scores indicating a high degree of correspondence. The observers' ratings are assumed to be more accurate because of the systematic observational method they used. The means of the difference scores can be found in Table 9.2. Analysis of these data indicate a tendency for significant differences between the workshop and control teachers over the year, $F(2, 74) = 2.10, p < .14$.

Workshop teachers increased their accuracy by the middle of the school year, becoming significantly more accurate than the control teachers, $t(37) = -3.01$, $p < .01$. This indicates that the ongoing workshops had been effective in improving their observational ability, which was felt to be an important prerequisite for successful use of behavior change skills. However, by the follow-up period, the workshop teachers were no longer significantly better than control teachers, $t(37) = -1.14$. The major part of the decreased accuracy of workshop teachers at this point was due to a fourfold increase in their overestimation of the on-task behavior of the target pupils. Several possible explanations exist for this increased overestimation. The overestimation may be representative of a

TABLE 9.2
Means of Absolute Value Difference Scores between Teachers' Estimates and Observers' Ratings of Pupil On-Task Behavior

Time	Workshop teachers	Control teachers
Early workshops	12.9	18.1
Later workshops	4.6	14.9
Follow-up	12.8	16.7

"thank you" effect to the consultant, in which the workshop teachers could have intentionally increased their reports of the favorability of their pupils' behavior. A related explanation would suggest that the teachers increased their overestimations unintentionally, as a result of their increased expectancies that the target pupils would perform better because of the teachers' efforts. In actuality, both reasons probably contributed to the increased overestimation.

In summary, over the course of the school year the consultee teachers tended to increase their verbal reinforcements and decrease their nonverbal attention behavior to their pupils. In addition, the consultees significantly increased their accuracy of estimating their pupils' level of appropriate behavior during the year while they attended the workshops, but their accuracy had eroded by the follow-up period.

Effects of Workshop Training on Pupil Behavior

Direct Tertiary Prevention Effects

The most direct test of the efficacy of the behavior modification workshops is the degree to which the specifically treated target pupils changed their behavior in a desirable direction over the course of the three time periods encompassing baseline, treatment, and follow-up, which were investigated. Using the BOSPT, successful tertiary prevention was shown by the significant 10.5% increase in the on-task appropriate behavior of the target pupils at the treatment period, while the matched control pupils remained at baseline levels, $F(1, 25) = 5.21, p < .04$, as seen in Table 9.3. Descriptively, the target pupils maintained their improved behavior reasonably well over a follow-up phase in which no workshop-organized modification projects were executed, demonstrating only a 1.3% decrease from their previously significant high level. In fact, while the target pupils were almost 13% worse than the nondesignated (nondisruptive) pupils on the on-task category at baseline, by follow-up the target pupils and nondesignated pupils had nearly identical on-task behavioral levels, with the target pupils then performing as well as the rest of their classmates (see Fig. 9.1).

However, at the follow-up period there was only a low tendency toward statistical significance for the difference between improvement of target pupils and of matched control pupils, $F(2, 50) = 1.78, p < .18$. Two factors that contributed to the failure to find a statistical significance at follow-up were: (1) a 2% increase in appropriate behavior of the matched control pupils, and (2) increased variability in the behavior of matched control pupils. It must also be noted that the BOSPT was a general rating scale and was not specific to the particular target behaviors changed. Therefore, the BOSPT results may well have underestimated the real effects of the target children's specific changes of behavior.

With regard to the general types of off-task behavior that were changed, the target pupils significantly decreased their passive off-task behavior, $F(1, 25) =$

TABLE 9.3
Mean Percentage of BOSPT On-Task Ratings of Pupils during Baseline, Workshop, and Follow-Up Periods

Experimental group	Baseline	Treatment	Follow-up
Workshop teachers' classes	81.7	— [a]	80.3
versus			
Control teachers' classes	82.1	—	80.8
Workshop designated pupils	74.4	82.7	81.1
versus			
Control designated pupils	78.0	75.9	77.8
Target pupils	71.0	81.5	80.2
versus			
Matched control pupils	69.2	69.5	72.0
versus			
In-class control pupils	74.2	83.6	80.3
Nondesignated pupils	83.9	—	80.3

[a] Observations on entire classes were not collected at this time.

4.50, $p < .05$. and tended to decrease their aggressive off-task behavior, as Table 9.4 indicates, $F(1, 24) = 3.20$, $p < .09$. Passive off-task behaviors were more affected by the teachers' direct modification efforts than were disruptive off-task behaviors, primarily because most of the modification projects were directed at the increase of such positive behaviors as the completion rate of daily class lessons. Therefore, the reinforcement contingencies were generally connected with the attentive, on-task behavior of pupils, rather than with specific disruptive acts. Winett and Winkler (1972) have criticized behavior analysts for usually defining the inappropriate behaviors that they decrease in children only as behaviors that interfere with order, quiet, and stillness in the classroom. Behavior change agents were thus seen as creating passive automatons out of children. However, the results of this present study demonstrate that workshop teachers, acting as behavior analysts, increased those behaviors of their pupils that often involved active verbal cooperation with fellow classmates, and de-

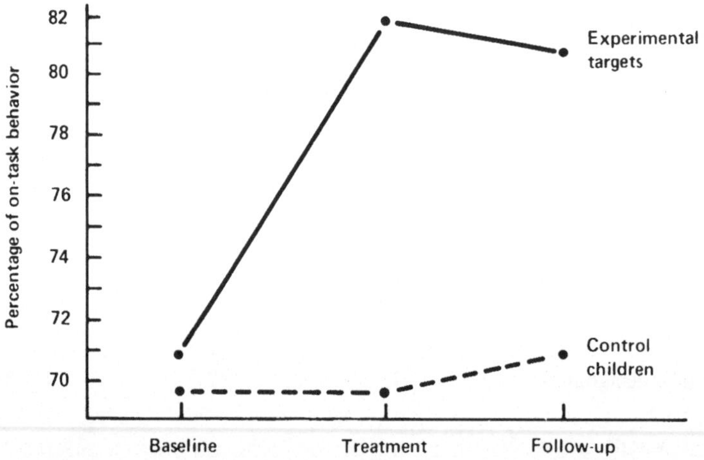

FIG. 9.1 Percentages of observed on-task behaviors emitted by target children and matched control participants.

creased those behaviors that involved students being passive, orderly, and quiet, yet also inattentive.

No significant differences were found between the behaviors of target pupils and in-class control pupils at any of the time periods investigated. Since the in-class control pupils were also members of the workshop teachers' group of "designated pupils," a discussion of the improvement of the behavior of in-class control pupils is subsumed in a following discussion of the radiating effects on designated pupils.

Workshop Teachers' Reports of Their Modification Attempts

It is important to note that the workshop teachers were not attempting to modify the broad classes of behavior assessed by the BOSPT, but rather they

TABLE 9.4
Mean Percentage of BOSPT Off-Task Ratings of Target and Matched Control Pupils during Baseline, Workshop, and Follow-Up Periods

Time	Target pupils			Matched control pupils		
	Passive off-task	Disruptive off-task	Aggressive off-task	Passive off-task	Disruptive off-task	Aggressive off-task
Baseline	17.3	11.3	0.4	16.8	14.1	0.0
Treatment	10.9	7.5	0.1	17.7	12.6	0.4
Follow-up	11.8	7.8	0.4	15.9	12.0	0.1

were changing specific kinds of behaviors such as the number of inappropriate verbalizations or the number of daily assignments completed. In their required modification reports, the workshop teachers reported marked changes in most of their target pupils for the specific behaviors modified. A portion of one of the teachers' reports is included below as an illustration.

Behavior Change Report

Target child and setting. Joanne[1] is a ten-year-old fourth grader. Throughout her school career she has been characterized by her teachers and other school personnel as being a "withdrawn" child. Social interaction with her peers had been difficult for Joanne, and although she has seemed to enjoy the attention of her teachers when given on a one-to-one basis, she has not participated well in whole class or small-group activities in the classroom. It is important to note that Joanne has begun to make friends during the current academic year. However, at the time behavior modification work was implemented with Joanne, she was still not participating in any class discussion. Academically Joanne functions somewhat below grade level. She is a conscientious worker, and she frequently enjoys success, especially in math.

The math class in which Joanne's behavior modification program was implemented is usually conducted in a conventional manner, with a formal lesson and class discussion occurring before an assignment of independent work is made. On one day of the week, the children work on completing assignments and are tested on number facts. On this day there is no large-group activity conducted in the classroom.

It was observed that although written assignments were usually completed by Joanne with a minimum number of errors, she never contributed to class discussion on a voluntary basis. Systematically taken baseline data showed that no voluntary contributions were made by Joanne during class discussions. The goal of behavior modification work with Joanne, therefore, became to have her make one oral contribution during each class discussion.

How behavior was measured. Baseline data on the frequency of contributions Joanne was making during discussions was made by simply counting the number of contributions made.

Behavior change technique and results. To initiate Joanne's behavior modification program, Joanne met with me during a recess period. We discussed Joanne's hesitancy to participate in class discussions. Joanne agreed that she found it difficult to speak up in the classroom and also indicated that she would like to be able to do so with ease. Joanne agreed that she would be willing to try making one contribution during each class period in the classroom with some friends of her choice. Our agreement became effective as of the next math class. Joanne's success in living up to her part of the bargain has been overwhelming. She has made at least one oral contribution during each class in which the opportunity to do so has presented itself (an average of 4.1 contributions per class). Other teachers report that her willingness to contribute has carried over in the other classes.

To provide a flavor of other specific modification projects initiated by the teachers, three case summaries will be presented here.

[1] Children's names have been changed to protect confidentiality.

One target child was a 9-year-old boy who was reported as being argumentative and defensive and as having very poor work habits. His teacher established a contract with him in which he was checked five times every math class to see if he was attending to his work. If he was behaving appropriately, he would receive a check mark on an index card taped to his desk. If he received 20 points per week, then he was allowed to have some free time to visit the school's resource room. During the 10-day baseline period, this target child spent an average of 35% of his time behaving attentively, but during the first three weeks of the treatment period, his average had almost doubled to 66%.

Another 9-year-old male target child was generally recognized by school personnel as being one of the most disruptive children in the school. He had been openly hostile with teachers and other pupils, although many times his negative behaviors appeared to be attempts to gain teacher attention. Previous attempts to get psychological help for the boy were rebuffed by his apparently uncooperative parents. The boy had a history of poor academic achievement despite an excellent verbal vocabulary. The teacher decided to give contingent verbal praise to the successful completion of daily assignments, while shaping his behavior to accomplish increasingly complex assignments. While the target child did not finish his assignment on any of the 5 baseline days, he was able to complete his assigment on 64% of the treatment days. His teachers reported that his hostility toward them had decreased, and he expressed overt enjoyment for their praise.

While social reinforcement proved to be a significant motivator for this boy, another teacher found that her initial attempts to use praise alone to increase the positive attending behavior of her 10-year-old target child was not sufficient. This girl was well adjusted socially and did not present a discipline problem, but she lacked interest in all the academic aspects of school. Her teacher finally devised a contract in which she observed the girl five times daily, and if the target child was behaving appropriately at those times, she was allowed to fill in squares on a card at her desk. When she had completed ten squares, she was allowed to come in during recess to do an art project. During 10 baseline days, the target child behaved appropriately 48% of the time that she was observed, but during her first 11 measured days of treatment, her appropriate behavior had increased to a 91% level.

Radiating Effects of Consultation

The significant increase of the on-task behavior of the designated (disruptive) pupils in workshop teachers' classes, as compared to the designated pupils of control teachers' classes, $F(2, 152) = 6.68$, $p < .003$, substantiated the hypothesis that changes in workshop teachers' behaviors would have positive radiating effects even on those problematic pupils who were not specifically treated (see Fig. 9.2). These radiating effects proved to be durable ones that were maintained strongly even over the follow-up period, as can be seen in Table 9.3 by the 7% increase in on-task scores. These results demonstrate that the workshops were

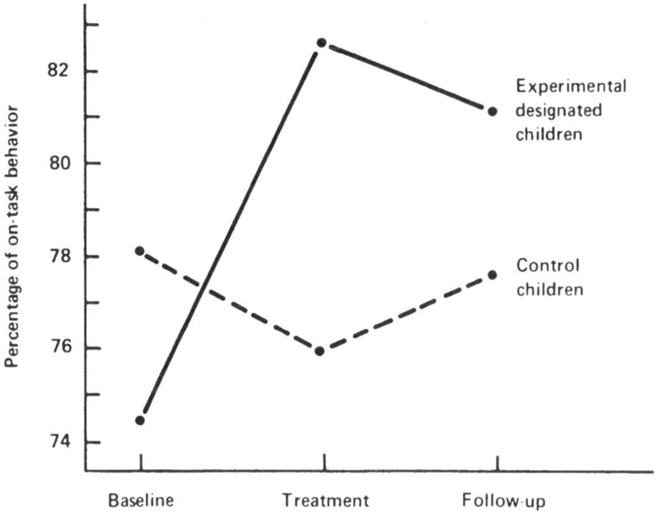

FIG. 9.2 Percentages of on-task behaviors emitted by designated problem children and matched control participants.

indeed a form of consultee-centered consultation, since the specifically treated pupils were not the only members of workshop classes who improved their on-task behavior levels. Even when the target and matched control pupils were statistically removed from the total sample of designated pupils, the nontargeted disruptive pupils in workshop classes still evidenced significantly greater improvement over the year than did similar pupils in control classes, $F(2, 98) = 5.08$, $p < .01$. The workshop teachers apparently used increased verbal social reinforcements and knowledge of such techniques as the Premack principle to modify the disruptive off-task behavior of the designated pupils. The improvement of the nontreated disruptive pupils may have also been partially due to their modeling of the more appropriate behavior of the target students.

The improvement of on-task attentive behavior for nontargeted designated pupils in workshop classes was accompanied by a significant 5% decline in disruptive off-task behavior for these pupils in relation to the control students, as indicated by Table 9.5, $F(2, 98) = 6.77$, $p < .003$. Although the target pupils had shown most of their improvement by decreasing their passive off-task behaviors, the behavioral improvement of the other designated pupils in the experimental classes principally involved a reduction in inappropriate behaviors that caused a distraction to other pupils. There were no significant changes in the other two off-task categories.

Except for a moderate decrease in the aggressive off-task behavior of workshop teachers' classes over time, $F(1, 11) = 2.29$, $p < .16$, no differences in behavior levels were found between classes of workshop teachers and those of control teachers. These results indicate that while the behavior of minimally to moderately problematic pupils can be affected by the radiating effects of teacher

TABLE 9.5
Mean Percentage of BOSPT Off-Task Ratings of Workshop Designated and Control Designated Pupils during Baseline, Workshop, and Follow-Up Periods

Time	Workshop designated pupils			Control designated pupils		
	Passive off-task	Disruptive off-task	Aggressive off-task	Passive off-task	Disruptive off-task	Aggressive off-task
Baseline	13.9	11.3	0.4	12.4	9.9	0.0
Treatment	10.7	6.3	0.2	12.3	11.7	0.2
Follow-up	12.2	6.4	0.3	11.5	10.5	0.1

behavior change, the behavior of nonproblematic students was affected very little.

Teacher Ratings of Pupils

There were no significant differences in improvement scores between experimental groups on either the Walker Problem Behavior Identification Checklist (WPBIC) total score or the two analyzed WPBIC subscales of acting-out and distractibility. In general, all teachers rated their pupils worse at posttreatment than at pretreatment on the WPBIC, even though there was little actual change in the behavior of the classes, and some individuals, such as most of the target pupils, markedly improved over the year. Despite the fact that the WPBIC was intended to provide a rating of relatively specific behaviors over a set time period, even the workshop teachers were not sensitive to positive pupils behavioral change. In a correlational analysis, the total score and two subscales of the WPBIC related in a low and unsystematic manner with BOSPT pupil behavior categories. Teacher ratings of students improvement (or more correctly, lack of improvement) on this measure paralleled those impressions obtained from teachers who rated socially withdrawn children, as reported in Chapter 8. The explanations of this phenomenon provided in the previous chapter seem equally applicable here.

Predictor Variables of Teacher Success

An effectiveness score was constructed for each workshop teacher by computing the average change in BOSPT-measured on-task behavior for her target pupils from baseline to follow-up. The mean effectiveness scores for the workshop teachers are included in Table 9.6, along with the values for the potential predictor variables. Analyses of the relationships between the nine predictor variables and teacher effectiveness by means of Kendall's tau statistic (Siegel,

TABLE 9.6

Means of Effectiveness Scores and Predictor Variable Values for Workshop Teachers

Teacher	Effectiveness scores (%)	Organizational ability	Social reinforcement value (pretest)	Expectancies for success	On-task behavior in workshops (%)	Yawns in workshops	Questions asked in workshops	Questions answered in workshops	Statements made in workshops	Average global rating of workshop behavior
1	−7.0	5	15.3	2	87.9	5	20	15	16	3.7
2	−1.8	3	16.4	1	96.9	2	9	18	14	3.8
3	6.5	4	17.0	2	96.9	24	11	14	19	3.7
4	7.5	2	19.8	1	86.1	2	3	8	2	2.4
5	20.8	2	16.8	1	97.4	0	7	5	7	3.0
6	35.4	1	17.0	2	98.0	0	0	6	5	2.6

1956) indicated the existence of six at least marginally reliable correlations, four of which were in the expected direction. Principal ratings of teacher organizational ability were positively ($T = .80, p < .04$) related, and the frequency of yawns during workshop lectures ($T = -.67, p < .10$) was negatively related to improvement in classroom decorum. In the same manner, a teacher's social reinforcement value ($T = .53, p < .15$) and her level of on-task behavior in the workshops ($T = .53, p < .15$) were highly correlated on a descriptive level with effectiveness, but these two correlations were not statistically significant, partially because of the small size of the workshop teacher sample.

The number of questions that teachers asked ($T = -.87, p < .02$) and answered ($T = -.73, p < .06$) in the workshops were also significantly correlated with teacher effectiveness, but in the opposite direction to what was originally expected. These results might be understood, however, by considering that all the workshop participants were at least moderately motivated, as shown by their volunteer status and by their expressed expectancies for success with the behavior modification techniques. With a motivated group like this, quietness on the part of the participants appeared to reflect silent attentiveness rather than unconcerned distraction or daydreaming. Those teachers who asked the most questions may have done so because they had the most trouble in perceiving the practical applications of the reinforcement approach. A possible implication of this finding is that more time should be spent in behavior change workshops with those people who ask the most questions. Further research might indicate that these individuals may not prove to be good prospects for a large-scale workshop approach since they do not get as much individual attention as they might need, despite their best efforts to do so.

Keeping in mind the small sample used in this investigation and the possibility that these results might have limitations on their general applicability, it appears that the more effective teachers have greater organizational ability, ask and answer fewer questions in a workshop-format consultation, and emit fewer signs of boredom, such as yawns, in a workshop. In addition, several other variables, such as the teachers' social reinforcement value and their level of on-task behavior in the workshop, warrant further investigation.

Nonbehavioral Trait Assessment of Pupils

Many of the global self-report measures, subscales, and items completed by the pupils, the WPBIC ratings completed by the teachers, and the BOSPT ratings made by undergraduate observers, all proved to differentiate at pretest those pupils who were designated by their teachers as most problematic from those pupils who were not so-designated. Specific items and subscales were chosen for investigation because of their apparent relevance to the behavioral changes examined. The average scores are presented in Table 9.7. The designated pupils demonstrated 8% less on-task behavior than nondesignated students, thus indi-

TABLE 9.7
Means of Designated Pupils and Nondesignated Pupils
for Self-Report Tests and WPBIC Ratings at Pretreatment

Measure	Designated pupils N=36	Nondesignated pupils N=42
Locus of control	17.4	16.6
Level of aspiration	13.3	9.0
Self-esteem total	59.1	63.0
Self-esteem, school-academic subscale	4.4	4.9
Sociometric	31.4	29.1
Teacher attitudes total	17.2	17.9
Teacher attitude No. 3	2.0	2.2
Teacher attitude No. 6	1.9	1.9
Teacher attitude No. 8	2.2	2.4
School attitude No. 1	3.0	4.2
School attitude No. 3	5.2	5.7
WPBIC total	186.4	145.2
WPBIC acting-out	53.9	38.6
WPBIC distractability	38.4	27.2

cating the validity of teacher nomination of problem pupils. The designated pupils were rated significantly worse than nondesignated pupils on the WPBIC total score ($t(311) = 8.04$, $p < .001$); acting-out subscale ($t(311) = 7.65$, $p < .001$); and distractibility subscale ($t(311) = 9.96$, $p < .001$). These latter findings were expected, since the same teachers who designated the pupils as problematic, also completed the WPBIC forms on the pupils. In relation to nondesignated pupils on the self-report measures, the designated pupils were found to have significantly (1) less school-related self-esteem ($t(296) = -1.97$, $p < .05$); (2) fewer friends ($t(320) = 3.11$, $p < .003$); (3) stronger feelings of being disliked by their teacher (Item 8, Teacher Attitude Scale, $t(278) = -1.98$, $p < .05$); (4) more dislike of school (Item 1, School Attitude Scale, $t(280) = -3.90$, $p < .001$); and (5) a reduced belief that they do well in school (Item 3, School Attitude Scale, $t(280) = -2.26$, $p < .03$). In addition, the designated pupils tended to have a more external locus of control ($t(307) = 1.44$, $p < .15$); lower overall self-esteem scores ($t(295) = -1.81$, $p < .08$); and also they tended to report less enjoyment in talking to their teachers (Item 3, Teacher Attitude Scale, $t(281) = -1.60$, $p < .12$). These results give a clear idea of the multitude of trait and attitude deficiencies that are related to significant levels of disruptive and inappropriate classroom behavior.

Although they served as good discriminators of designated pupils at pretest, the self-report measures (with the exception of the attitude questions) were generally unaffected at posttest by the pupils' behavior changes that had begun to occur two months earlier. These findings parallel the results of Ward and Baker (1968), and Buys (1972), as well as those reported in Chapter 8. Although there were some indications of mean improvements for workshop-designated pupils on some measures, the increases were not reliably different from the increases of control groups. On the sociometric measure, there was a tendency for the control classes' members to like each other more by posttest than did the workshop classes' pupils, $F(1, 60) = 3.70$, $p < .10$. Evidently, changes in personality traits are not immediate and can occur only after some time has lapsed since the initiation of positive behavior changes. This period of time may allow the individual to determine if his confidence and ability to maintain his new behavior is permanent.

With regard to changes in the five specifically examined attitude statements as related to various experimental breakdowns of the classes, the children of workshop teachers' classes came to feel that they were doing better in school (Item 3, School Attitude Scale, $F(1, 60) = 4.51$, $p < .05$), and the workshop-designated pupils came to like their present teacher more (Item 6, Teacher Attitude Scale, $F(1, 72) = 5.23$, $p < .03$). Evidently these simple attitude statements were more sensitive to change over this time period than were more formally measured personality constructs. The resultant attitude changes suggest that a "good behavior spiral" had started, with both teachers and pupils becoming increasingly reinforcing to each other in their behaviors and attitudes.

Teacher Evaluations of Workshop Efficacy

Workshop teachers were asked to give a subjective estimate of the amount and direction of the behavioral change they produced in each of their target pupils. Of the target pupils, 33.3% were viewed as having improved a significant amount, 41.7% a moderate amount, and 25.0% to a slight extent. These self-reported estimates are remarkably similar to the ratings made by teachers who attended the behavior modification workshop reported by Andrews (1970). The same estimates made by Andrews' teachers were, respectively, 36.5%, 37.3%, and 18.3%. These convergent results across two studies suggest that workshop teachers believed that roughly one-third of the pupils they modified improved significantly, one-third improved moderately, and one-third improved slightly or not at all.

The workshop teachers all emitted very high initial ratings of their expectancies to change their students' behavior and of their attitudes about their job satisfaction and teaching role. As a result, there were no improvements after the workshops on these expectancies and attitudes, as assessed in the questionnaires administered in the workshops.

Suggestions for Implementation and Evaluation of Future Workshops

To summarize the results of this level of intervention, consultee-centered behavior modification consultation in a workshop format demonstrated at least moderate efficacy in training teachers to influence behavioral changes in pupils. There were individual differences in how much the teachers benefited from the workshops, and future research should investigate in a more systematic fashion the presently reported suggestive findings concerning the predictive variables of teachers' success as behavior analysts. As a related issue, future research should investigate the relative merits of workshop consultation versus individual consultation, particularly for different types of teachers.

Because of the strong evidence for the radiating effects of teacher intervention on their pupils, the generalized preventive effects of teacher behavior on nontargeted pupils should be increasingly emphasized in teacher consultation projects. Moreover, further research should examine and verify the role of teachers' contingent social reinforcement in the production of behavior change in mildly problematic and normal children who are not being specifically treated by the teachers. The suggestion is, of course, based on the assumption that even the subtle, unplanned effects of social reinforcement procedures are quite powerful.

Since this evaluation was of a project that was primarily meant to provide a mental health service to an elementary school, it is appropriate to end this discussion with several service-oriented concerns. Some practical suggestions for maximizing the benefits of behavior modification workshops were gained from the teachers' postworkshop questionnaires and from the experience gained from interacting with the elementary school teachers. Following are four suggestions for increasing the practicality of interventions of this type:

1. Be more practically oriented to teachers' specific pupils, even in early workshops when general principles are discussed.
2. Have the workshop sessions before school or, if possible, during school, rather than after school when teachers are fatigued and less enthusiastic.
3. Attempt to compress the early workshops and to complete them all in as short a time as possible, so as to avoid being interrupted by long school vacations or by the school's natural high-stress periods for teachers, such as grade report times.
4. Minimize the disruption and suspiciousness caused by the classroom and workshop observations of behavior necessary for evaluation puposes, by clearly outlining the purpose and importance of the observations and by gaining general permission from the participants to initiate the observations.

In summary, in order to produce maximum teacher behavior change, it is extremely important to be consistent in applying reinforcement principles even to the consultation relationship with the consultee, making the workshop intervention as reinforcing as possible to the participating teachers.

Part IV

LARGER SOCIAL AND ETHICAL ISSUES

10

Community Interventions Today and Tomorrow: The Challenge and the Promise

This final chapter has a fourfold purpose. The first is to consider the impact of the program on the structural organization of the school system. There were several major effects of the intervention that transcended statistical summaries of group changes, and these are highlighted in the initial section. We next consider two of the more important unresolved concerns of the present effort that require further study: namely, the lack of long-term follow-up and the nonconverging nature of our dependent measures. The third section deals with what we perceive to be the future of prevention efforts. This includes speculation on the role of preventive endeavors within the larger societal framework, as well as more specific suggestions for preventive programs in the school. Finally, we address vitally important general ethical issues surrounding intervention efforts and research in community settings.

The Impact of the Program on the School System

In a sense, all of the changes in the functioning of the target children had impact on the functioning of the school system. This section summarizes some changes in the organizational structure of the school and discusses role changes of key staff members that resulted from the intervention. Both of these forms of change have more potential permanence than the previously described results, as changes in staff emphasis may continue through the years. These changes may ultimately have more impact on the psychosocial well-being of the children. One or two classes trained in social problem solving, for example, will have relatively little impact compared with successive classes of children trained each year using a constantly improving problem-solving curriculum. These self-perpetuating alterations in the operation of the school system may, in turn, stimulate subsequent innovations over time.

Most of these "system changes" and their effects could be operationalized and quantified (for example, amount of time spent developing problem-solving curricula, number of "problem" children retained in classes, and so on). Others are more subtle, reflecting attitudinal shifts and changing orientations resulting from a recognition of the increased effectiveness of the staff in enhancing the positive development of their children. All are considered extremely important results of this and any future intervention.

The most important program outcome from the overall perspective of the school system was the adoption of the program and its continuation in the ongoing functioning of the school through subsequent years. This assimilation process is very important because it signifies several system changes. On the most general level, it indicates that school personnel will devote a certain portion of their time and efforts to systematic programs designed to enhance the psychosocial well-being of the students.

A preventively oriented program has been given legitimate status in the school. Key members of the system, including teachers, guidance personnel, and the principal, now consider the implementation of such preventive endeavors as one of the formal tasks of the organization. Class time has been set aside for social problem-solving training, unit meetings have been spent determining which children might best be helped by companions, and teachers have begun to implement projects of their own design to help disruptive and academically deficient children.

This adoption was facilitated by four factors. The first was our attempt to build the intervention so that it would be compatible with the existing operation of the school. As we described in Chapter 1, this is a critically important aspect of successful societal intervention. The second factor was the mode of developing liaisons between the experimental team and the school, as outlined in Chapter 2. The third was the success of the program, both as perceived experientially and as documented by our empirical findings. The fourth was ensuring that resources necessary for continuation of the program were developed in the school. We left behind a substantial pool of teachers who could serve as trainers for behavior analysis projects or implement the problem-solving curriculum. In addition, the school guidance counselor was able to supervise a companion program successfully. This wholehearted adoption of the program was one of its primary positive outcomes.

System changes in each of the specific interventions can also be delineated. For the social problem-solving project, a minimum of 30 minutes was put aside each week for further training, and additional divergent thinking exercises were introduced into many other classroom tasks. The teacher's role in the preventive process was thus legitimized and institutionally endorsed.

Problem solving had to be practiced in order to be taught; many of the teachers themselves probably became better problem solvers, although this very important benefit was not measured. Such skills could ultimately provide a secondary payoff in the increased efficiency of the organizational effectiveness of the teachers as a group. More direct problem-solving training for teachers (Schmuck *et al.*, 1972) would, of course, be a useful accompaniment to our intervention.

The companion project probably had the least generalization to the system since it relied primarily on outside nonprofessionals and was conducted during playground and recess periods and not in the classroom. However, as mentioned above, the school guidance counselor, a key member of the school's mental health team, played a major part in maintaining this project after our initial resources were expended. The program is now continuing under her supervision and includes greater participation from and coordination with the classroom teachers. Another important system effect is that college students, recruited each year from the university, are considered an important asset to the school's prevention team. They are described as working for the school. Their presence is encouraged, and their work on the playground is viewed as an important school function.

The behavior change project taught new conceptions about the etiology and maintenance of troublesome behavioral excesses and deficits to almost one-third of the teachers, and provided them with useful strategies for implementing change. Disruptive or academically deficient children no longer needed to be immediately sent out of the class for "treatment," or blamed for being "sick," "deviant," or "abnormal" as their difficulties multiplied. The teachers have come to view themselves as effective change agents and the first line of aid to the child in difficulty.

These major and minor changes accumulated to have a powerful effect on the climate and attitudes within a school system. The project at its best provides some promise that certain problems in children can be prevented or reduced before they become more serious. Moreover, the school itself can provide specific and effective services toward this goal. This positive climate of effectiveness, if maintained, can allow further program developments in prevention, thus beginning a constructive cycle of system change.

In addition to the service components, the research aspects of the intervention also had effects on the members and structure of the school system. In one sense, the very fact that school personnel not only tolerated but actually supported the large-scale nature of the research in the project is testimony to their serious commitment to developing health-promoting programs for the children. The research in its various phases meant hours of extra work for many teachers and other staff members. Teachers had to repeatedly open their classrooms for months of observations, many times without a complete knowledge of what was being observed. Besides commitment, such support is indicative of the high level of sophistication of many staff members who understand the need for control procedures and the necessity of unbiased ratings in our experimental procedures. The support also attests to the great level of trust that evolved between members of the school system and the authors.

The more general system implications lie in the fact that the school could open its doors to evaluation in the search for innovation. Very few other institutions, including most community mental health centers, would probably be so receptive to self-scrutiny and change. The project demonstrates to members of the school that research can be compatible with service. It also provides evidence to mental health professionals that evaluation does not have to be sacrificed to a strong service orientation.

Finally, the program demonstrates intersystem accommodation between the university and the elementary school. The two institutions can establish an effective and productive partnership for the mutual benefit of both. This last point has especially important implications as universities come under increasing pressure to provide highly visible service projects that have impact on those who influence funding priorities.

Problems Requiring Further Study

Two main problems will be addressed in this section. The first is the necessity for long-range follow-up of prevention projects. The second deals with the lack of convergence of multiple outcome indicators and the implications of this methodological difficulty. There are different issues involved in each of these two areas and they will be discussed separately.

This study was developed using intermediary criteria, although our ultimate interest is the long-term consequences of such efforts in reducing "pathology" and promoting more adaptive societal functioning. The intermediate criteria developed for the project are considered an important conceptual advance because these dimensions allowed us to develop a specific, short-term project that embodied experimental control and empirical analysis within a relatively brief period. The total operating time of the project from initial contact with the school to final evaluation was about 18 months.

We believe that carefully chosen intermediate criteria are sufficient for preliminary investigations such as this one, and we encourage other researchers to base their preventive endeavors on these or similar criteria. There is certainly a strong need for health promotion studies of all types in psychology.

However useful such face valid indices are, their ultimate utility will only be determined by long-range follow-up investigations. Such a follow-up is vital and will be facilitated by more studies involving larger numbers of participants. Without a follow-up, several crucial questions will remain unanswered. Can we reduce incidence rates of variously defined types of "deviance" with these types of programs? Which adaptive consequences on the subsequent development of the children result from such endeavors? Is one year of training enough, or should a multiple year sequence of intervention be planned? What organizational changes in the school structure result from successful collaboration in these projects? Would auxiliary programs in the home be necessary to support school programs? These and several other crucial questions remain to be answered by careful, long-range interventions that must and will inevitably be developed.

The other major methodological issue in the study is the lack of convergence in our outcome measures. Such inconsistency highlights the need for multiple outcome assessment as stressed in Chapter 2. Our direct behavioral observations generally provided us with the most supportive evaluative data. These measures were developed for group comparisons, primarily for assessing social interactions and classroom activity. They measured broader categories than the specific target behaviors being trained, but they were the most closely related measures to what we were specifically trying to change. However, improvement on these direct behavioral measures was not paralleled by positive changes on other global or self-reported assessment indices.

For example, teacher and peer ratings in this research endeavor were generally unrelated to independently measured changes in the academic or social functioning of the pupils. This lack of relationship is of special concern because Cowen *et al.* (1973) found that peer ratings were the best single predictor of subsequent psychological difficulty as indicated by listing on a county-wide psychiatric register. Retrospective reports of change, furnished by the companions in the present study, indicated dramatic improvement in the children, but these scores were again unrelated to the behavioral indices.

These nonconvergent findings are not surprising, as the independence of measures obtained through separate self-reported and behaviorally rated channels of assessment has been well documented (Goldfried & Sprafkin, 1974; Lang, 1968). The low degree of correspondence among these measures also points out a strength of the intervention. In Chapter 2, we argued that each channel of assessment contains inherent problems specific to that particular domain. If the outcomes of a therapeutic endeavor indicate that measures from different domains change in a consistent direction, the impact of the intervention is stronger than (1) if only a single measure changes and the others do not; or (2) if only highly intercorrelated measures change.

For example, if companion ratings and behavioral observations both point to improvement in socially isolated children, one can assume that the consequences of this program were more far reaching than if only one of these modes indicated positive change. As more studies employ direct behavioral observation, hopefully these sorts of relationships will become clarified.

Psychology needs more sophisticated measures for evaluating change in school and home settings. We especially need measures geared to assessing strengths and adaptive skills in naturalistic settings. Most of our traditional psychological assessment devices have been of a verbal nature and pathology oriented. The failure of some of our current evaluative devices should not be cause for despair but rather, ought to spur psychologists to develop more valid and useful measures of human functioning (Rotter, 1973).

One possible solution to the lack of adequate assessment devices is the further development of standardized behavioral situational tasks. The structured real-life situation developed for evaluation of problem-solving skills is one example of this type of device. Such measures would have the standardization features necessary for group comparisons and valid statistical treatment, yet would be closer to the natural behavioral tasks to which one wishes to generalize. Such standardized situational measurement devices, if developed to assess adaptive behaviors, may be one antidote to the biases created by the past array of measurement technologies in psychology.

The Future of Prevention Programs

It is our impression that the number of prevention-oriented, health-enhancing projects is going to increase considerably in the future. There are several reasons for this expectation, and some have already been mentioned in the first chapter. For purposes of our discussion, these reasons can be classified into two general groups. The first set clusters around a prevailing disenchantment with the state of our current approaches to psychological treatment. Community psychologists are probably more united in their general disenchantment with the reach and effectiveness of traditional clinical approaches, than in a common conception of constructive alternatives to improve them.

Most community psychologists agree that traditional approaches are focused on after-the-fact, piecemeal attempts to rehabilitate the "sick" individual with circumscribed, expensive, and time-consuming techniques. Unlike some of our more radically inclined colleagues, we believe that traditional psychotherapeutic techniques are at times appropriate for specific individuals who possess clearly delineated problems that can be treated by well-substantiated procedures. The difficulty with this strategy is that such approaches have been uncritically extended to social problems and populations for which they are simply not appropriate.

One does not have to be a skilled researcher to observe that traditional approaches have not been sufficient to meet the vast human problems of our time. The individually oriented, passive, rehabilitative approach seems to be an especially inept model for preparing psychologists to handle ever-increasing problems of the future. Moreover, traditional approaches ignore much that has been learned about human ecology and human behavior in organizational contexts. They also fail to incorporate recent knowledge about social and cognitive development.

In one sense, community psychology is a radical innovation in treatment approaches; in another, it is simply an attempt to bring our growing knowledge into the clinical arena. This second perspective provides a markedly positive impetus toward the development of new approaches in the helping services.

At the risk of being exceptionally simplistic, we are gradually coming to the realization that people are greatly affected by the social systems of which they are a part. Why not attempt, then, to improve these systems toward the ultimate enhancement of its members? We also know that social development is exceedingly complex and consists of specific skills that must be learned. If one can learn maladaptive social behaviors, why not attempt to teach specific, personally adaptive social skills? Disenchantment with past approaches and their empirical failures, coupled with the promise of new conceptions of human behavior, combine to justify a strong emphasis on the preventive approach.

We also predict that such preventive projects will assume an increasingly multidisciplinary focus in the future. Concern for and expertise in improving the human condition is expanding beyond traditional academic disciplines. Linkages between economists, psychologists, anthropologists, social planners, lawyers, and human development specialists are becoming both increasingly necessary and practicable, as interventions become more comprehensive and complex. We need to launch a concerted and aggressive effort toward promoting health; we must not settle for passive, fractionated rehabilitative attempts.

Such efforts must ultimately be addressed to constructive social change. We need to work, not only with our educational organizations, but also with labor, mental health, welfare, and other systems, toward the enhancement of human functioning in all of its manifold aspects. These new approaches will have to be explicitly linked to such values as equality, justice and opportunity within the structure of our society. From this broader perspective, many of the problems formerly considered to be in the realm of mental health are found to have roots in the current functioning of many of our social organizations. This realization will, hopefully, force today's mental health professionals to reconsider the utility of viewing human difficulties as involving psychic dysfunction. In the long run, adherence to the current conceptions of abnormality, deviance, and psychogenic illness will contribute to larger social problems, rather than reduce them.

We must, as Ryan (1971) has pointed out, be willing to look at the casualties of our society as "victims," rather than "deviants." At present, the burdens imposed by technological advancement fall on those members of society who have the fewest resources to deal with additional sources of stress. These groups include the poor and uneducated, as well as an increasingly growing number of other individuals, who experience alienation and frustration while being forced to accommodate themselves to questionable societal changes. Future strategies should be aimed at increasing the effectiveness of our social structures to the advantage of these groups.

Within the more narrow focus of this book, however, several possibilities exist for the expansion of the described intervention. These would include an experimental extension of the problem-solving curriculum to all elementary grade levels, similar to the programs developed by Ojemann (1969). Social problem solving offers a particularly useful focus for prevention efforts because it aims at enhancing personal self-esteem and specific social competencies, while recognizing and appreciating the diversity of human behavior. Interpersonal skill training, self-modification strategies (Watson & Tharp, 1972), and assertive training could profitably be included with social problem-solving training in experimental programs.

New teaching media and creative training techniques, including innovative uses of modeling and video presentations, could be developed to help in curriculum implementation. An interesting training adjunct might involve using parental volunteers as helpers in classroom training sessions. Extension of social problem solving to couples planning to have children might enhance the child's home environment, another important KISS system described by Bower (1972).

The continued use of college students and other community personnel such as senior citizens, housewives, and high schoolers holds promise as an important human resource. The involvement of such groups in meaningful roles in our school systems promotes the helper–therapy principle (Rappaport, Chinsky, & Cowen, 1971). These people may help socially deficient children while helping themselves in the process. Likewise, the use of behavioral techniques in the classroom seems to be a most effective way to change teachers' behaviors and, in turn, help children to better master the demands of their educational experiences. Given our current economic problems, large groups in society could be productively employed in service programs such as this one.

The integration of behavioral analysis and community psychology holds vast promise for improving the assessment and, therefore, the ultimate effectiveness of community programs. MacDonald, Hedberg, and Campbell (1974) call the use of behavioral analysis "a behavioral revolution in community mental health [p. 228]." Rather than a revolution, we consider the behavioral emphasis as part of a general evolutionary trend toward more precision and accountability in the mental health realm.

Chapter 1 discussed the marriage of community psychology and behavioral analysis. The subsequent chapters presented one of the products of such a union. Clearly, behavioral analysis' greatest contribution to community psychology is its methodological clarity. The literature is reflecting an increasing number of community projects incorporating this methodology (Fo & O'Donnell, 1974; Patterson, 1974), and we predict the appearance of even more such interventions in the future.

Ethical Issues in Community Involvement

Social scientists interested in preventive interventions in the community are presented with a curious dilemma. They clearly recognize that human suffering from psychogenic sources has not been diminished by traditional techniques. Indeed, population density seems to have added additional difficulties, such as urban stress, unemployment, alcoholism, and child abuse, to the apparently ever-increasing list of human problems. Intervention in the community, particularly by altering our KISS systems, seems to be a promising approach toward aggressively challenging these problems.

However, community intervention poses value conflicts and confusions of its own. Four vitally important classes of ethical concern can be delineated, relating to privacy, freedom of participation, behavior control, and experimentation. Special ramifications that influence the operation of the community interventionist are descibed for each of these areas in turn.

Privacy issues are not typically of concern in traditional mental health practices, as the individual actively seeks help in ameliorating his or her psychological difficulties. Providing informed consent for the collection and utilization of personal information by the therapist is part of the therapeutic contract within this traditional model. Preventive approaches, on the other hand, cannot employ all of the information-gathering strategies that are used in most current mental health treatment endeavors, since those practicing prevention seek out *potentially* problematic situations. This orientation implies that gathering data after obtaining the informed consent of those seeking treatment will be possible in only a small number of cases. The community psychologist will therefore be forced to use information gathered from unusual sources, such as peer ratings and school records. Since the focus is on potential problems, the necessity of information of this type is not readily apparent to those who will be asked to provide it. The relationship between an individual's right to keep these sources of information private and the community interventionist's need to access is presently ambiguous and in need of clarification.

There is a second aspect to the privacy problem. The reliance on paraprofessional personnel in community endeavors suggests that more individuals will have access to potentially damaging information than is the case in traditional helping endeavors. We have no simple solutions to this complex problem, although two suggestions seem feasible. Community psychologists should operate under a clearly explicated and widely publicized code of ethics. This code should include provisions for examining conflicts about privacy and should also contain a mechanism for redressing legitimate grievances. The second suggestion involves the type of information that should be made available to the paraprofessionals who participate in preventive programs. Stuart (1970) has pointed out that general descriptive labels (for example, psychotic, minimally brain damaged) are more harmful than specific descriptions of behavior. We suggest that disseminating the latter is ethically more justifiable, and more useful, than utilizing the potentially more stigmatizing labels.

Traditional mental health providers have been necessarily concerned with an individual's right to refuse treatment only when the change effort is required for the general good of society (for example, ordering psychiatric treatment for a convicted child molester in lieu of a prison sentence). The self-selection of most outpatients for psychotherapy is an indicant of the patient's freedom of choice.

The preventive nature of many community mental health endeavors makes freedom of participation a complex ethical issue. Prevention implies the amelioration of *potential* problems, which the general populace would find difficult to thoroughly comprehend. The power and status of the interveners, in combination with the ambiguity of referents that define the potential problematic condition, increase the likelihood of participation in preventive programs without the fully informed consent of the individuals involved.

Once again, there are no easy answers to this dilemma. We believe, however, that mental health professionals have the obligation to increase the freedom of all that they have contact with. We agree with Skinner (1971) in defining freedom as the number of behavioral alternatives open to an individual at any particular time. Within this framework, the question of requiring involvement devolves into balancing the economic, social, and psychological costs of uninformed participation against the probable benefits that derive from the intervention. These factors can only be accurately aligned if they are measurable. We have argued in previous chapters that the use of intermediate criteria of adjustment provide preventive programs with a higher degree of visibility than they would otherwise enjoy. Intermediate criteria can serve as stable and comprehensible guidelines against which the merits and liabilities associated with participation in preventive endeavors can be rationally and ethically explored.

The third issue, namely, the specter of behavior control, is usually raised only after particular psychotherapeutic interventions have been proven to be effective. It is notable that concern with such control was not a salient issue in the public forum before the advent of the psychothechnology known as "behavior modification." Many well-intentioned individuals have expressed deep concern over what they perceive as uncontrolled growth in the power of behavioral technologists. What both proponents and detractors of the behavior modification position fail to recognize, however, is that the so-called "laws" of human behavior must be operationalized by employing concrete procedures in specific settings. As Reppucci and Saunders (1974) point out, the behavioral engineer exerts a very weak and tenuous form of control over social systems. The technologist can gain access to social settings and employ his change strategies effectively *only* with the cooperation of those to whom the procedures are directed.

We must admit that any potentially powerful behavior change strategy can be misused by unscrupulous practitioners. However, much recent research indicates that the specific behavior change operations within this framework are not particularly effective unless the individual expects them to be. Outside of total treatment institutions, the effectiveness of behavior modification techniques is reduced to the extent that the change agent neglects the development of a mutually satisfying relationship. In fact, the manipulative and callous use of behavior change procedures in a coercive manner may well foster a backlash of reactance that would ultimately destroy the effectiveness of the behavior modifier.

We realize that issues relating to "behavior modification," especially in a school system, are emotionally laden ones. Our hope is that readers will honestly attempt to understand the spirit as well as the procedures of our intervention, and not condemn our advocacy of the behavior analytic approach because of its connotative overtones of coercion and control. The essential theme of our approach is to apply knowledge of behavior influence processes toward the development of increasingly humane social systems.

Requiring a code of ethics for community psychologists and behavior change agents is one method of preventing abuses in the employment of increasingly more sophisticated intervention procedures. An even more effective method of insuring the proper use of behavior control strategies is to disseminate information concerning their operation as widely as possible (London, 1969). No psychotherapeutic procedure, including our social problem-solving curriculum, is value free. The clash between *publicly proclaimed* values is the essence of ethical discourse and, ultimately, understanding. The danger of malevolent outside behavior influence is heightened by ignorance or fear. If all participants in mental health facilitation programs are taught to apply general strategies of behavior change to improve their own life situations, the possibility of behavioral control being exerted by external agents is reduced.

Finally, it seems especially unfortunate that, just when many researchers are willing to attempt socially innovative research, public distrust has focused on the "experimental" aspect of this involvement. "Innovation" and "change" generally have positive connotations, but "research" and "experimentation" seem to be considered with some disfavor. To counter this negative reaction, we must begin to develop a constructive dialogue with public and governmental groups to explain the need for researching the impact of our interventions. Rational change with experimental evaluation, though raising concerns of privacy and personal rights, is ultimately less dangerous to our democratic way of life than is random and nonplanned change without evaluation (Campbell, 1969b).

Because of the legitimate concerns for the rights of all participants, researchers are obligated to ensure that no damage or misunderstanding results from their work. Interventions must be carefully selected and planned to ensure that only positive or neutral effects are likely to occur. Communication with both the host agencies and participants must be continuous and completely honest for the duration of any project. Results must be empirically obtained and must also be as widely disseminated as possible, so as to ensure maximum information for future researchers and social planners.

The difficulties of conducting prevention-oriented research are numerous, but this form of intervention is vital to the ultimate well-being of our society. Considering the vast problems of the contemporary age, experimentation consistent with the practical and ethical values of society seems far less harmful than the immorality of noninvolvement.

APPENDIX

Social Problem-Solving Curriculum: A Workbook

This section presents the problem-solving curriculum in a more detailed and integrated form than was possible in the text. Its purpose is twofold. The first is to provide more information to readers interested in understanding the nature of our intervention more completely. The second, and equally important objective, is to serve as a resource for other professionals in education and mental health who wish to develop their own training programs in problem solving.

This section is *not* presented as a "cookbook" or "blueprint" to be followed verbatim in order to create a problem-solving curriculum. We do not presume to have the final and finished product for such a task. Moreover, a cookbook approach is contrary to the basic tenets of both creative problem solving and our orientation toward implementing school interventions. As discussed in Chapters 1 and 2, such interventions must be established collaboratively with school personnel and will therefore be unique to each setting. Thus, we are not emphasizing carbon-copy replicas of our program but, rather, individual programs linked by a common objective and rationale: the development of effective school-based programs aimed at enhancing the psychological development of children.

In order to assist those developing their own programs, we have included some examples of additional techniques introduced during a second year of the problem-solving program with similarly effective results (McClure, 1975).

In this section we will first describe some of the general training approaches and principles used in teaching the problem-solving curriculum. Next we will discuss the workshop method used to develop the collaborative approach with the teachers. This is followed by a description of the classroom formats used in problem-solving training. The section concludes with a reveiw of the basic units of the curriculum and sample exercises that we have found to be useful.

Basic Training Principles and Techniques

Our general emphasis in teaching social problem-solving skills is to encourage trainers to use a wide range of instructional strategies. Emphasis is given to innovative, experienced-based learning rather than the more traditional didactic classroom format. Experiential techniques are considered vital in training complex social skills such as successful interpersonal problem solving. For this reason, whenever possible, learning experiences and situations were created so the child could participate directly.

Teachers were oriented to several training principles and procedures in light of this experiential emphasis. Most of these principles are based on observational and reinforcement strategies discussed in detail by Bandura (1969) and on the techniques to foster divergent and creative thinking developed by Renzulli (1970).

Modeling. Frequently, the quickest way to learn a skill is to observe someone else. Children learn to imitate the behaviors of adults and other children early in life. Providing a model becomes a powerful means for increasing the frequency of present behaviors and for the development of new behaviors. As a result of this principle, videotape modeling played a central role in the present problem-solving curriculum. The videotapes permit the children to observe a peer model in the process of solving a actual problem. Showing the videotapes on television monitors tended to increase student interest and enhance the "gamelike" enjoyment of the learning experience. Many of the exercises were structured for group problem solving, and these group activities also allow the less creative problem solvers to model their more able peers.

Reinforcement and shaping techniques. In simplest terms, the notion of reinforcement is that people will keep doing whatever you reward them for doing. If children are rewarded by the teacher for producing a variety of different ideas or strategies, then this behavior will increase. The importance of the teacher's social praise in reinforcing creative problem-solving behavior is crucial. Further, the teacher's role in shaping problem-solving behaviors of less creative children is stressed in small-group activities. In such activities the teachers can use shaping techniques with individual children by reinforcing each small step that approximates the target behavior. Often the teacher can use prompting questions to elicit the behavior.

Other children in the classroom are also an important source of reinforcement. Utilization of gamelike activities with peers can reward children for creative problem solving. As Silberman (1970) indicates, gamelike activities are the "work" of the child and are a principal way to motivate children to become involved in learning experiences.

Role playing and behavioral rehearsal. As mentioned above, stress is placed on learning by doing. Children can have a lot of fun in role playing or skitlike activities. We included some role playing in our concluding exercises, and McClure (1975) developed additional role playing techniques for use throughout the curriculum. Teachers usually did not need to force anyone into role playing, and the children generally loved it. Children usually had a chance to play several parts during the course of the program. Observers (children not role playing) are given active roles by being instructed to pay attention to the feelings of the role players and are asked for their participation during discussions of the role playing. During role playing, teachers avoided any evaluation of the quality of the child's *performance* in the role and encouraged all children to become involved. In addition to generating a high level of interest, the role-playing activities provided the children with an opportunity to rehearse the component behaviors of the problem-solving process.

Brainstorming techniques. Often the first solution that is generated for a problem is not always the best. Brainstorming techniques encourage children to consider as many solutions to a problem as possible. The best way to promote brainstorming is to reinforce the child for quantity of ideas and withhold criticism and evaluation until after the students have presented a wide range of possible solutions to the presented problem. Activities that stress group problem solving also help youngsters to see the benefits of several minds working together generating multiple solutions to a given problem. Brainstorming stresses a divergent approach in looking for answers and reduces premature criticism of creative alternatives.

Workshops for Teachers

The teachers in our program were trained in the problem-solving curriculum through workshops conducted in the school. These workshops were held weekly during the program and lasted about 40 minutes to one hour. They were scheduled during the school day during periods set aside by the school for planning and curriculum development. Scheduling workshops in this way reduced the placement of additional work on participating teachers.

Rather than being presented with a completed "package" of problem-solving exercises, the teachers were given a workbook that outlined the basic objectives of the curriculum, the principles or techniques thought to be the most effective, and the suggested classroom formats. From this outline, *the consultant and teachers worked as a team in the development of specific exercises for classroom use*. Opportunity was also provided for the teachers to give the consultant feedback concerning the previous exercises. This process frequently resulted in modification of the structure or format of the exercises developed during that workshop.

For example, at the beginning of the workshop the previous exercise or two would be reviewed. Matters such as the children's interest and grasp of the material, as well as the classroom workability of the exercise, would be discussed. If necessary, this feedback could lead to additional exercises within that unit of the curriculum. For example, this occurred after a vacation period when the teachers felt the children has forgotten material from the previous exercise. This feedback was also very useful when the children especially enjoyed a particular exercise or technique.

After this review, the workshop would focus on the next set of objectives in the curriculum and would design an exercise using the Exercise Worksheet as a guide (See Table A.1). This part of the workshop focused on the goal or objective of the exercise and the development of suggestions by the teachers regarding specific instructional methods. The role of the teacher in the classroom exercise and the use of potential methods of reinforcement were discussed. Arrangements for obtaining the necessary materials were also made.

A list of social and interpersonal problems actually generated by eight-, nine-, and ten-year-old children was used as a source of sample problems for the classroom exercises. This list was continually supplemented during the program with additional problems discussed by the children in training. This list was expanded during the second year to include unfinished story stems from problems contained in work by Shaftel and Shaftel (1967).

The worksheets also provided for the teacher's own evaluation of the exercise. These exercise worksheets were kept by the teachers in their own notebooks over the course of the program and could be used as the core of their own future problem-solving curriculum.

Classroom Format

The arrangement of children into small or large learning groups depends on the size of the classroom, the number of children in each class, and the number of teaching staff available. The teacher's experiences with large- or small-group instruction is obviously also important. We were able to use teacher aides and selected undergraduate student aides to supplement the teaching staff during problem-solving training sessions. This allowed for the presence of at least two adults during the training procedure and permitted the frequent use of small-group exercises.

The small-group arrangement is considered ideal for learning social problem solving. However, some parts of our program were designed to be presented to the whole class at one time. Examples of specific exercises used during large- and small-group formats are discussed below.

Large-group format. Most of the curriculum units began with the students in the classroom in one large group. This format made extensive use of the

TABLE A.1
Exercise Worksheet

Class: ______________________ Date: ____________ Time: ____________

Unit Objective:

Exercise Objective:

Instructional Method:
Classroom format

Directions, probes

Method of reinforcement

Necessary materials

Sample Problems:

Teacher Evaluation of Exercise & Comments:

modeling techniques described above. In some units the teacher would model or demonstrate the behavior for the students. In other units videotaped peer models demonstrated the particular problem-solving behavior of the unit. Reinforcement and shaping techniques were often used in the large group as well. For example, the teacher may reinforce a particular child who responds with the desired behaviors during the demonstration. There were also several pauses in the videotapes during which the teacher elicited specific responses from individual children as to what they would do next if they were in the position of the video model. The pauses in the videotape allowed for the active participation of the children in the sequence being taught.

Small-group format with teacher. After presenting the orienting exercise to the whole class, the next exercise in each unit generally consisted of having the children work in small groups with the teacher. Usually the teacher and an aide would spend 10–15 minutes with each group of children. Most groups consisted of four or five children, but some were smaller. While the teacher may have modeled the behavior again in these small groups, she normally made more extensive use of shaping and reinforcement with individual children.

The small group allowed for more participation by each child in the creative problem-solving process, and the teacher's presence helped to ensure that each child had a chance to contribute. There was also opportunity with the small group for children to model the behavior of their more successful peers.

Small-group format without teacher. After a few exercises, the children often learned the basic aspects of the task and were able to practice the behaviors alone in their group. Using this format, the teacher would monitor progress of several groups simultaneously and intervene where necessary with specific children who need help. Self-directed groups could also employ gamelike activities in which the children could compete with each other to generate the "most original" solution or the greatest number of solutions to a given problem. The teachers often gave out prizes and social praise during these activities, and reported that they were highly successful with the children.

Again it is important to stress that there is no *fixed* classroom design to be followed in using the curriculum. While generally one format may be used for an exercise on a given day, there are situations where a variety of arrangements can be mixed together in the same exercise. For example, an exercise may include starting in the large group with an unfinished story depicting a problem situation, breaking up into small groups to discuss problem-solving strategies, and reforming into a large group to share the different strategies developed. In many of the small-group exercises, the teachers found it helpful to appoint a "secretary" to list the various points discussed by the group. This secretary also helped the groups stay on-task when working without the teacher.

While the use of small groups in problem-solving training is considered most effective, we realize that limited budgets and personnel shortages are often the common situation in many school systems. *One excellent alternative solution to this problem is to use selected volunteer parents in auxillary teaching roles. This would facilitate bringing families and the community into training programs.* If small groups cannot be established, modification of any of the exercises to the large-group format is quite appropriate, and successful training in large classes has been reported.

SOCIAL PROBLEM-SOLVING CURRICULUM: SAMPLE EXERCISES

The curriculum is presented here to refresh the reader's memory and to show its integration with the specific techniques and exercises presented as examples. The curriculum was separated into units, each of which had specific objectives. Although the children were trained in the units sequentially, this did not imply that the child had to solve problems in a fixed sequence. Rather, it was felt that a sequential unit approach would help to specify curriculum objectives in terms of operational and trainable problem-solving behaviors.

Divergent Thinking Unit

This unit provides an opportunity to have the children experience group problem-solving and brainstorming techniques. Specific objectives include the generation of new ideas from given information and divergent thinking. It is during this unit that teachers begin to stress the child's creative role in problem solving.

This unit was included to set the tone for the kind of creativity hoped for during the rest of the social problem-solving curriculum, as well as to provide the children with experience in group problem-solving and brainstorming techniques. The children frequently seemed quite familiar with the small-group techniques and were able to generate creative ideas. Therefore, during the second year of the program, fewer exercises were planned for this unit and greater emphasis was placed on *increasing the children's expectancies that problems can often be solved as a result of their own efforts.* This increased expectancy is considered a crucial first step in successful problem solving.

Exercise example 1. The teacher presents a problem to the class and models brainstorming by generating an "original" or "way-out" solution to the problem. A good problem to start off this exercise with is "all possible ways you might have come to school this morning." The teacher also encourages imagination and withholds evaluation or criticism of ideas. As each child generates an idea, it is written on the blackboard regardless of how silly or "way-out" it may seem. Every idea is reinforced with enthusiastic comments, and the teacher should refrain from statements such as, "a good idea *but*. . . ."

Exercise example 2. The teacher works in small groups with the children trying to involve all the members of the group, using encouragement and prompting where needed. A good problem for divergent thinking is alternate uses for objects other than those they are normally used for. The object can be combined with another object, or it can be changed or modified in form if the child wishes. Again the teacher withholds criticism, since the focus is on the generation of new ideas. After the group begins to master the task, the teacher can move to another group.

Exercise example 3. An interesting variation of the above exercise has the teacher begin with the children in a large group. They brainstorm a list of all discarded objects in the house. This list is written on the board. Then in small groups the children generate as many alternative uses for these objects as possible. After 20 minutes the groups report their ideas back to the large group. The teacher then gives a prize to the group with the most ideas, as well as the group with the most original idea.

Problem Identification Unit

The goal of this unit is to teach the child the importance of identifying and defining the problem, and the importance of setting long-term and short-term goals. The specific objectives are that the child recognize a problem situation when it occurs, identify the problem, and specify a desirable outcome. For many children this unit was relatively easy, but some children had trouble with the recognition and definition of a problem situation, and training was crucial to further progress. Again, this unit stressed the positive expectancy that problems are solvable, and provided a structured opportunity for the teachers to elicit feedback from children concerning problems they face.

Exercise example 1. The teacher orients the class to the fact that all people have problems and that if they work at them they can usually solve them. Using some sample problems, the teacher demonstrates that the first thing necessary for solving a problem is identifying the problem and defining the goal. Emphasis is placed on separating the relevant from the irrelevant aspects of the problem. Problems are selected from a list of sample problems (for example, a child won a box of candy and others want to share it, but the child wants to show it to his family; a child is fooling around at the end of the day and misses her bus, and her mother works; a child wants to join a game at recess, but the sides are already even). For the last half of the session the children are asked to brainstorm a list of problems that they encounter. This part of the exercise asks children to apply problem identification to their own problems and thus helps to get feedback from children concerning problems they face. A useful technique for this part of the exercise is to have the children each write down a problem situation and then discuss the problems without identifying the author.

Exercise example 2. The teacher works in small groups with the children practicing the identification of the problem. Problems used in this exercise can be selected from unfinished problem stories (for example, Shaftel & Shaftel, 1967) or selected by the teacher from the list of problems generated in the previous exercise. The teacher helps the group work toward a clear definition of the problem and the goals of each character. The teacher can ask the following questions as probes to elicit discussion in the small group: "What is the problem as (name of character) sees it?" "What does (name of character) want to happen?" "Can each of the characters in the problem reach their goals?" Using these probes the teacher attempts to elicit the participation of each child in the small group.

Exercise example 3. An interesting variation of the above exercise developed by McClure (1975) uses role-playing techniques. The teacher presents a problem story to the children. The teacher helps the children to explore their different views of the problem situation by reenacting the same scene several times and changing actors in the key roles. During the role playing, the teacher can ask the same probing questions discussed above. After role playing a few enactments, the children discuss how different ways of seeing the problem affect the problem definition and goals. They also note how vaguely defined goals make problem solving difficult.

Alternative Solutions Unit

The primary objective of this unit is that the child generate several alternate solutions to a problematic situation. Here the divergent thinking and brainstorming techniques are applied to social problems. The rationale is that brainstorming many possible alternative solutions will increase the likelihood that the most effective solution will be available to the child. The teacher defers judgement of the solutions and encourages the children to generate as many solutions as possible. The goal here is to establish an orientation that looking for alternatives will maximize problem-solving effectiveness. This is one of the most important units of the curriculum and one that has demonstrated the most effective results.

Exercise example 1. A videotaped peer model is shown attempting to solve a problem. The model generates a variety of alternative solutions to the problem (for example, an eight-year-old girl loses her lunch money at school and approaches her peers and teacher for help in solving her problem; a nine-year-old boy considers many alternatives with his brother trying to solve the problem of getting a new bicycle). During pauses in the tape, the teacher asks the children what other options the problem solver should consider, reinforcing children for the consideration of alternatives. The teacher also asks whether the model should give up, again praising children for their persistance and the generation of more alternatives.

Exercise example 2. In this exercise the teacher works in small groups with a list of unfinished problem stories. The teacher encourages each of the children in the small group to participate in the problem-solving process. Often the teacher can select problems from the list of problems generated by the children during the problem identification exercises. The teacher can prompt individual children with questions: "How can you. . . ?" "What else can you do?" "What other ways can you think of?" It is probable that the group will want to discuss the consequences of various solutions, especially when a solution is antisocial. The teacher can turn discussions of consequences into another opportunity to generate more alternative solutions by saying, "Since this solution may cause a problem, what other solutions can you think of that won't cause this problem?"

Exercise example 3. A variation of the above exercise has the children work in small groups without the teacher. The teacher gives the groups two problems, one at a time. For example, how can a child get into a secret neighborhood club? Or, what do you do if you borrowed a bike, left it in the street, and someone's car rode over it? After 20 minutes, the group with the most original solution wins a prize. Also the group with the most alternatives wins a prize. This intergroup gamelike activity seems especially successful in motivating the children to consider multiple alternatives.

Exercise example 4. McClure (1975) has also designed an exercise for role playing alternative solutions. The teacher gives the children an unfinished problem story after first allowing the group to generate a number of alternative solutions. Then the teacher selects a negative or ineffective solution for the first enactment. The teacher stops the enactment when he or she feels that the negative proposal has been adequately presented. The teacher probes the children to consider whether the solution has solved the problem and whether there are other solutions (emphasizing alternative solutions, rather than lengthy discussions of consequences), again turning such discussion into opportunity to role play other solutions.

Consideration of Consequences Unit

The objective of this unit is that the child consider the relevant outcomes, obstacles, or consequences that are possible for any given solution to a problem. By helping the child to consider potential consequences of particular solutions, potentially more effective or adaptive solutions are possible. A primary objective is that the child will consider what will happen before taking action.

Exercise example 1. A videotape model is used showing peers considering the possible consequences to solutions that they generated to the problem (for example, a child wants to watch a favorite television show and also has some competing obligation to complete homework or a chore). At pauses in the videotape, the teacher can ask the students what the possible consequences or obstacles were for solutions presented. The teacher asks what will happen if a particular solution is used, what other solutions are possible, and what the consequences are of these new solutions. Finally, the teacher asks the class for the selected course of action given the potential consequences.

Exercise example 2. The teacher works in small groups with the children using unfinished problem stories. The teach discusses the importance of looking for the possible consequences to solutions and also emphasizes that there is often more than one possible consequence to a particular solution. The children go through a list of possible solutions to a problem and identify both those most likely and those least likely to be effective. The teacher can probe the group by asking these questions: "What will happen if. . . ?" "What will happen in the short run?" "What will happen in the long run?"

Exercise example 3. A variation of the above exercise has the teacher give the children a problem and seven potential solutions. The children work in small groups and are asked to list the possible consequences for each solution. After each group discusses the potential consequences, they pick the best and poorest solution. They then return to the large group and explain their choices. This exercise works best with social problems in which several solutions have comparable consequences (for example, trying to join a particular group that plays together at recess every day. Potential solutions: sit next to the group at lunch, invite some of the group members over on Saturday, ask them to let you play, interfere with their game so you can play, wait to be invited, tell the teacher you want to play in that group, have a party and invite members of the group).

Exercise example 4. The role-playing exercise developed by McClure (1975) begins with having the teacher select a ineffective solution to a problem for the first enactment. The teacher probes the group to consider the consequences of the solution, including how the characters feel about particular solutions. If possible, teachers select children for roles they have little opportunity to play in real life. The aggressive child plays a shy role and the timid child plays a leader. The teacher concludes the exercise with a discussion of the best or most effective solutions enacted.

Elaboration of Solutions Unit

This unit focuses the child on expanding and elaborating a particular solution, giving the steps necessary to carry out or implement the solution or strategy. The stress is on maximizing the effectiveness of the solution by elaborating the step-by-step means necessary to achieve the goal. The crucial point is that it is necessary to make concrete step-by-step plans in order to effectively implement a good solution. Emphasis is placed on the interpersonal aspects of the solution that will maximize its success.

Exercise example 1. A videotape is shown of a model in the process of solving a problem (for example, a child wants to get permission from his parents to go camping over a holiday; two sisters want to have a party so they can get more friends in school). During pauses in the tape, the teacher asks children what steps the model could take to maximize the effectiveness of the solutions presented. The teacher also reviews other possible solutions and their consequences during the pauses.

Exercise example 2. In this exercise, the teacher works in small groups, discussing how the effectiveness of a solution is maximized by considering the details involved in implementing the solution (for example, the timing of a solution, interpersonal approach or style, the moods and feelings of the other person). The teacher elicits discussion of the potential steps or elaborations to a series of problems (for example, how to get the teacher to have a nature walk, how to get a friend to play a certain game when he doesn't want to, how to set up a new craft club at school). The teacher can probe the discussion by saying, "Given, we have picked this solution, what is the first thing that we must do?" The children can then work in small groups, making a list of the steps necessary to implement their solutions.

Exercise example 3. This exercise, developed by McClure (1975) uses role playing to practice the elaboration of solutions. After discussing the various suggestions concerning how to implement a particular solution to a problem, the teacher allows the children to enact the solutions until they are unable to continue. The inadequacies of their plans are usually readily apparent during the enactments. If not, the teacher stops the enactments and discusses potential problem areas and specific steps that can be taken to maximize the effectiveness of the solutions.

Integration of Problem-Solving Behaviors Unit

Exercises during this unit stress the integration and linkage of the problem-solving behaviors into a set. The objective is for the child to link the generation of a new solution to the consideration of possible outcomes for that solution and the elaborations necessary to implement the solution. During this unit the children have additional experience seeing how these problem-solving behaviors can be acted out in a real-life situation. Role playing and skitlike activities are especially useful in this aspect of training.

Exercise example 1. A videotape model is used to show peers using all of the component problem-solving behaviors in the solution of a problem (for example, a series of scenes dealing with the problem of not having friends in school are presented, including classroom and recess situations). During pauses in the tape, the teacher asks the children for possible alternative solutions ("What else can he or she do?"), potential consequences to these solutions ("What will happen if. . . ?"), and elaborations to the solutions ("How can he or she carry out this solution?"), and encouarages class input and discussion.

Exercise example 2. The teacher first reviews the component parts of the problem-solving process with the large group. Then the children discuss in small groups a problem they will enact in subsequent exercises (for example, you want to befriend an unpopular kid whom your friends usually tease, how you handle a bully on the playground, what you do if you get a good (or poor) paper and other children tease you). The children plan the various solutions they will enact to the problem situation.

Exercise example 3. In this exercise the children role play the problem discussed in the previous exercise before the rest of the class. Periodically during the enactment, the teacher stops the group and allows for discussion by the whole class of other strategies the characters might consider, potential effectiveness of solutions enacted, and the feelings of the characters involved in the role playing.

References

Abidin, R. R. What's wrong with behavior modification. *Journal of School Psychology,* 1971, 9, 38–42.

Abidin, R. R. A psychosocial look at consultation and behavior modification. *Psychology in the Schools,* 1972, 9, 358–364.

Aldous, J., Condon, T., Hill, R., Strauss, M., & Tallman, I. (Eds.), *Family problem solving: A symposium on theoretical, methodological, and substantive concerns.* Hinsdale, Illinois: Dryden Press, 1971.

Alinsky, S. D. *Rules for radicals: A practical primer for realistic radicals.* New York: Vintage, 1972.

Allen, G. J. Case study: Inplementation of behavior modification techniques in summer camp settings. *Behavior Therapy,* 1973, **4**, 570–575.

Allen, K. E., Hart, B., Buell, J. S., Harris, F. R., & Wolf, M. M. Effects of social reinforcement on isolate behavior of a nursery school child. *Child Development,* 1964, **35**, 511–518.

Allinsmith, W., & Goethals, G. W. *The role of schools in mental health.* New York: Basic Books, 1962.

Anderson, C. Nonintellective correlates of originality. *Behavioral Science,* 1966, **11**, 282–294.

Andrews, J. K. The results of a pilot program to train teachers in the classroom application of behavior modification techniques. *Journal of School Psychology,* 1970, **8**, 37–42.

Andrews, L. M., & Karlins, M. *Requium for democracy?* New York: Holt, Rinehart, & Winston: 1971.

Bach, G. R., & Wyden, P. *The intimate enemy.* New York: William Morrow, 1968.

Bandura, A. *Principles of behavior modification.* New York: Holt, Rinehart & Winston, 1969.

Becker, W. C., Madsen, C. H., Arnold, C. R., & Thomas, D. R. The contingent use of teacher attention and praise in reducing classroom behavior problems. *Journal of Special Education,* 1967, **1**, 287–307.

Bennis, W. G. *Changing organizations.* New York: McGraw-Hill, 1966.

Bernstein, D. A., & 'Allen, G. J. Fear survey schedule (II): Normative data and factor analyses based upon a large college sample. *Behaviour Research and Therapy,* 1969, 7, 403–407.

Biber, B. Integration of mental health principles in the school setting. In G. Caplan (Ed.), *Prevention of mental disorders in children.* New York: Basic Books, 1961.

Blackwood, R. O. The operant conditioning of verbally mediated self-control in the classroom. *Journal of School Psychology,* 1970, **8**, 251–258.

Bower, E. Primary prevention of mental and emotional disorders–a frame of reference. In N. Lambert (Ed.), *The protection and promotion of mental health in the schools.* Bethesda, Maryland: Department of Health, Education and Welfare, Public Service Publication No. 1126, 1965.

Bower, E. M. *Early identification of emotionally handicapped children in school.* (2nd ed.) Springfield, Illinois: Thomas, 1969.

Bower, E. M. Education as a humanizing process and its relationship to other humanizing processes. In S. E. Golann & C. Eisdorfer (Eds.), *Handbook of community mental health.* New York: Appleton, 1972.

Bower, E. M. Community psychology and community schools. In W. L. Claiborn & R. Cohen (Eds.) *School intervention: Vol. I of a continuing series in community–clinical psychology.* New York: Behavioral Publications, 1973.

Bower, E., Shellhamer, T. A., & Dailey, J. M. School characteristics of male adolescents who later become schizophrenic. *American Journal of Orthopsychiatry,* 1960, **30**, 712–729.

Brammer, L. M. *The helping relationship: Process and skills.* Englewood Cliffs, New Jersey: Prentice-Hall, 1973.

Brennan, E. C. College students and mental health programs for children. *American Journal of Public Health,* 1967, **57**, 1767–1771.

Breyer, N. L., & Allen, G. J. Effects of implementing a token economy on teacher attending behavior. *Journal of Applied Behavior Analysis,* 1975,

Breyer, N. L., & Calchera, D. J. A behavioral observation schedule for pupils and teachers. *Psychology in the Schools,* 1971, **8**, 330–337.

Breyer, N. L., Calchera, D. J., & Cann, C. Behavioral consulting from a distance. *Psychology in the Schools,* 1971, **8**, 172–176.

Bringman, W. G. Re-examination of ethnocentrism and problem-solving rigidity. *Psychological Reports,* 1967, **20**, 1069–1070.

Broden, M., Hall, R. V., & Mitts, B. The effect of self-recording on the classroom behavior of two eighth-grade students. *Journal of Applied Behavior Analysis,* 1971, **4**, 191–200.

Broskowski, A., & Smith, T. P. Manpower development for human service systems. In D. Harshbarger & R. F. Maley (Eds.), *Behavior analysis and systems analysis: An integrated approach to mental health programs.* Kalamazoo, Michigan: Behaviordelia, 1974.

Brown, J. C., Montgomery, R., & Barclay, J. R. An example of psychologist management of teacher reinforcement procedures in the elementary classroom. *Psychology in the Schools,* 1969, **6**, 336–340.

Brownbridge, R., & VanVleet, P. (Eds.) *Investments in prevention: The prevention of learning and behavior problems in young children.* San Francisco: Pace I. D. Center, 1969.

Buckley, N. K., & Walker, H. M. *Modifying classroom behavior.* Champaign, Illinois: Research Press, 1970.

Buell, J., Stottard, P., Harris, F. R., & Baer, D. M. Collateral social development accompanying reinforcement of outdoor play in a preschool child. *Journal of Applied Behavior Analysis,* 1968, **1**, 167–173.

Bushell, D., Jr., Wrobel, P. A., & Michaelis, M. L. Applying group contingencies to the classroom study behavior of preschool children. *Journal of Applied Behavior Analysis,* 1968, **1**, 55–61.

Buys, C. J. Effects of teacher reinforcement on elementary pupils' behavior and attitudes. *Psychology in the Schools.* 1972, **9**, 278–288.

Campbell, D. T. Prospective: Artifact and control. In R. Rosenthal & R. Rosnow (Eds.), *Artifact in behavioral research.* New York: Academic Press, 1969. (a)

Campbell, D. T. Reforms as experiments. *American Psychologist,* 1969, **24**, 409–429. (b)

Campbell, D. T., & Stanley, J. C. *Experimental and quasi-experimental designs for research.* Chicago: Rand-McNally, 1963.

Caplan, G. Types of mental health consultation. *American Journal of Orthopsychiatry,* 1963, **33**, 470–480.

Caplan, G. *Principles of preventive psychiatry.* New York: Basic Books, 1964.

Cartwright, R., & Biber, B. The teacher's role in a comprehensive program for mental health. In R. Ojemann (Ed.), *The school and the community treatment facility in preventive psychiatry.* Ames, Iowa: State University of Iowa Press, 1965.

Casey, J. P. Creativity and the solving of social problems. *Journal of Educational Research,* 1965, **54**, 154–159.

Chinsky, J. M. Collaborative interventions in community mental health: A personal perspective. In S. E. Golann & J. Baker (Eds.), *Current and future trends in community psychology.* New York: Behavioral Publications, 1975.

Chorover, S. L. Big brother and psychotechnology. *Psychology Today,* 1973, **7**, 43–57.

Clarizio, H. F. (Ed.) *Mental health and the educative process.* Chicago: Rand-McNally, 1969.

Clement, P., & Milne, D. C. Group play therapy and tangible reinforcers used to modify the behavior of 8-year-old boys. *Behavior Research and Therapy,* 1967, **5**, 301–312.

Clement, P. W., Roberts, P., & Lantz, C. Social models and token reinforcement in the treatment of shy, withdrawn boys. *Proceedings of the 78th Annual Convention of the American Psychological Association,* 1970, **5**, 515–516.

Commission to Study the Consolidation of Children's Services. *A plan to transfer psychiatric and related services for children to the Department of Children and Youth Services.* Hartford, Connecticut: Council on Human Services, 1975.

Cook, P. E. *Community psychology and community mental health.* San Francisco: Holden-Day, 1970.

Coopersmith, S. *Antecedents of self-esteem.* San Francisco: W. H. Freeman, 1967.

Cossairt, A., Hall, R. V., & Hopkins, B. L. The effects of experimenter's instructions, feedback, and praise on teacher praise and student attending behavior. *Journal of Applied Behavior Analysis,* 1973, **6**, 89–100.

Cowen, E. Emergent approaches to mental health problems: An overview and directions for future work. In E. Cowen, E. A. Gardner, & M. Zax (Eds.), *Emergent Approaches to Mental Health Problems.* New York: Appleton-Century-Crofts, 1967.

Cowen, E. Coping with school adaptation problems. *Psychology in the Schools,* 1971, **8**, 322–329.

Cowen, E. L. Social and community interventions. *Annual Review of Psychology,* 1973, **24**, 423–472.

Cowen, E. L., Carlisle, R. L., & Kaufman, G. Evaluation of a college student volunteer program with primary graders experiencing school adjustment problems. *Psychology in the Schools,* 1969, **6**, 371–375.

Cowen, E. L., Dorr, D., Trost, M. A., & Izzo, L. D. A follow-up study of maladapting school children seen by nonprofessionals. *Journal of Consulting and Clinical Psychology,* 1972, **39**, 235–238.

Cowen, E. L., Leibowitz, E., & Leibowitz, G. Utilization of retired people as mental health aides with children. *American Journal of Orthopsychiatry,* 1968, **38**, 900–909.

Cowen, E. L., Pederson, A., Babigian, H., Izzo, L. D., & Trost, M. A. Long-term follow-up of early detected vulnerable children. *Journal of Consulting and Clinical Psychology,* 1973, **41**, 438–446.

Cowen, E. L., Zax, M., & Laird, J. D. A college student volunteer program in the elementary school setting. *Community Mental Health Journal,* 1966, **2**, 319–328.

Cutler, R. L. A research evaluation of an action approach to school mental health: IV: Research evaluation of a school mental health program. *American Journal of Orthopsychiatry,* 1961, **31**, 339–346.

Davis, S. G. Current status of research and theory in human problem solving. *Psychological Bulletin,* 1966, **66**, 36–54.

Davison, G. C. The training of undergraduates as social reinforcers for autistic children. In L. Ullmann & L. Krasner (Eds.), *Case studies in behavior modification.* New York: Holt, Rinehart & Winston, 1966.

Deibert, A. N., & Harmon, A. J. *New tools for changing behavior.* Champaign, Illinois: Research Press, 1970.

Dollard, J. & Miller, N. *Personality and psychotherapy.* New York: McGraw-Hill, 1950.

Dorr, D. An ounce of prevention. *Mental Hygiene,* 1972, **56**, 25–27.

Doyal, G. T., Ferguson, J., & Rockwood, I. A group method for modifying inappropriate aggressive behavior in the elementary school. *American Journal of Orthopsychiatry,* 1971, **41**, 311–312.

Duncan, C. P. Human problem solving: Recent research. *Psychological Bulletin,* 1959, **56**, 397–429.

Dunham, H. W., & Weinberg, S. K. *The culture of the state mental hospital.* Detroit: Wayne State University Press, 1960.

Dunlop, T. W. *Behavioral observations: Fact and artifact.* Unpublished Master's thesis, University of Connecticut, Storrs, 1974.

Dunn, L. M. *Expanded manual for the Peabody Picture VocabularyTest.* Minneapolis, Minnesota: Circle Press, 1965.

D'Zurilla, T., & Goldfried, M. Problem solving and behavior modification. *Journal of Abnormal Psychology,* 1971, **78**, 107–129.

Fairweather, G. W. *Methods for experimental social innovation.* New York: Wiley, 1967.

Fairweather, G. W. *Social change: The challenge to survival.* Morriston, New Jersey: General Learning Press, 1972.

Feldhusen, J. F. Problem solving and the abstract-concrete dimension. *Gifted Child Quarterly,* 1975, **19**, 122–129.

Feldhusen, J. F., Houtz, J. C., & Ringenbach, S. E. The Purdue Elementary Problem-Solving Inventory. *Psychological Reports,* 1972, **31**, 891–901.

Feldhusen, J. F., Thurston, J. R., & Benning, J. J. Longitudinal analysis of classroom behavior and school achievement. *Journal of Experimental Education,* 1970, **38**, 4–10.

Flanagan, J. C. Evaluation and validation of research data in primary prevention. *American Journal of Orthopsychiatry,* 1971, **41**, 117–12.

Fo, W. S. O., & O'Donnell, C. R. The buddy system: relationship and contingency conditions in a community intervention program for youth with professionals as behavior change agents. *Journal of Consulting and Clinical Psychology,* 1974, **42**, 163–169.

Garmezy, N. Vulnerability research and the issue of primary prevention. *American Journal of Orthopsychiatry,* 1971, **41**, 101–110.

Giebink, J. W., Stover, D. O., & Fahl, M. A. Teaching adaptive responses to frustration to emotionally disturbed boys. *Journal of Consulting and Clinical Psychology,* 1968, **32**, 366–368.

Gildea, M. C-L., Glidewell, J. C., & Kantor, M. B. The St. Louis Mental Health Project: History and evaluation. In E. L. Cowen, E. A. Gardner, & M. Zax (Eds.), *Emergent approaches to mental health problems.* New York: Appleton-Century-Crofts, 1967.

Gile, L., Neth, B., & Shack, D. M. *Behavior modification workshop I: An introduction to the behavioral process.* Unpublished manuscript, Education Department, University of Connecticut, Storrs, 1972.

Glidewell, J. C. Studies of mothers' reports of behavior symptoms in their children. In S. B. Sells (Ed.), *The definition and measurement of mental health.* Washington, D. C.: National Center for Health Statistics, 1968.

Glynn, E. L. Classroom application of self-determined reinforcement. *Journal of Applied Behavior Analysis,* 1970, **3**, 123–132.

Goffman, E. *Asylums.* Garden City, New York: Anchor, 1961.

Golann, S. *A coordinate index reference guide to community mental health.* New York: Behavioral Publications, 1969.

Goldfried, M. R., & Sprafkin, J. N. *Behavioral personality assessment.* Morristown, New Jersey: General Learning Press, 1974.

Goldner, R. H. Individual differences in whole–part approach and flexibility–rigidity in problem solving. *Psychological Monographs,* 1957, **71** (Whole No. 60).

Goodman G. *Companionship therapy.* San Francisco: Jossey-Bass, 1972.

Goodwin, D. L. Collaboration between the university and the school: A joint venture–one view: Innovation and behavior change through collaboration with a school staff. *Journal of School Psychology,* 1970, **8**, 209–214.

Gordon, S., Berkowitz, M., & Cacace, C. Discovering and meeting the mental health needs of emotionally disturbed elementary school children: With emphasis on children whose parents are inadequate. *Mental Hygiene,* 1964, **48**, 581–586.

Gottlieb, J., & Howell, R. The concepts of prevention and creative development as applied to mental health. In R. Ojemann (Ed.), *Four basic aspects of preventive psychiatry.* Ames, Iowa: State University of Iowa Press, 1957.

Greenberger, E., O'Connor, J., & Sorensen, A. Personality, cognitive and academic correlates of problem-solving flexibility. *Developmental Psychology,* 1971, **5**, 416–424.

Greiger, R. N., Mordock, J. B., & Breyer, N. General guidelines for conducting behavior modification programs in public school settings. *Journal of School Psychology,* 1970, **8**, 259–266.

Guilford, J. P. *The structure of intellect model: Its uses and implications.* Los Angeles: University of Southern California Press, 1960.

Guilford, J. P. *The nature of human intelligence.* New York: McGraw-Hill, 1967.

Hall, R. V. *Behavior modification: Applications in school and home.* Lawrence, Kansas: H&H Enterprises, 1971 (a).

Hall, R. V. *Behavior modification: The measurement of behavior.* Lawrence, Kansas: H&H Enterprises, 1971. (b).

Hall, R. V., Fox, R., Willard, D., Goldsmith, L., Emerson, M., Owen, M., Davis, F., & Porcia, E. The teacher as observer and experimenter in the modification of disputing and talking-out behaviors. *Journal of Applied Behavior Analysis,* 1971, **4**, 141–149.

Hall, R. V., Lund, D., & Jackson, D. Effects of teacher attention on study behavior. *Journal of Applied Behavior Analysis,* 1968, **1**, 1–12.

Hall, R. V., Panyan, M., Rabon, D., & Broden, M. Instructing beginning teachers in reinforcement procedures which improve classroom control. *Journal of Applied Behavior Analysis,* 1968, **1**, 315–322.

Hamburg, D. A., & Adams, J. E. A perspective on coping behavior. *Archives of General Psychiatry,* 1967, **17**, 277–284.

Harris, F., Johnston, M., Kelley, C. S., & Wolf, M. Effects of positive social reinforcement on regressed crawling of a nursery school child. *Journal of Educational Psychology,* 1964, **55**, 35–41.

Harshbarger, D., & Maley, R. F. *Behavior analysis and systems analysis: An integrative approach to mental health programs.* Kalamazoo, Michigan: Behaviordelia, 1974.

Hart, B. M., Reynolds, N. J., Baer, D. M., Brawley, E. R., & Harris, F. R. Effect of contingent and noncontingent social reinforcement on the cooperative play of a preschool child. *Journal of Applied Behavior Analysis,* 1968, **1**, 73–76.

Heilbrun, A. Counseling readiness and the problem-solving behavior of clients. *Journal of Consulting and Clinical Psychology,* 1968, **32**, 396–399.
Hereford, C. F. *Changing parental attitudes through group discussion.* Austin, Texas: University of Texas Press, 1963.
Heyder, D. W., Strickland, C., & Hayes, S. *Problem solving in retarded adolescents and young adults: Findings of a group psychotherapy program.* Norfolk, Virginia: Tidewater Association for Retarded Children, 1970. (ERIC Document Reproduction Service No. ED 044 868.)
Hinton, B. L. Personality variables and creative potential. *Journal of Creative Behavior,* 1970, **4**, 210–217.
Hinton, B. L. Personality factors and resistance to the effects of frustrations on creative problem-solving performance. *Journal of Creative Behavior,* 1971, **5**, 267–269.
Hoffman, L. R. Group problem solving. In L. Berkowitz (Ed.), *Advances in experimental social psychology.* Vol. 2. New York: Academic Press, 1965.
Hollister, W. The concept of "strens" in preventive interventions and ego-strength building in the schools. In N. Lambert (Ed.), *The protection and promotion of mental health in the schools.* Bethesda, Maryland: Department of Health, Education, and Welfare Report No. 1126, 1965.
Holzberg, J. D., Knapp, R. H., & Turner, J. L. College students as companions to the mentally ill. In E. L. Cowen, E. A. Gardner, & M. Zax (Eds.), *Emergent approaches to mental health.* New York: Appleton-Century-Crofts, 1967.
Homme, L. E. *How to use contingency management in the classroom.* Champaign, Illinois: Research Press, 1970.
Hops, H. The school psychologist as a behavior management consultant in a special class setting. *Journal of School Psychology,* 1971, **9**, 473–483.
Horn, R. E. Experiment in programmed learning. In P. Runkel, R. Harrison, & M. Runkel (Eds.), *The changing college classroom.* San Francisco: Jossey-Bass, 1969.
Houtz, J. C., Ringenbach, S. E., & Feldhusen, J. F. Relationship of problem solving to other cognitive variables. *Psychological Reports,* 1973, **33**, 389–390.
Howe, M. J. Repeated presentation and recall of meaningful prose. *Journal of Educational Psychology,* 1970, **61**, 214–219.
Hunt, H. A. The American school system: A possible locus for a national mental health program. *Psychology in the Schools,* 1968, **5**, 35–40.
Iscoe, I., Pierce-Jones, J., Friedman, S. T., & McGehearty, L. Some strategies in mental health consultation: A brief description of a project and some preliminary results. In E. L. Cowen, E. A. Gardner, & M. Zax (Eds.), *Emergent approaches to mental health problems.* New York: Appleton-Century-Crofts, 1967.
Jahoda, M. *Current concepts of positive mental health.* New York: Basic Books, 1958.
Jamieson, G. H. Prior learning and response flexibility in two age groups. *Journal of Gerontology,* 1969, **24**, 174–183.
Kaplan, A. *The conduct of inquiry.* San Francisco: Chandler, 1964.
Kellam, S. G., Branch, J. D., Agrawal, K. C., & Grabill, M. E. Woodlawn Mental Health Center: An evolving strategy for planning in community mental health. In S. E. Golann & C. Eisdorfer (Eds.), *Handbook of community mental health.* New York: Appleton, 1972.
Kelly, J. G. The quest for valid preventive interventions. In G. Rosenblum (Ed.), *Issues in community psychology and preventive mental health.* New York: Behavioral Publications, 1971.
Kennedy, D. A., & Seidman, S. B. Contingency management and human relations workshops: A school intervention program. *Journal of School Psychology,* 1972, **10**, 69–75.
Kent, R. N., O'Leary, K. D., Diament, C., & Dietz, A. Expectation biases in observational evaluation of therapeutic change. *Journal of Consulting and Clinical Psychology,* 1974, **42**, 774–780.

Kirby, F. D., & Toler, H. C. Modification of preschool isolate behavior: A case study. *Journal of Applied Behavior Analysis,* 1970, **3**, 309–314.

Klien, D. An example of primary prevention in the schools. In N. Lambert (Ed.), *The protection and promotion of mental health in the schools.* Bethesda, Maryland: Department of Health, Education, and Welfare, Public Service Publication No. 1126, 1965.

Kurz, R. B., & Capone, T. A. Cognitive level, role taking ability and the Rorschach human movement response. *Perceptual and Motor Skills,* 1967, **24**, 657–658.

Lachenmeyer, C. W. Experimentation–A misunderstood methodology in psychological and social-psychological research. *American Psychologist,* 1970, **25**, 617–624.

Lambert, N. *The protection and promotion of mental health in the schools.* Bethesda, Maryland: Department of Health, Education, and Welfare Report No. 1126, 1965.

Lang, P. J. Fear reduction and fear behavior: Some problems in treating a construct. In J. M. Schlien (Ed.), *Research in psychotherapy.* Vol. 3. Washington, D.C.: American Psychological Association, 1968.

Larcen, S., Spivack, G., & Shure, M. *Problem-solving thinking and adjustment of dependent–neglected preadolescents.* Paper presented at Eastern Psychological Association, Boston, 1972.

Levine, M., & Graziano, A. M. Intervention programs in elementary schools. In S. E. Golann & C. Eisdorfer (Eds.), *Handbook of community mental health.* New York: Appleton, 1972.

Levitt, E. L. Research on psychotherapy with children. In A. Bergin & S. L. Garfield (Eds.), *Handbook of psychotherapy and behavior change.* New York: Wiley, 1971.

Loeber, R. Engineering the behavioral engineer. *Journal of Applied Behavior Analysis,* 1971, **4**, 321–326.

London, P. *Behavior control.* New York: Harper & Row, 1969.

Long, B. E. A model for elementary school behavioral science as an agent of primary prevention. *American Psychologist,* 1970, **25**, 571–574.

Lorion, R. P., Cowen, E. L., & Caldwell, R. A. Problem types of children referred to a school-based mental health program: Identification and outcome. *Journal of Consulting and Clinical Psychology,* 1974, **42**, 491–496.

Louttit, C. M. *Clinical psychology: A handbook of children's behavior problems.* New York: Harper, 1936.

Lovitt, T. C. Behavior modification: The current scene. *Exceptional Children,* 1970, **37**, 85–91.

Lovitt, T. C., Guppy, T. E., & Blattner, J. E. The use of a free-time contingency with fourth graders to increase spelling accuracy. *Behavior Research and Therapy,* 1969, **7**, 151–156.

Lundsteen, S. W. *Promoting growth in problem solving in an integrated program of language skills for the fifth grade.* Dayton, Ohio: Charles S. Kettering Foundation, 1970. (ERIC Document Reproduction Service No. ED 045 304.)

MacDonald, K. R., Hedberg, A. G., & Campbell, L. M. A behavioral revolution in a community mental health. *Community Mental Health Journal,* 1974, **10**, 228–235.

MacDonald, S., & Gallimore, R. Introducing classroom behavior management skills to experienced teachers. *The Journal of Educational Research,* 1972, **65**, 420–424.

Madsen, C. H., Becker, W. C., & Thomas, D. R. Rules, praise, and ignoring: Elements of elementary classroom control. *Journal of Applied Behavior Analysis,* 1968, **1**, 139–159.

Madsen, C. H., Madsen, C. K., Saudargas, R. A., Hammond, W. R., Smith, J. B., & Edgar, D. E. Classroom RAID (rules, approval, ignore, disapproval): A cooperative approach for professionals and volunteers. *Journal of School Psychology,* 1970, **8**, 180–185.

Maley, R. F., & Harshbarger, D. The integration of behavior analysis and systems analysis: A look at the future? In D. Harshbarger & R. F. Maley (Eds.), *Behavior analysis and systems analysis: An integrated approach to mental health programs.* Kalamazoo, Michigan: Behaviordelia, 1974.

Malott, R. W. A behavioral-systems approach to the design of human services. In D. Harshbarger & R. F. Maley (Eds.), *Behavior analysis and systems analysis: An integrative approach to mental health programs.* Kalamazoo, Michigan: Behaviordelia, 1974.

Martin, F. The effects of a creative problem-solving workshop upon the cognitive operations of verbal classroom interactions in primary school grades. *Psychology in the Schools,* 1972, **10,** 126–130.

Matarazzo, J. D. The practice of psychotherapy is art and not science. In A. R. Mahrer & L. Pearson (Eds.), *Creative developments in psychotherapy.* New York: Jason Aronson, 1973.

McClure, L. *Social problem-solving training and assessment: An experimental intervention in an elementary school setting.* Unpublished Doctoral dissertation, University of Connecticut, Storrs, 1975.

McWillians, S. S., & Finkel, N. J. High school students as mental health aides in the elementary school setting. *Journal of Consulting and Clinical Psychology,* 1973, **40,** 39–42.

Meacham, M. L., & Wiesen, A. E. *Changing classroom behavior.* (2nd ed.) New York: Intext Educational Publishers, 1974.

Mendelsohn, G. A., & Gall, M. D. Personality variables and the effectiveness of techniques to facilitate creative problem solving. *Journal of Personality and Social Psychology,* 1970, **16,** 346–351.

Minuchin, P., Biber, B., Shapiro, E., & Zimiles, H. *The psychological impact of school experience.* New York: Basic Books, 1969.

Mischel, W. *Personality and assessment.* New York: Wiley, 1968.

Mitchell, W. E. Amicatherapy: Theoretical perspectives and an example of practice. *Community Mental Health Journal,* 1966, **2,** 307–314.

Mordock, J. B., & Phillips, D. R. The behavior therapist in the schools. *Psychotherapy: Theory, Research and Practice,* 1971, **8,** 231–235.

Morton, R. An experiment in brief psychotherapy. *Psychological Monographs,* 1955, **69,** Whole No. 686.

Murrell, S. A. *Community psychology and social systems: A conceptual framework and intervention guide.* New York: Behavioral Publications, 1973.

Nelson, D. E. *Experimental evaluation of methods of teaching students to consider alternative problem solutions.* Stanford, California: American Institute for Research in the Behavioral Sciences, 1970. (ERIC Document Reproduction Service No. ED 040 475.)

Newton, M. R., & Brown, R. D. A preventive approach to developmental problems in school children. In E. Bower & W. Hollister (Eds.), *Behavioral science frontiers in education.* New York: Wiley, 1967.

Nichtern, S., Donahue, G. T., O'Shea, J., Marans, M., Curtis, M., & Brady, C. A community educational program for the emotionally disturbed children. *American Journal of Orthopsychiatry,* 1964, **34,** 705–713.

Nowicki, S., & Strickland, B. R. A locus of control scale for children. *Journal of Consulting and Clinical Psychology,* 1973, **40,** 148–154.

O'Connor, R. D. Modification of social withdrawal through symbolic modeling. *Journal of Applied Behavior Analysis,* 1969, **2,** 15–22.

O'Connor, R. D. Relative efficiency of modeling, shaping, and the combined procedures for modification of social withdrawal. *Journal of Abnormal Psychology,* 1972, **79,** 327–334.

Ojemann, R. Basic approaches to mental health–The human relations program at the State University of Iowa. In J. Seidman (Ed.), *Educating for mental health: A book of readings.* New York: T. Crowell, 1963.

Ojemann, R. *Developing a program for education in human behavior.* Cleveland, Ohio: Educational Research Council of Greater Cleveland, 1969.

Ojemann, R., Levitt, E., Lyle, W., & Whiteside, M. The effects of a "causal" teacher-training program and certain curricular changes on grade school children. *Journal of Experimental Education,* 1955, **24**, 95–114.

Ojemann, R. H., & Snider, B. Effects of a teacher-training program in behavioral science on changes in causal behavior scores. *Journal of Educational Research,* 1964, **57**, 255–260.

O'Leary, K. D., & Drabman, R. Token reinforcement programs in the classroom: A review. *Psychological Bulletin,* 1971, **75**, 379–398.

O'Leary, K. D., & Kent, R. N. Behavior modification for social action: Research tactics and problems. In L. Hamerlynck, L. C. Handy, & E. J. Mash (Eds.), *Behavior change: Methodology, concepts and practice.* Champaign, Illinois: Research Press, 1973.

O'Leary, K. D., Kent, R. N., & Kanowitz, J. Shaping data collection congruent with experimental hypotheses. *Journal of Applied Behavior Analysis,* 1975, **8**, 43–52.

Orne, M. T. On the social psychology of the psychological experiment: With particular reference to demand characteristics and their implications. *American Psychologist,* 1962, **17**, 776–783.

Osborn, A. F. *Applied imagination: Principles and procedures of creative problem solving.* (3rd ed.) New York: Schribner, 1963.

Packard, R. G. The control of "classroom attention": A group contingency for complex behavior. *Journal of Applied Behavior Analysis,* 1970, **3**, 13–28.

Pagano, D. F. Effects of test anxiety on acquisition and retention of material resembling the content of college courses. *Journal of Experimental Research in Personality,* 1970, **4**, 213–221.

Parnes, S. J., & Meadow, A. Effects of "brainstorming" instructions on creative problem solving by trained and untrained subjects. *Journal of Educational Psychology,* 1959, **50**, 171–176.

Patterson, G. R. Interventions for boys with conduct problems: Multiple settings, treatments and criteria. *Journal of Consulting and Clinical Psychology,* 1974, **42**, 471–480.

Patterson, G. R., & Reid, J. B. Reciprocity and coercion: Two facets of social systems. In C. Neuringer & J. L. Michael (Eds.), *Behavior modification in clinical psychology.* New York: Appleton-Century-Crofts, 1970.

Patterson, N. B., & Patterson, T. W. A companion therapy program. *Community Mental Health Journal,* 1967, **3**, 133–136.

Paul, G. L. Behavior modification research: Design and tactics. In C. M. Franks (Ed.), *Behavior therapy: Appraisal and status.* New York: McGraw-Hill, 1969.

Platt, J., & Spivack, G. Problem-solving thinking of psychiatric patients. *Journal of Consulting and Clinical Psychology,* 1972, **39**, 148–151. (a)

Platt, J., & Spivack, G. Social competence and effective problem-solving thinking in psychiatric patients. *Journal of Clinical Psychology,* 1972, **28**, 3–5. (b)

Platt, J., & Spivack, G. Studies in problem-solving thinking of psychiatric patients: Patient-control differences and factorial structure of problem-solving thinking. *Proceedings of the 81st Annual Convention of the American Psychological Association,* 1973, **8**, 463–464.

Poser, E. The effect of therapists' training on group therapeutic outcome. *Journal of Consulting Psychology,* 1966, **30**, 283–289.

Powers, E., & Witmer, H. *An experiment in the prevention of delinquency: The Cambridge–Somerville youth study.* New York: Columbia University Press, 1951.

Rabkin, J. G. Opinions about mental illness: A review of the literature. *Psychological Bulletin,* 1972, **77**, 155–171.

Rappaport, J., & Chinsky, J. M. Models for delivery of service from a historical and conceptual perspective. *Professional Psychology,* 1974, **5**, 42–50.

Rappaport, J., Chinsky, J. M., & Cowen, E. L. *Innovations in helping chronic patients: College students in a mental institution.* New York: Academic Press, 1971.

Reid, J. B. Reliability assessment of observational data: A possible methodological problem. *Child Development,* 1970, **41**, 1143–1150.

Renzulli, J. S. *The Connecticut Mark I Creativity Program.* University of Connecticut, Storrs, 1970.

Reppucci, N. D., & Saunders, J. T. Social psychology of behavior modification: Problems of implementation in natural settings. *American Psychologist,* 1974, **29**, 649–660.

Robins, L. N. *Deviant children grown up.* Baltimore, Maryland: Williams & Wilkins, 1966.

Roen, S. R. Primary prevention in the classroom through a teaching program in the behavioral sciences. In E. Cowen, E. Gardner, and M. Zax (Eds.), *Emergent approaches to mental health problems.* New York: Appleton-Century-Crofts, 1967.

Rosenthal, R. *Experimenter effects in behavioral research.* New York: Appleton-Century-Crofts, 1966.

Ross, D. M., Ross, S. A., & Evans, T. A. The modification of extreme social withdrawal by modeling with guided participation. *Journal of Behavior Therapy and Experimental Psychiatry,* 1971, **2**, 273–279.

Rotter, J. B. *Social learning and clinical psychology.* Englewood Cliffs, New Jersey: Prentice-Hall, 1954.

Rotter, J. B. Generalized expectancies for internal versus external control of reinforcement. *Psychological Monographs,* 1966, **80**(1, Whole No. 609).

Rotter, J. B. The future of clinical psychology. *Journal of Consulting and Clinical Psychology,* 1973, **40**, 304–312.

Rotter, J. B. *Generalized expectancies for problem solving and psychotherapy.* Paper presented at XV Interamerican Congress of Psychology, Bogota, Colombia, 1974.

Rotter, J. B., Chance, J. E., & Phares, E. J. *Applications of a social learning theory of personality.* New York: Holt, Rinehart & Winston, 1972.

Rotter, J. B., & Rafferty, J. E. *The manual for the Rotter Incomplete Sentences Blank: College Form.* New York: The Psychological Corporation, 1950.

Rucker, C. N. Acceptance of mentally retarded junion high children in academic and non-academic classes. Unpublished doctoral dissertation, University of Iowa, 1967.

Ryan, W. *Blaming the victim.* New York: Pantheon, 1971.

Sarason, S. B. *The culture of the school and the problem of change.* Boston: Allyn & Bacon, 1971.

Sarason, S. B., Levine, M., Goldenberg, I. I., Cherlin, D. L., & Bennett, E. M. *Psychology in community settings: Clinical, educational, vocational, social aspects.* New York: Wiley, 1966.

Schiff, S., & Kellam, S. A community-wide mental health program of prevention and early treatment in the first grade. *Psychiatric Research Reports,* 1967, **21**, 92–104.

Schmidmeyr, B., & Weld, R. Attitudes of institution employees toward resident-oriented activities of aides. *American Journal of Mental Deficiency,* 1971, **76**, 1–5.

Schmuck, R. A., Runkel, P. J., Saturen, S. L., Martell, R. T., & Derr, C. B. *Handbook of organization development in schools.* Palo Alto, California: National Press Books, 1972.

Schroder, H. M., & Rotter, J. B. Rigidity as learned behavior. *Journal of Experimental Psychology,* 1952, **44**, 141–149.

Schwartz, D. A. Community mental health in 1972: An assessment. In H. H. Barten & L. Bellak (Eds.), *Progress in community mental health.* Vol. 2. New York: Grune & Stratton, 1972.

Scott, W. Concepts of normality. In E. Borgatta & W. Lambert (Eds.), *Handbook of personality theory and research.* Chicago: Rand-McNally, 1968.

Shaftel, F. R., & Shaftel, G. *Role playing for social values and decision making in the social studies.* Englewood Cliffs, New Jersey: Prentice-Hall, 1967.

Shore, N., Milgram, N., & Malasky, C. The effectiveness of an enrichment program for disadvantaged young children. *American Journal of Orthopsychiatry,* 1971, **41**, 441–449.

Shure, M., & Spivack, G. Means–ends thinking, adjustment, and social class among elementary school-aged children. *Journal of Consulting and Clinical Psychology,* 1972, **37**, 389–394. (a)

Shure, M., & Spivack, G. *Problem solving thinking: a preventive mental health program for preschool children.* Paper presented at EPA, Boston, April, 1972. (b)

Shure, M., Spivack, G., & Jaeger, M. Problem-solving thinking and adjustment among disadvantaged preschool children. *Child Development,* 1971, **42,** 1069–1075.

Siegal, S. *Nonparametric statistics for the behavioral sciences.* New York: McGraw-Hill, 1956.

Silberman, E. E. *Crisis in the classroom: The remaking of American education.* New York: Random House, 1970.

Simon, H. A., & Newell, A. Human problem solving: The state of the theory in 1970. *American Psychologist,* 1971, **26**, 145–159.

Skinner, B. F. *Science and human behavior.* New York: Macmillan, 1953.

Skinner, B. F. Teaching machines. *Science,* 1958, **128**, 969–977.

Skinner, B. F. A case study in scientific method. In S. Koch (Ed.), *Psychology: A study of a science* (Vol. 2). New York: McGraw-Hill, 1959.

Skinner, B. F. *The technology of teaching.* New York: Appleton-Century-Crofts, 1968.

Skinner, B. F. *Beyond freedom and dignity.* New York: Bantam, 1971.

Smith, D. C. *A community helper program for children with behavioral and learning disorders.* Columbus: Ohio State University, 1969. (ERIC Document Reproduction Service No. ED 040 557.)

Solomon, R. L. An extension of control group design. *Psychological Bulletin,* 1949, **46**, 137–150.

Spano, B. J. Causal thinking, adjustment and social perception as a function of behavior science concepts in elementary school children. Unpublished Doctoral Dissertation, University of Gainsville, Florida: Florida, 1965.

Speedie, S. M., Houtz, J. C., Ringenbach, S. E., & Feldhusen, J. F. Abilities measured by the Purdue Elementary Problem-solving Inventory. *Psychological Reports,* 1973, **33**, 959–963.

Spivack, G. *A conception of healthy human functioning* (Research and Evaluation Report No. 15). Philadelphia: Department of Mental Health Sciences, Hahnemann Medical College and Hospital, 1973.

Spivack, G., & Levine, M. *Self-regulation in acting-out and normal adolescents.* Washington, D.C.: Report to NIMH, M-4531, 1963.

Spivack, G., & Shure, M. *Social adjustment of young children.* San Francisco: Jossey-Bass, 1974.

Spivack, B., & Spotts, J. The Devereux Child Behavior Scale: Symptom behaviors in latency age children. *American Journal of Mental Deficiency,* 1965, **69**, 839–853.

Stanwyck, D. J. Creative problem solving: What of its affect? In J. K. Davis and J. F. Feldhusen (Chair), *Creative problem solving–Theory, research and training procedures.* Symposium presented at meeting of American Psychological Association, New Orleans, 1974.

Stennett, R. G. Emotional handicap in the elementary years: Phase or disease? *American Journal of Orthopsychiatry,* 1966, **36**, 444–449.

Stern, C., Nummedal, S., & Brussell, S. *Therapeutic interventions with emotionally-disturbed preschool children.* Los Angeles: U.C.L.A., 1971. (ERIC Document Reproduction Service No. ED 058 945.)

Stevenson, H. W., Hale, G. A., Klein, R. E., & Miller, L. K. Intercorrelations and correlates in children's learning and problem solving. *Monographs of the Society for Research in Child Development,* 1968, **33,** 1–68.

Stone, G., Hinds, W., & Schmidt, G. Teaching mental health behaviors to elementary school children. *Professional Psychology,* 1975, **6,** 34–40.

Stuart, R. B. *Trick or treatment: How and when psychotherapy fails.* Champaign, Illinois: Research Press, 1970.

Suinn, R. M. Changes in non-treated subjects over time: Data on a fear survey schedule and the test anxiety scale. *Behaviour Research and Therapy,* 1969, **7,** 205–206.

Sulzer, B., & Mayer, G. R. *Behavior modification procedures for school personnel.* Hinsdale, Illinois: The Dryden Press, 1972.

Susskind, E. C. Questioning and curiosity in the elementary school classroom. Unpublished doctoral dissertation, Yale University, 1969.

Thomas, D. R. Preliminary findings on self-monitoring for modifying teaching behaviors. In E. A. Ramp and B. L. Hopkins (Eds.), *A new direction for education: Behavior analysis, 1971.* Lawrence, Kansas: University of Kansas Press, 1971.

Thomas, D. R., Becker, W. C., & Armstrong, M. Production and elimination of disruptive classroom behavior by systematically varying teachers' behavior. *Journal of Applied Behavior Analysis,* 1968, **1,** 35–45.

Toffler, A. *Future shock.* New York: Bantam, 1970.

Torrance, C. D. *Guiding creative potential.* Englewood Cliffs, New Jersey: Prentice-Hall, 1962.

Trickett, E. J., Kelly, J. G., & Todd, D. M. The social environment of the high school: Guidelines for individual change and organizational redevelopment. In S. E. Golann and C. Eisdorfer (Eds.), *Handbook of community mental health.* New York: Appleton, 1972.

Tucker, L. R., Damarin, F., & Messick, S. A base-free measure of change. *Psychometrika,* 1966, **31,** 457–473.

Ullmann, L. P. *Institution and outcome.* New York: Pergamon, 1967.

Umbarger, C. C., Dalsimer, J. S., Morrison, A. P., & Breggin, P. R. *College students in a mental hospital.* New York: Grune & Stratton, 1962.

Van Antwerp, M. The route to primary prevention. *Community Mental Health Journal,* 1971, **7,** 183–188.

Walker, M. *Walker Problem Behavior Identification Checklist Manual.* Los Angeles: Western Psychological Services, 1970.

Ward, M. H., & Baker, B. L. Reinforcement therapy in the classroom. *Journal of Applied Behavior Analysis,* 1968, **1,** 323–328.

Walzer, S., Richmond, J. B., de Buno, T. Epidemiology and disordered learning. In I. N. Berlin (Ed.), *Advocacy for child mental health.* New York: Brunner/Mazel, 1975.

Watson, D. L., & Tharp, R. G. *Self-directed behavior: Self-modification for personal adjustment.* Monterey, California: Brooks/Cole, 1972.

Watt, N. F., Stolurow, R. D., Lubensky, A. W., & McClelland, D. C. School adjustment and behavior of children hospitalized for schizophrenia as adults. *American Journal of Orthopsychiatry,* 1970, **40,** 637–657.

Webb, E. J., Campbell, D. T., Schwartz, R. D. & Sechrest, L. B. *Unobstrusive measures: Nonreactive research in the social sciences.* Chicago: Rand-McNally, 1966.

Westman, J. C., Rice, D. L., & Bermann, E. Nursery school behavior and later school adjustment. *American Journal of Orthopsychiatry,* 1967, **37,** 725–731.

Winett, R. A., & Winkler, R. C. Current behavior modification in the classroom: Be still, be quiet, be docile. *Journal of Applied Behavior Analysis,* 1972, **5,** 499–504.

Wood, W. S., & Bland, C. Some suggested guidelines for intervention with public schools. In E. A. Ramp & B. L. Hopkins (Eds.), *A new direction for education: Behavior analysis, 1971.* Lawrence, Kansas: University of Kansas Press, 1971.

Zax, M., & Cowen, E. L. *Abnormal psychology: Changing conceptions.* New York: Holt, Rinehart & Winston, 1972.

Zax, M., Cowen, E. L., Izzo, L. D., Madonia, A. J., Merenda, J., & Trost, M. A. A teacher-aide program for preventing emotional disturbances in young schoolchildren. *Mental Hygiene,* 1966, **50,** 406–415.

Zax, M., Cowen, E. L., Rappaport, J., Beach, D. R., & Laird, J. D. Follow-up study of children identified early as emotionally disturbed. *Journal of Consulting and Clinical Psychology,* 1968, **32,** 369–374.

Zax, M., & Specter, G. A. *An introduction to community psychology.* New York: Wiley, 1974.

Zimmerman, J., Zimmerman, E., Rider, S. L., Smith, A. F., & Dinn, R. Doing your own thing with precision: The essence of behavior management in the classroom. *Educational Technology,* 1971, **11,** 26–32.

Subject Index